THE CONSEQUENCE OF INNOVATION:
21ST CENTURY POETICS

THE CONSEQUENCE OF INNOVATION:
21ST CENTURY POETICS

➤

Edited by Craig Dworkin

ROOF BOOKS
NEW YORK

ISBN: 978-1-931824-29-3
Library of Congress Catalog Card Number: 2008921463

Cover Art by Bruce Pearson
Encyclopedia 3 (relative calm sounds of gunfire and footsteps sadly familiar
sheds some light), 2005. Copyright: Bruce Pearson
Photo: Alan Zindman
Courtesy: Ronald Feldman Fine Art, New York

This book was made possible, in part, with public funds from the
New York State Council on the Arts, a state agency.

Roof Books are distributed by
Small Press Distribution
1341 Seventh Street
Berkeley, CA. 94710-1403
Phone orders: 800-869-7553
www.spdbooks.org

Roof Books are published by
Segue Foundation
300 Bowery
New York, NY 10012
seguefoundation.com

Contents

Seja Marginal

Craig Dworkin

For however insignificant a role the word "poet"
may play in the intellectual history of our time,
future generations will find its unexpected, albeit
inextinguishable, traces in our economic history.
                                        —Robert Musil

One day, towards the end of the 1980s, Eliot Weinberger picked up a copy of the *Directory of American Poets* to find a disquieting statistic:

> 4,672 poets, all of them published, and all of them, incred-
> ibly, approved by a committee which determines that they
> are, in fact, poets. To read only one book by every living
> American poet—at the rate of one book a day, no holi-
> days—would take 13 years, during which time another few
> thousand poets would have appeared.[1]

Weinberger was struck by the difference between the rates of publish-ing during his own post-modern moment at the close of a dark decade and the height of high modernism two generations earlier. Looking back at a survey by the journal *Accent*, which had set out to take stock of the literary 1930s, he discovers that "there were only 151 American poets, and they published 264 books of poetry. If one read only two books a month in that decade, one would have read every new book of American poetry."[2] Times change, but neither of the periods Weinberger focuses on were exceptional; the publication of poetry increased steadily and exponentially—year by year—over the course of the twentieth century, and that trend continues, unchecked, into the new millennium.

Some of the force of Weinberger's rhetoric depends on the absurd precision of his figures, but the comparison of even roughly figured quantities—or simply orders of magnitude—is worth considering. While any precise statistics are in fact quite difficult to correlate, given the number of variables and the assumptions made by different sources (above all, what counts as "poetry," as well as what kind of publishers or publications are included), the general outlines are strikingly clear, and the consequences for any consideration of what "contemporary poetry" might mean are unavoidable. In the period since Weinberger's essay was published the number of poetry books in print has doubled, the number of publishers has increased by almost 80%, and there are nearly half again as many poetry magazines in circulation. None of these statistics accounts for the explosion in on-line publishing.[3] Which means that the practical task of thinking about "contemporary poetry" is even more daunting now than it was for Weinberger. The Poets House (New York), which aspires to acquire every book of poetry published in America, excluding vanity press publications, has shelved over 20,000 volumes from between the years 1990 and 2006.[4] According to Bowker, the leading data provider to the publishing industry (the same company that assigns ISBN numbers), there were 37,450 poetry and drama titles between 1993 and 2006. Considering only books published during the last year: Poets House catalogued 1,971 titles with a 2006 copyright; Bowker registered 5,486 new titles under the category of poetry; and Amazon lists 9,444 poetry titles with that publication date for sale.[5] As they stand, these numbers are significant for anyone interested in the rhetoric of "poetry"—that is, in the range of quite different texts that fall under that single capacious category—but they are easily reduced, at least to some degree, for the reader not interested in certain genres: nursery rhymes and children's books; "inspirational" verse; collections of song lyrics; reissues of public domain classics; thematic collections of light verse (there are hundreds of titles, for instance, that feature poetry about cats). Even after eliminating what Weinberger terms "nonliterary poetry," and discarding reissues or reprints of older texts, one is still faced with a staggering number of new books of poetry. A thousand new poetry books a year? Two thousand? Ten? As we'll see, the difference—for all practical purposes—is moot.

Whatever the exact numbers, their implications are startling. Perhaps most surprising is the deduction that in an economy of massive production without mass consumption, many more people write poetry than read it. Or, to be more cautiously precise: more people submit their poetry for publication than purchase the publications of others. Charles Molesworth long ago noticed that even "a small magazine of modest reputation, *Poetry Northwest*, considers forty thousand poems a year, though the magazine has fewer than one thousand subscribers."[6] In the decades since, that discrepancy has become standard. Submissions to *Poetry* magazine are approaching one-hundred thousand per year, some ten times the journal's circulation, and the same ratio holds for first book contests: the number of manuscripts submitted to such contests is far greater—by an order of magnitude—than the number of copies sold by the winner. If other cultural spheres behaved like the poetry world, it would be as if the only visitors to art museums were themselves exhibiting painters, the only radio listeners were themselves recording musicians, all filmgoers actors. The practice of publication aside, the psychological economy of poetry under conditions of such excess pits reading and writing against one another; the activities—once two sides of the same commitment to poetry—are now in competition with one another. Given that simply keeping abreast of new poetry publications requires an all-consuming dedication, every minute spent writing a poem is time that the conscientious poet could be using to read.

Another implication of the trend in contemporary poetry publishing bears on every reader, poet or not. Poetry faces a Malthusian limit. Bound by discrepant rates of production and consumption, the readerly economy of poetry in the twenty-first century cannot avoid a catastrophic calculus: the rate of consumption quickly hits an arithmetic limit (any one person can only read so much), but the rate of production is increasing geometrically. Even the partisan reader who wants to keep up with a particular niche within the broad field of contemporary poetry faces an overwhelming task. Consider, for instance, a reader interested in the kind of poetry published by Roof Books. The distributor for Roof, Small Press Distribution, handles around six-hundred new poetry titles a year. Excluded from that figure are chapbooks and "little magazines," which happen to be the venues for some of the most innovative new writing, and which would add at least five-hundred other relevant titles. University presses publish another several hundred new titles annually. The larger independent and commercial presses add far fewer, perhaps another hundred. So without bothering to look on-line, and without worrying about books from other countries, or in languages other than English, or anything published last year, the reader in search of one slice of new American poetry has to sift through well over a thousand relevant titles—a number already narrowed from the five to ten thousand published annually. Part of Weinberger's incredulity at the fact that those in the *Directory of American Poets* had been "approved by a committee" is clearly disdain at the bureaucratization of poetry, but part is also surely the realization that those thousands of poets had *already* been winnowed from the tens of thousands of people writing poetry and not publishing in sufficient quantities or in the proper venues to be confirmed by the *Directory*. The hypothetical reader interested in the kind of poetry published by Roof faces the same realization; even after substantially narrowing the field by some kind of editorial vetting—whether it be Small Press Distribution's decision to adopt a press or the vote of the board of a university press to publish a manuscript—the number of relevant books is staggering. Now admittedly not all of those books need to be read very carefully to have a sense of what they are like (though even a quick glance at a thousand books is no small commitment—the cost alone would be prohibitive for most readers), but one could expect the serious and dutiful student of contemporary poetry to read two to three poetry books a day.[7] Every day. And then, if trends continue as they have for over a century, to read even more next year—just to keep up.

Whether one views these conditions as a glut or a renaissance, the corollaries are worth considering. To begin with, it follows that views of the contemporary are necessarily narrow, and only ever partial. Quite simply: no one knows what is going on. There are no experts in contemporary poetry, no one with a clear overview of the field or the range of current trends. However little Weinberger could have learned about the poetry published in 1990, we know even less about the poetry of our current day, and can expect to know still less about whatever is published next year. Or, to be more optimistic: even assuming that somewhere—with lonely bloodshot eyes—a handful of obsessive readers are in fact managing to keep up with their two or three books per day, they have precious little time to do the additional reading that would put those books in context: no time to read up on poetry from the previous year, or the previous decade, or the last century, or from other traditions—no time for reading in any other genre, or, moreover, for communicating what they have learned from their intensely myopic study. Even if there were experts in contemporary poetry, that is, they could not put their expertise into context, and they would be hard pressed to find the time to write about what they knew.

The problem is certainly not unique to contemporary poetry. The scholar of Victorian literature, for instance, faces a similar dilemma. Tens of thousands of novels were published in Britain during Victoria's reign. One figure widely cited by historians estimates as many as sixty thousand novels in volume format alone, with far more appearing in periodical installments.[8] Whether surveying twenty-first-century poetry or nineteenth-century fiction, the difficulties involved in reading so many books are the same, but the differences are telling. Most importantly, the dissimilarities between undertaking contemporaneous and retrospective projects—that is, between trying to come extemporaneously to terms with the literature of one's own time and looking back over more than a century's intervention of scholarly, commercial, and popular vetting—has allowed the institutions and disciplines that emerged around the two literatures to develop quite differently. Despite the vast number of titles, the canon of Victorian fiction is relatively small and enjoys a broad consensus about its core texts. A comparison of Ph.D. exam lists and syllabi from various literature departments reveals a surprising constant roster with only minor fluctuations (*Tess* rather than *Jude*, Stevenson rather than Stoker, *et cetera*). Reforms and upheavals certainly occur over time; Olive Schreiner, for instance, was absent from such lists not long ago but is now a mainstay and more likely to appear than Trollope. But at any given moment the sense of the field, presented by Victorianists *as a field*, is consistent. For contemporary poetry, the inverse holds: from course to course or list to list one or two authors might haphazardly repeat—the only statistically probable name turns out to be John Ashbery—but the rosters are otherwise unpredictable. To put this another way, a graduate reading list in twentieth-century poetry which does not include Gertrude Stein or Charles

Olson or Bruce Andrews can still seem unremarkable and responsible, whereas an exam list in nineteenth-century fiction that did not include Thackeray or Eliot or Brontë would seem radical. The former seems to merely make assumptions, while the latter seems to be making a point.[9]

Moreover, debates about modern and contemporary poetry display a far more contentious set-theory mentality. The Victorian canon (to stay with that comparison) is of course open to revision and reassessment and idiosyncratic emphases: should religious tracts be included in a consideration of Victorian fiction? should one read Charles Kingsley's *Hypatia* rather than Charles Dickens' *Bleak House*? Lady Jane Wilde rather than Oscar Wilde? However heated such debates might be, no one opposed to replacing Edward Bulwer-Lytton with Wilkie Collins protests by dismissing *The Moonstone* with the declaration "that's not fiction!" In contrast, works that leading scholars of poetry would hold to be key canonical texts might not even qualify as "poetry" for others: is *Tender Buttons* the foundational poem of modernism or not poetry at all? Is John Cage one of the central figures of post-war poetry or not a poet at all? I remember leaving a reading by Kenneth Goldsmith (one of the contributors to the present volume and a writer discussed in the essay by Sianne Ngai) and overhearing a conversation in which one of the most prominent critics of American poetry was asked what he thought of the poetry reading. His reply: "What poetry reading?" Such disagreements are one distinctive facet of the discourse around contemporary poetry, which lacks consensus not merely on critical assessments, aesthetic valuations, and canonical choices, but on the very contours of the field from which a canon can begin to be drawn.

That fundamental divide—or rather, merely the reader's knowledge that such categorical disagreements exist—points to another difference between contemporary poetry and other fields: how genres and sub-genres come to be mapped. New titles in the various categories of genre fiction ("horror," "science fiction," "westerns," "romance," *et cetera*) are also published annually in the thousands. Film genres are another case in point. While the reviewer of commercial Hollywood studio films could watch a movie every other day and easily keep up on all the new theatrical releases, the viewer interested in Bollywood films would need to watch two or three films every day (assuming that screenings could be found); but for the cineaste interested in the type of independent films submitted to the Sundance Film Festival there are simply not enough hours in the day: the Festival received over 8,000 films last year. Contemplating such figures reveals the assumptions and prejudices we have about different cultural categories. Genre fiction, by definition, is formulaic; one assumes that variations among the several thousand "fantasy" novels published each year will be minor. Sub-genres of poetry are presumably equally formulaic, but the category as a whole is far too broad to be handled in the same way as "true crime." Similarly, do we imagine that the conventions of Indian cinema are more strict than "indie" film conventions? Does the viewer who sees only a fraction of Hindi releases have a better sense of that genre than the viewer who sees a similar percentage of documentaries? And which viewer is closer to the position of the reader of contemporary poetry? The point is that no one will ever know: a claim for the vast uniformity of contemporary poetry could never be confirmed, just as, conversely, Bollywood cinema might display a radical formal diversity unseen by any given viewer who just happens to see the hundreds of films that are very much alike but who has missed the hundreds of others pioneering unimagined new cinematic directions.

One obvious implication of these considerations is that the umbrella term "poetry" may not be very useful. Worse yet, it may well lead to the kind of confusions Ludwig Wittgenstein termed "grammatical errors." Because we have a single term, we imagine that all of the things designated by that term share a family resemblance. The category of "poetry" inclines us to forget that one "poem" may have much more to do with a film, or a musical composition, or something else entirely than with another text that also happens to be called a poem. More troubling, a further implication of these figures is that the models we have for literary knowledge and expertise, as well as the kinds of activities that we imagine to constitute scholarship, need to be radically revised or entirely replaced. Surveys, broad synoptic claims, arguments based on norms, strong accounts of large-scale historical change, and other modes of inquiry by individual readers based on comprehensive knowledge and global perspectives can no longer be maintained. At least two alternatives present themselves.

On the one hand, even greater distance and further abstraction: rather than a series of evaluative close readings, critics might assemble data about work that could be analyzed—either collectively or mechanically—at some remove. Instead of attempting to account for individual books, the task would be to graph and model the complex poetic ecosystem itself, or to map data in ways that their composite assembly would reveal new information. Rather than look at discrete texts, criticism would turn to charting the relations among texts and visualizing those networks themselves. Franco Moretti has suggested a similar solution to the problem of trying to come to terms with the field of nineteenth-century European novels: "a field this large cannot be understood by stitching together separate bits of knowledge about individual cases, because it *isn't* a sum of individual cases: it's a collective system, that should be grasped as such, as a whole."[10] Such an approach is analogous to what Lev Manovich has called the database logic of new media, where the focus is not on the production of new data, but on new ways of accessing, ordering, and displaying large quantities of already accumulated data. Close readings and explications would give way to an activity more like tagging.

On the other hand, criticism might abandon the dream of comprehensive knowledge altogether, as well as the values of totality and mastery it implies. Surrendering to the impossibility of understanding any field so vast, critical inquiry would be confined to accounting for isolated singularities, exceptions, idiosyncrasies and minute particulars. A criticism ever more local, focused, specialized, and *ad hoc* would allow scholars to continue to read texts in more or less the same ways, but require that they be careful to frame their readings in very precise terms, without making more generalized claims. Furthermore, part of the task of criticism under these conditions would shift to more emphatically communicating the essence and necessity of poems that the critic's audience may never have heard about, much less read. Not just analyses and readings of particular passages or poems, but quick and rich descriptions of what it means for the text in question to be considered a poem; not just a persuasive argument about a text but a persuasive evaluation of its urgency: given all the other poems one might instead be reading, why this one? Without needing to convince people to think in new ways about a poem they know and have already read, the force of critical rhetoric comes to bear instead on the value of talking about a poem, *any poem*, at all. Instead of being organized around common texts, discussions of poetry would have to cohere around a common interest in the critical arguments that can be made about poems, around a commitment to speak to the contemporary. Without shared assumptions, canonical texts, coherent traditions or standard references, the critical discourse around contemporary poetry would thus become not so much a traversal of common ground as reports from distant frontiers that define a foreign, uncharted space; an aggregation of distinct, discontinuous and widely separated points rather than a congruence of overlapping planes; pizzicati rather than chords. The character of critical conversations thus transforms from more public to more private discourses, from continuous dialogue toward a series of discrete monologues, from the mode of debate toward the mode of the manifesto. Criticism in this new dispensation would be all the more intently focused on the specifics of the individual, particular poem, but with no regard for "poetry" *en masse*—even as a commitment to "contemporary poetry," in the abstract, and as an ideal, must come to supercede collective allegiance to any particular canon of poems.

• • •

But wait a minute. Too *much* poetry? This vision of excess runs diametrically counter to one of the first *idées reçues* of contemporary literature: that there is not enough poetry; that its miniscule share of the cultural landscape renders it insignificant and invisible—that poetry is so marginal it doesn't matter. "'The Marginalization of Poetry'—it almost/ goes without saying," as Bob Perelman acknowledges.[11] And indeed, statistics also support this view of draught and scarcity. In comparison with total book production, poetry accounts for only about one percent of all new titles. A National Endowment for the Arts survey in 2004 found that only 12% of adults had read any poetry in the previous year.[12] These statistics of fractions and modesty can be reconciled with the sense of excess if one remembers the absolute terms of their scale (12% of adult Americans is still some 25 million readers), but looking at any particular book, the picture is inescapably bleak. The typical print run for a book of small press poetry, somewhere between 200 to 1,000 copies, is almost always optimistic, determined more by volume breaks in production costs for cover printing and binding than by any realistically projected sales.[13] Only a very small handful of those poetry books, somewhere less than half of one percent of one percent, will ever sell more than a thousand copies, or go into a second printing. To assign a book of small press poetry in an undergraduate class can instantly double its sales. Repeating the class once or twice can send that title out of print. Under the best conditions (a publisher able to both sell directly and also through a reliably accessible, stable, well advertised and easily found distributor willing to warehouse a title for more than a decade), the typical book of small press poetry—over the course of ten or twenty years—will sell a hundred copies. Which returns us to the same predicament in which excess left us. Not only could no individual read all of the books of contemporary poetry, but any individual book of contemporary poetry is likely to have been read by only a very few people. The dream of a common text has long been lost to poetry. If you have read a book of small press poetry, you are likely to constitute one or two percent of its total readership. Moreover, with a print run of a thousand copies, a book of poetry aims, hubristically, at around .008%—*less than one percent of one percent*—of the American poetry-reading public.[14] An exceptionally successful book of contemporary poetry might attain a readership equivalent to a mid-sized high school. The most wildly popular, runaway bestseller might aspire to the readership of a billboard in a small rural town.

As with the figures of excess, these numerical indications of scarcity and scatter have implications as well, especially for attempts to measure the value of poetry. In an economy predicated on mass consumption and subscribed to the neo-liberal ideologies of a *soi-disant* "free market," the easy reasoning surmises that if poetry is so little read, it must not be very good; if poetry were better, some suspect, it would be more popular. A quick look at the *most* popular might raise some suspicion about that logic—*American Idol*; the *High School Musical Soundtrack*; *Pirates of the Caribbean 2*; *The Da Vinci Code*; *Morrigan's Cross*—as should any specific comparison (was Super Bowl XVI better than Super Bowl XVII because it was watched by a larger percentage of households, or was XVII better because it had a larger total number of viewers?).[15]

The absurdity of bluntly equating popularity with value does not really need emphasizing, however much the recurrent suspicion unconsciously lingers, but the point is that such comparisons immediately throw one back onto the definitions of "value" itself—a category, like "poetry," that is too various and broad to be used without qualification or explanation. When the fundamental character of works is radically diverse, criticism needs to make not only its argument, but also a case for the value of its selective attentions. Depending on assumptions about what films ought to do, for example, *Pirates of the Caribbean* is obviously a much better film than, say, Nathaniel Dorsky's *Song and Solitude* (one of the less commercial and more critically acclaimed films of 2006). *Pirates* is clearly better at exploiting conventions of novelistic narrative, exploring the limits of celebrity appeal and traditions of the stage, employing illusionistic sound and availing itself of special effects, generally offering itself to escapist fantasy entertainment, and so on. *Song*, on the other hand, is clearly the better film when judged on other criteria: exploiting the meditative potential of projector mechanics (the work is shot on 16mm film and meant to be projected at 18 frames per second); exploring the logic of the shot rather than the scene; capturing and printing the nuances of light; generally offering itself to formal analysis and intellectual reflection; and so on. Questions of value always return one to further questions, which cannot be indefinitely postponed and which cannot, in any event, be answered by the number of books or tickets sold.[16]

The converse assumption—whether it takes the form of a smug coterie belief that the small audience for poetry certifies its value, or the presumption that a small audience condemns poetry as elitist—is no more tenable and no less persistent. One scarcely needs to refute the first version of that assumption, familiar in its inverse formulation from Chamfort's maxim, wittily presented as a widely held received idea in its own right: "Il y a à parier que toute idée publique, toute convention reçue, est une sottise, car elle a convenu au plus grand nombre [one wagers that any popular idea, any received wisdom, is a stupidity, because it is held by so many]."[17] The second version of the assumption, the sanctimonious charge of elitism, however, has been recently taken up not only by the enemies of poetry, but by its supposed defenders as well. Among the spokespeople for dominant cultural institutions, one of the catchphrases of twenty-first-century poetics has been "accessibility." Trumpeted most loudly by the new century's Poet Laureates (Billy Collins [2001-2003] and Ted Kooser [2004-2006]), "accessible," "democratic" poetry—an invitingly familiar, plainspoken, pre-modernist lyric—has been pitted against the perceived elitism of restive, cryptic, experimental, incoherent, or formally challenging texts. Contemporary poetics has thus returned to a version of the twelfth-century contest between the *trobar leu* and the *trobar clus*. Echoing the mantra of the National Endowment for the Arts Chairman Dana Gioia, whose widely cited and reprinted 1991 essay "Can Poetry Matter?" ends with a plea to *"expand the art's audience,"* these Laureates bemoan the small readership for poetry, and they have paradoxically sought to "expand the art's audience" by denigrating one entire segment of readers and dismissing the traditions of the difficult.[18]

The virtues of competing aesthetics (not to mention the validity of characterizations such as "accessible" and "difficult") can of course be debated, but rather than take up the argument at those levels I merely want to point out the fundamental difference between the Laureates' strategy and other attempts to reconcile issues of audience and difficulty in other cultural spheres. Contemporary physics, for just one comparison, is notoriously difficult and has a noticeably small audience of initiates and enthusiasts; the response, however, has not been to call for a return to simplified Newtonian mechanics because they are more "accessible" than sub-atomic models, just as no one would accuse Calculus of being "undemocratic" because it is more difficult and less popular than simple arithmetic. In the spheres of math and science, the response to questions of audience and difficulty is educational. The call has been to better educate students, training them to have the requisite skills for understanding more advanced concepts. Or, similarly, rather than scrap String Theory as a mandarin pursuit in which physicists are writing only for other physicists, science writers are tasked with better explaining the relevance and workings of the theory to non-scientists. Accordingly, those concerned with the challenging difficulty of some poetry might make it more accessible not by changing the poetry itself, but rather by changing the education of its potential readership and honing the critical discourse about poetry.

The second discrepancy between the recent discourse around poet-

in fact adventurous, idiosyncratic, and diverse. Moreover, contrary to the culture-war mindset that imagines a mainstream opposed to the margin, the statistics of the long tail suggest that consumers typically purchase *both* popular superstar titles as well as obscure niche titles. Tastes turn out to be far less exclusive than partisans on either side of the popular divide suppose. Not only are the purchasers of the most obscure products more enthusiastic about the mainstream products that still constitute the majority of their purchases, but habitual consumers of mainstream products stray increasingly from popular titles the more they are permitted to explore, and then the further they depart from the short head of the sales graph the more obscure titles they purchase.[22]

Assuming that poetry follows the same pattern as other cultural commodities, one might thus predict that the Laureates—rather than pushing for more popular mainstream poetry "hits" to replace unpopular experiments under the false impression that unpopular works diminish the readership for poetry—would be better off advocating the obscurities of the long, tapering small-press tail. The lesson for poetry, in the event, is to make a greater variety of poetry both more easily available and more easily discoverable. Digital distribution aids the former task, and my own experience with archiving digital versions of out-of-print books indicates that at the very least there is an audience for the most restive poetry that the initial print runs of those books did not exhaust.[23] The task of making the varieties of poetry more discoverable, however, has been rendered all the more difficult and necessary in the twenty-first century, not only because of the geometric increase in publication but because in just the last few years, for reasons Jed Rasula identifies in his essay for this volume, the traditional indicators of aesthetic affiliation—such as publishers with aesthetically consistent and narrowly edited lists—have become increasingly blurred.

So once again, the conditions for poetry in the twenty-first century put increased pressure on its paratexts, those extra-poetic texts that can filter and link even part of the bewildering precession of published titles. That pressure comes to bear on criticism as well—a criticism, as we have seen, that needs to adjust its focus (whether closing in on the linguistic surface of a discrete text or pulling out to view the system of literary activity as a whole), to address the uninitiated, to educate as well as persuade its readers, and, more than ever, to stake its claims with a scrupulously open clarity. The aim of this collection, which gathers essays from the last decade about poetry from the last decade, is to present versions of such criticism. Because they are coeval with their subjects, these essays are like topographies of actively volcanic islands; the ground they map will undoubtedly look very different in even the near future, perhaps disappearing altogether, as the genuine eruptions and terrain-changing earthquakes come to be distinguished through the sound and fury of what is otherwise so much steam and sulfurous smoke. Real-time satellite snapshots rather than retrospective documentaries, they are, however, no less accurate for that.

Most of the writing about contemporary poetry takes the form of short reviews, often no more than extended blurbs, or artists' statements about their own practice. In selecting the following essays I have avoided both genres, though with obvious exceptions; the rule of thumb was more prejudice than stricture. Although the collection was not intended to be thematic, I was interested to find that critics have recently returned again and again to issues of gender, technology, and politics—often, indeed, the interrelation between the three. Nor was this collection meant to be a representative survey (a manifestly impossible goal given the publication statistics cited in the beginning of this essay), and it is frankly partisan in its limited scope. Partisan, but not necessarily advocating. While I predict that some of the poetry discussed in the following pages will eventually be considered defining events of literary history, massive Krakatoas of the word, others will turn out to be no more than small tremors of tectonic quirks, hazards thrown up as the plates of literary cultures collide and readjust, soon to be submerged and forgotten—seamount atolls of colorless reef sunk back beneath the sea of irrelevancy.

Above all, the selections were made with the hope that they would be of use and interest to readers who are *not* necessarily so partisan—a choir of voices singing to outriding circuit preachers rather than preachers turning to the choir. Instead of seeking the last word on any particular poet, I looked for essays that would open the way for the *first* words on some of the hundreds of thousands of poems from the last decade never mentioned in the following pages. My hope is that readers will be able to take these essays as models for engaging those works, as well as future works, and further, as a spur to keep reading deep into the immense expanse of uncharted publications, knowing they are unlikely to ever meet the handful of others who might have chanced to open the same book.

Knowing too that the vast majority of the publications they encounter will be inevitably unreadably awful. Most poetry sucks (to borrow *Coagula*'s tag-line phrasing for their assessment of the art world), and this is equally true of small press poetry; the avant-garde, as Hugh Kenner once said, can be just as boring as anything else. On occasion, of course, some of it will be astonishing. But the gleam of the rare gem should not blind us to the even more important and fabulous lesson of all the silted mud and gravel. That seemingly formless excess of endless granular particulates reveals, on inspection, infinite varia-tions—pyrite and mica in quiet eddies at the bank, to be sure—fools' gold in glitter—but beneath them always another configuration of sur-face and structure, another shifting of metamorphic silicates in unstrat-ified till, no matter how far down you dig or how vigorously you sift— the mere knowledge of those other, as yet uncovered grains, each with the unlikely but unshakeable possibility of taking some radical new form, however slight in its variance, should be seen as an incontestable proof that something else can always be done, the glint of difference giving onto a glimpse of the beach beneath the rubble of the paving stones. Proof, more importantly, that something else *is* being done, both far more inaccessible and much much closer than you think. And if most of that obscure and unseen activity experiments from known results with fabricated data, plagiarizes in order to be expressive, slav-ishly imitates under the banner of innovation, jockeys with naked careerism, ornaments itself to fads with no sense of fashion, and fran-tically waves the fallen banner of the very avant-garde it most basely betrays, it sometimes—if only for the space of a few words—gives way to the inassimilable: a barely audible glitch, a nearly invisible fleck of paint spackling in abstraction on an illusionistic canvas, a flicker in the frame, an anomalous phenomenon, a punctum. In an atypically opti-mistic passage, Paul Mann writes of those moments:

> We must entertain—doubtless the right word—the sheer possibility
> that what we encounter here is not just one more margin or one
> more avant-garde, however impossible it will be to avoid all the

orders and terms attendant upon those venerable and ruined cultural edifices. We must remain open to the possibility that this stupid underground poses all the old questions but a few more as well, that it might suggest another set of cultural arrangements, other topographies and other mappings, however unlikely that might be.[24]

Or simpler still: one insists on alternatives—on revolution, to give it its fancy name—because the *status quo*, in whatever arrangement of our everyday life, is unacceptable. Refusing, safely complacent, to read beyond it is one small part of the unexamined pantomime of criminal silence. Heroic silence, in contrast, always refuses to speak from the wings: "seja marginal," in Hélio Oiticica's appositive imperative, "seja herói."[25]

➤

Free (Market) Verse

Steve Evans

Ten years ago, when the *New York Times Magazine* set out to caricature the leading tendencies in the poetry world, it used the occasion of James Merrill's death to file an obituary for the "poetry establishment" as a whole. Without that elegant poet's inherited millions (his father was the Merrill in Merrill Lynch), which had trickled down to fellow poets via the Ingram Merrill Foundation, the clubby uptown world of old-style patronage—donor readings at J.P. Morgan's former home, easy access to the pages of *The New Yorker*, cushy tenured chairs, guaranteed publication by FSG and Knopf, and a monopoly on prestige- and cash-conferring prizes—was fast unraveling. Barbarians of various descriptions—Language Poets, Hip Hop Poets, Neo-Formalists, Surrealists, and Nuyorican slam poets—were assembling at the gate. And it wasn't another exquisitely crafted, emotionally muted, slyly allusive poem—such as Merrill had made his reputation on—that they were clamoring for.

If there was no trace in the magazine's cartoon gallery of a cohort of midwestern white guys with business backgrounds aspiring to write instantly "accessible" poems about authentic American life for the amusement and improvement of semi-literate "regular" folks, that's because it would take a presidency as benighted and hokey as that of George W. Bush to bring such a group to prominence. Through men like Dana Gioia, John Barr, and Ted Kooser, Karl Rove's battle-tested blend of unapologetic economic elitism and reactionary cultural populism is now being marketed in the far-off reaches of the poetry world. A curiously timed gift from a pharmaceutical heir who, before slipping into four decades of crippling depression, had submitted a pseudonymous item or two to Chicago's *Poetry* magazine, which politely rejected them, has bankrolled the unlikely effort.

What interested most people about Ruth Lilly's hundred-million-dollar gift to *Poetry*, publicly announced in the late fall of 2002, was the sheer size of the sum. Though she bestowed even more money on an organization called Americans for the Arts, the idea that a quaintly penurious outfit like *Poetry* should come into such unexpected riches appealed to the journalistic imagination. The charming, Dickensian narrative involved shabby, sunless quarters in a library basement inhabited by a chain-smoking, lunch-skipping editor who had for two decades heroically sacrificed all to the culling—from ninety thousand submissions a year—of the few poems good enough to earn their two dollars a line and be brought before the eyes of the magazine's subscribers. Now, through her mysterious beneficence, Lilly had lifted *Poetry* from this place of squalor and cultural obsolescence: from a grandparent warehoused in a seedy retirement home, it had been transformed into the newest and richest kid on the block, its financial capital now far exceeding the dwindling symbolic capital it had been husbanding since the days of first-wave modernism.

Poetry may be "news that stays news," as Ezra Pound, an early contributor to the magazine, once asserted, but it has a hell of a time cracking into an actual news cycle. That the story of the Lilly bequest had such tremendous newsworthiness was no doubt due to the way it fused two terms held to be incompatible since at least the Romantic period: poetry and money. The novelty of the conjunction, and the eccentric manner in which it came about—the frail and reclusive Lilly, most of whose life has been spent under psychiatric care, had her lawyer handle everything, reminding some of the old television series *The Millionaire*—made for good, or rather feel-good, copy.

The good feelings might have been harder to sustain if any of the journalists covering the bequest back in November 2002 had bothered to connect it to another bit of news concerning Eli Lilly & Co., a long-standing supporter of Republican politicians as well as an indirect backer, through the Lilly Endowment, of the usual conservative causes. If your recollection of the fall of 2002 has dimmed, perhaps it is because you have blocked out the memory of the mid-term elections that were seen as legitimizing both Bush's initial appointment to the presidency and his post-9/11 makeover into a wartime commander in chief. Shortly after the results were in, four paragraphs were append-ed—no one could say by whom—to the 475-page Homeland Security Bill then under consideration in Congress, paragraphs that exempted the Lilly Company from lawsuits (the American Prospect foresaw a "torrent" of them) related to the manufacture of Thimerosal, a preser-vative added to vaccines and thought by some to be a cause of autism.

How bulletproofing a Big Pharma concern made the homeland safer, again, no one could say. But the action could not have come at a better time for Lilly. Having lost its bid to extend the patent on Prozac when the Supreme Court rejected its appeal without comment, the company stumbled badly in the first quarter of 2002. Faced with com-petition from generic alternatives for the first time since its introduction to the US market, Prozac sales had dropped off by seventy percent. With no blockbusters anywhere near introduction, and with the threat of litigation over Thimerosal growing more serious, Lilly's share price had taken a serious downturn.

In fact, between January 2002, when Ruth Lilly revised her estate plan and funded the bequest to *Poetry*, and December 2002 (just weeks after the bequest was publicly announced), the 3.8 million shares of Lilly stock that formed the basis for the gift had declined in value by thirty-six percent. Worse news still for *Poetry*, National City Bank of Indiana, which handled the trusts that funded the bequest, botched the sell-off of the stock so badly that Americans for the Arts first filed a fed-eral suit against the bank and then, when that failed on procedural grounds, the lawyers for *Poetry* joined them in legal action, alleging neg-ligence and breach of fiduciary duty.

There are several facts to hold onto here. First, the heartwarming story of Ruth Lilly's handout to *Poetry* magazine was at least in part timed to draw attention away from the scandalous political payoff that had been snuck into the Homeland Security Bill and hurriedly signed into law by Bush. Second, the bequest itself was already, by the time it was made public, the object of bitter litigation nowhere discussed in the press coverage.

Poets for Bush

Several other developments around that time rhymed with the *Poetry* bequest. In September of 2002, the poet Ed Hirsch was picked to preside over the John Simon Guggenheim Foundation, effectively putting him in charge of about $7 million in grant monies per year. The following month, the neo-formalist businessman poet Dana Gioia, who takes credit for revitalizing the sales of Jell-O and Kool-Aid during his stint in the marketing department at General Foods, was named to head the NEA, which distributes about $100 million in grants to organizations, state agencies, and a dwindling number of individual artists each year.

Each man interpreted his ascension as a sign that reason was slowly being restored to a poetry world that had addled its collective brain in academic workshops, bogged itself down with postmodern claptrap, and attended for far too long to degrees and CV-lines in default of its duty to be "accessible." Hirsch, an aesthetically conservative poetry insider who left the University of Houston to take up the Guggenheim post, lamented his genre's self-inflicted wounds. "Poetry hasn't been well-served by poets who fled to the margins," he told the *New York Times*, exhibiting a handy knack for construing effects (poetry's marginal status in the capitalist infotainment order) as causes (it's poets who fled to the margins). Gioia's fame stems more from an attack he launched on the inbred subculture of academic poetry in 1991 than from any serious interest in his own verse, and he has continued to trumpet accessibility ever since. "I still write more for my old fellow workers" at General Foods, he has said, "who will never read my poems, than for the literati." He is also—at least according to the magazine *Workforce Management*—a welcome "corrective contrast to the tired stereotype of an eccentric or anti-establishment artist."

According to a squib in *Variety*, "some Washington insiders speculated that first lady Laura Bush, an avid supporter of the arts and letters, had a hand in tapping Gioia." If that was the case, Gioia kept mum about it in public. One suspects the cause was less modesty than the nearly universal loathing for the Bush administration felt by poets in those days when the president was forcing his battle plans for Iraq down an unwilling world's throat. Indeed, Gioia's confirmation to his post came from the Senate on January 29, 2003, just two weeks before a gala dinner at which the first lady had hoped to demonstrate her admiration for the rhyming arts in the company of culture-war hawk Lynne Cheney and a group of poets that included Sam Hamill. When the militant pacifist (and ex-Marine) Hamill not only declined to attend but decided to counter-program a "day of poetry against the war," the East Wing event—which may have been intended as a coming out party for Gioia—was summarily scrapped. As Hamill gathered thousands of anti-war poems for presentation to Congress (some 13,000 had come in by March 1st), Gioia spent the first months of his chairmanship dodging questions about the poetry community's broad-based rejection of Bush's drive to war. Even the politically quiescent Billy Collins, then serving as poet laureate, publicly expressed distaste for the gathering storm of "shock and awe." But Gioia stubbornly maintained his silence. When pressed, he'd respond with a defensive generalization, arguing that if poetry is considered "only as conceptual, ideological speech, it diminishes its role as art." It was amusing, in a way, to see the bright-eyed champion of clarity, accessibility, and familiar forms being driven into the arms of aesthetic indeterminacy by a spontaneous and overwhelming outbreak of plain-speaking dissent.

Deregulating Poetry

The tiny but powerfully placed band of businessmen poets continued to grow when, in February 2004, the organization established to administer *Poetry* magazine's Prozac millions named an investment banker, John Barr, to be its new president. (Joseph Parisi, the long-time editor of the magazine, had been set to lead the foundation, but he returned from a vacation in the summer of 2003 apparently thinking better of it.) Like Gioia—described by Barr as a "kindred spirit" with whom he bonded "because we could both read balance sheets and had this love for poetry"—Barr leans heavily on his dual background when speaking to reporters, whose fawning stories always seem to run under half-clever headlines like "A Passion for Poetry, and Profits," or "Invested in Poetic Currency," or "Dollars and Sense," or "Poetry and Investment Banking: It's All About Risk." Swooning is routine when reporters encounter the charismatic Mr. Barr. Consider the following, which actually appeared in the respectable pages of the *Christian Science Monitor*:

> When John Barr, president of the Poetry Foundation, enters a room, the image that comes to mind is "live wire." Make that "power line,"

since Barr, formerly an investment banker known for structuring complex utility deals, seems to have great energy beneath a cool exterior. His quick smile and striking white hair add to the impression that he doesn't just occupy a room, he commands it.

At least all those electricity metaphors underscore the fact, usually overlooked by reporters at cultural desks, that Barr made his fortune in the business sector whose leading light was Enron. Indeed, Barr was one of the founders of Enron's chief competitor, Dynegy, which followed the leader into complex but questionable utility deals and then into a near-catastrophic tailspin, with its share price falling 95% in 2002. Barr does not himself appear to have participated in any Enron-style looting of consumers, investors, and municipalities. But his ability to surf the waves of energy deregulation, first at Morgan Stanley, then in his "boutique" mergers-and-acquisitions firm Barr Devlin, does testify to an apparent love for the game of privatizing public resources, minimizing citizen oversight of decisions that affect them, and exporting the laissez-faire model abroad. "I think poets should be imperialists," Barr once told an interviewer, "I think they should be importers; I think they should be exploiters of external experience, without apology. I don't see that kind of thinking very often in the poetry world."[1]

Are the skills that allow one to extract profits from a newly deregulated field also useful in the world of poetry? Does the argot of mergers and acquisitions have any purchase in the thickly populated and relatively decentralized territory of twenty-first-century verse? It takes but a small feat of metaphorical imagination to get to yes. And it is here that the MBA poets, like Gioia and Barr, have shown some flashes of brilliance largely absent from their poems. For when they cast a cold eye over the poetry industry, over the toilers who staff the increasingly routinized creative-writing programs, churning out two or three thousand MFAs in poetry per annum, they see a market in need of shaking up.

In "Can Poetry Matter?," the 1991 blueprint for deregulating poetry that Gioia took with him to the NEA, Gioia castigates the artificially propped-up institutional market for poems: "Like subsidized farming that grows food no one wants, a poetry industry has been created to serve the interests of the producers and not the consumers." And just as David Horowitz enlists the language of civil rights in his struggle to end college campus discrimination against God-fearing white kids, Gioia swipes a page from the opposition by converting anti-academicism—usually the weapon of bohemians, avant-gardists, and other writers from the social margins—to his own purposes. He even cites Karl Marx as his authority for the following nugget of class-conscious analysis: "In poetry's case [...] socioeconomic changes have led to a divided literary culture: the superabundance of poetry within a small class and the impoverishment outside it. One might even say that outside the class-room—where society demands that the two groups interact—poets and the common reader are no longer on speaking terms."

Over at the Poetry Foundation, Barr parrots Gioia's critique of academia, backing it up with some hands-on experience that may prove even more important than his familiarity with deregulation: Back in 1994, when serving as chairman of Bennington College's board of trustees, Barr drove through a plan to eliminate tenure at that institution and to fire two dozen full-time faculty members who had previously enjoyed the protection of it. The censure his actions brought upon the college from the American Association of University Professors seems neither to bother Barr, nor to be remembered by those who profile him in the media. But as an example of his contempt for the professoriat, and as a taste of the designs he may have on academia, where a modicum of autonomy from market forces can still be found, the Bennington purge speaks volumes.

The deregulation of Bennington was carried out under the guise of fiscal necessity, but to lend it legitimacy a pedagogical "philosophy" was concocted as well. So while they crushed faculty governance structures, Barr and Co. also floated the slogan that instructors should henceforth "practice what they teach," meaning that those who worked with mediated knowledge (an art historian, for instance, rather than a studio artist, or a literary scholar who refrained from writing novels) were non-productive parasites who deserved their pink slips. A similar view informs Barr's view of the poetry world. In interviews, he speaks eagerly of the "hothouse" feel of much contemporary poetry, and of his desire to toss a brick through the glass. "There is great poetry being written in the academy," he told Kevin Larimer of *Poets & Writers*, "but we might get a broader experience base in poetry if people did things other than write and teach." Need a concrete example?

Here is Barr's favorite: "Ernest Hemingway. In 1933 he took his first safari [...] he shot lions and went home and wrote about it[...]. I don't know a lot of poets who do that."

Poetics of the Backlash

The distinctive project shared by Gioia at the NEA, Barr at the Poetry Foundation, and their partner in several recent projects, Ted Kooser, a former Nebraska insurance underwriter who became U.S. Poet Laureate in 2004, can be summarized rather simply: to deny, disrupt, and discredit existing networks of poetry production, which are seen as pathetically small, disgustingly smug, and—like subsidized farming—crypto-socialist, and to restore to his rightful place of preeminence the reader, referred to alternately as "common" or "general," who validates good poetry by actually paying for it on the open market and who never did have much use for the linguistic shenanigans of modernism and its successors. As Barr puts it: "by growing the universe of readers who will buy books of poetry, the Foundation hopes to bring economic as well as artistic life to the business of writing poetry."

The assertion upon which the whole program rests—namely that poetry has somehow shrunk to become the exclusive property of the same latté-sated, wind-surfing, advanced-degree-holding snobs who voted for Kerry—is a fabrication so flimsy as to border on hallucination. But the hallucination is expressive. What it says is that Gioia, Barr, and Kooser, not to mention the folks at the *Washington Times*, *Weekly Standard*, and *New Criterion* who celebrate the poetic regime change, all very much wish that the large and diverse audience for poetry that manifestly does exist today would disappear, so that it could be replaced with a more docile and homogeneous one of their own choosing.

Just imagine. Gone would be the many poets and readers of poetry who relished the explosive growth and democratization of the art in the Sixties, a decade that rekindled a longstanding alliance between poetry and social progress after it had been smothered by Cold War academics. Forgotten would be the advent first of mimeograph magazines, then xerox ones, then web-based ones, which have irrevocably decentralized the world of poetry by taking the power of publication out of the hands of a few authoritative editors and presses and giving it directly to poets themselves, who often choose gift economies over profit-driven ones as they weave together strands of an alternative—and sometimes quite radicalized—form of communication in sharp contrast to the uncritical monopoly media. All traces of the social movements that made such vigorous use of poetry to articulate their aspirations and their anger would be erased: gone the feminists, gone the gay writers and readers, gone the advocates of civil rights and multiculturalism. Gone, finally, and most satisfyingly, the cities—New York and Brooklyn, San Francisco and Berkeley, Chicago, Boston, Atlanta, Los Angeles, Detroit—unpredictable points of contact and collision that inspire vernacular poetries, cosmopolitan avant-garde poetries, and everything in between.

And what is the market force previously and unjustly neglected by the nation's literati, that vast untapped dynamo of poetic renewal envisioned by verse's self-appointed deregulators? Is it the barn and tractor set, as Kooser sometimes suggests? The recently bereaved or betrothed, desperate for a serviceable sentiment? The grandchildren of Nixon's silent majority, with a craving for rhymed quatrains? John Barr worries that "commuters, travelers in hotel rooms who would love to see an anthology at night, airplane travelers," are not getting their daily verse. The deepest desire of our businessmen poets, it seems, is for a twentieth-first century poetry reader who has been resurrected directly from the nineteenth, a Lazarus innocent of Ezra Pound, a Rip van Winkle whose eyes open on the same page of Longfellow he'd been reading before dozing off, a sleeping beauty unacquainted with the temptations of Gertrude Stein.

And Deliver Us from Modernism

After a year of quiet deliberation and strategic planning, the Poetry Foundation began in the spring of 2005 to publicize the uses to which it will put Ruth Lilly's millions. Naturally there will be a website. And henceforth poets will receive $6 a line rather than $2 for publishing in the redesigned pages of *Poetry*. Some new prizes have been concocted: one for a neglected master, one for humor, one for a slow starter who publishes his or her first volume after the age of fifty. Of course there will also be a poll—perhaps, more accurately, a market survey—to determine American attitudes toward poetry (Barr predicted to the *New York Times* that it would be "a major reality check" that should "tell us exactly what's going on out there").

There are also two collaborative projects underway, one with poet-laureate Kooser, the other with "kindred spirit" Dana Gioia. Both express a yearning for the pre-modernist nineteenth century, when verse flourished in newspapers, as Kooser will strive to make it do again; and when school children were force-fed poems for memorization and recitation, as Gioia wishes them again to do in national "recitation bees" judged on the four criteria of accuracy, eye contact, volume, and understanding of the poem.

Despite the sporadic, half-hearted attempts he makes to seem open to poetry's "exploratory" or experimental side, it is clear that what John Barr loves best are poems he can "parse," poems that, as he puts it, "go from A to B to C" and continue "a tradition that has existed for hundreds of years" that he calls "the poetry of the rational or the didactic." So it is no surprise that these are just the kind of poems that Ted Kooser has good-naturedly offered to deliver in free weekly installments to editors of some 40,000 mid-sized and rural newspapers across the country, with a dedicated website built and operated by the Poetry Foundation for further dissemination of Kooser's "product."

In introducing his newspaper column, "American Life in Poetry," Kooser likes to emphasize the home states of the versifiers he has chosen: there are South Dakota poets and Kentucky poets and Minnesota poets and Nebraska poets and Ohio poets and Washington state poets and Illinois poets and Texas poets. And he tries to connect with his readership through earnest opening gambits like: "Perhaps your family passes on the names of loved ones to subsequent generations." He keeps the poems ultra brief and relentlessly "accessible," favoring inconspicuous free-verse narratives with one or two rhymed things thrown in for fun. It is never hard to "parse" them, true, but it is also hard to imagine getting interested in or excited by them either.

Here's how a glum four months of Kooser's column parses out: A speaker observes an alienated couple as they dourly squirt Windex at each other's faces from opposite sides of a pane they're cleaning. A speaker assists minimally in the burial of an acquaintance. A speaker recalls buying red shoes for a woman who hasn't been seen since. A speaker feels remorse for having a crippled piglet put down. A speaker observes a neighbor hauling bales to his barn as autumn descends. A speaker employs end rhyme to convince himself to give up booze. Biting into a potato, a speaker recalls his impoverished childhood. A speaker is reminded by moonflowers of her recently deceased mother. A speaker contemplates an elderly veteran in a parade. A speaker celebrates the arrival of spring. A speaker observes as a male peacock's ostentatious display fails to interest a female intent on food. A speaker named after his grandfather feels his forebear's presence while filling out forms and at supper. A tamed speaker recalls his youthful virility on the eve of his fortieth birthday. A speaker likens an elderly neighbor in a housecoat to a sunset. A speaker contemplates the life of an obsessive collector of Noah's Ark images and trinkets. A speaker likens love to salt.

Barr likes to say that "poetry's golden age will come when it is in front of a general audience." But no Midas could transform this meager stuff into good poetry. This is not because the poems Kooser selects are populist in intention. It is because they are almost entirely devoid of verbal wit, cognitive surprise, or strong passions. And if the businessmen poets think they will widen the market share for their products, perhaps it is time to reconsider just how much worldly savoir-faire they in fact possess: such poems barely compete for attention with a paleolithic comic strip like "Beetle Bailey," let alone Def Poetry Jam or the latest Clear Channel megahit. As for literary competence, Barr admits:

> I think that if I had been a subscriber to *Poetry* magazine in 1912, when it was founded, and Harriet Monroe picked poems by the unknown poets, T.S. Eliot, Ezra Pound, and others, I would not have understood them, and I wouldn't have known that they were to become known, a century later, as the great modern poets. I am a little bit humble about recognizing the next great talent when it shows up.

The next great talent in American poetry would be lucky not to be recognized by Barr and his friends at the NEA and Library of Congress, for there's no telling whether he or she would survive the attack this novum-phobic crew would no doubt launch in the name of rational didacticism and the beleaguered general reader. With hundreds of millions of private and federal dollars now at their disposal, the businessmen poets are positioned to administer serious damage to one of the liveliest, most democratized, and brilliantly articulate art forms in America. But it is doubtful that their curious amalgam of economic elitism, drowsy formalism, and right-wing populism will prove a match for the Whitmanic tradition of radical democracy, fearless formal investigation, and do-it-yourself ingenuity that has produced most of the country's greatest poetry. While the Poetry Foundation prescribes its Prozac poems to reluctant readers, the wide-awake poetry of the present can be expected to be everywhere otherwise occupied.

➤

The Task of Poetics, the Fate of Innovation, and the Aesthetics of Criticism

Charles Bernstein

Imagine poetry as a series of terraces, some vast, some no bigger than a pinprick, overlooking the city of language. The sound and light show begins in the dark: sentences dart by, one by one, forming wave after wave of the rag and boneshop of the quotidian, events passing before our eyes like the faint glimmer of consciousness in an alcoholic stupor. Facts, facts everywhere but not a drop to drink.

Language is an event of the world, just as, for language users, the world is an event of language. Even the world is a word.

All the signs say no passage; still, there must be a way.

To practice poetics is to acknowledge the inevitability of metaphor, the linguisticality of perception, the boundedness of thought, the passion of ideas, the beauty of error, the chains of logic, the possibilities of intuition, and the uncanny delight of chance. In contrast to the syllogistic rationality of expository writing, poetics is situational, shifts with the winds, courts contradiction, feeds on inconsistency.

I embrace a poetics of bewilderment. I don't know where I am going and never have, just try to grapple as best as I can with where I am. The poetry that most engages me is not theoretically perspicacious, indeed it has a poetics and an aesthetics but not a predetermining theory; it is multiform and chaotic, always reformulating and regrouping. Competence is less important to me than responsiveness; mobility, ingenuity and invention more important than solutions to predefined problems.

Alexandar Becanovic, the editor of *Monitor*, a Montenegrin journal, recently asked me (thinking of US poetry): "Can you find, in the massive plurality of recent American poetry, common reference points? Is there, in that 'cacophony,' some kind of harmony?"—It is always possible to find points in common just as it is always possible to find differences. As to the points in common, the question for American poetry—and it has been a question for a long time—is what are the terms of the common? Emerson imagines an America that is in process, where the commonness is an aspiration, not something that is a given social fact. Langston Hughes says we are a "people in transition." The "point" is not to hurry through this *going* because we never arrive. *Get used to it!* Perhaps this is what we have in common, the particularities that we cultivate within the same space: our simultaneous presence to, and difference from, one another. I worry that harmony would be too close to homogeneity. I go for a microtonal tuning where the music is discovered in the process of active (maybe activist?) listening, not given to, predetermined by, idealized scales. The sirens screeching in the night to take away the dead or wounded interrupt our quiet, refined mediations. I want a poetry that incorporates those interruptions without losing its own newly foundering rhythms.

Particulars and their constellation: mosaic, seriality. Imagination of the negotiation of democratic social space: the particular not consumed, not made into an abstraction nor into stone, not dominated.

Morality vs. aesthetics: I don't want to make poems that tell you what to think but that show a different order of thinking.

Fragments not as discontinuous but as overlays, pleats, folds: a chordal poetics in which synchronic notes meld into diachronic tones.

One of the two most important lessons of poetics is that the contemporary practice of poetry informs all readings of poetry. Poetry begins in the present moment and moves backwards and forwards from there. With no orientation in contemporary poetry and poetics, we remain ungrounded, as readers or as scholars, without a direct connection to how works of literature are engendered in our own time. Without this knowledge, it will be all the harder to understand the relation of older works to their own times or to ours, or, for that matter, future works to the times yet to come. The absence of this visceral connection to poetic practice may be disguised by the demeanor of disinterested or clinical professionalism, but it will be betrayed in the body of the text of any scholarship produced.

The second fundamental lesson of poetics is that literary works do not exist only, or even primarily, on the page. Alphabetic writing in books remains the dominant medium for poetry in our time, as it has over the past many hundreds of years; but there was poetry and poetics before the invention of the alphabet, just as new poetries and new poetics will emerge from our post-alphabetic environment of digital and electronic language reproduction. Indeed, the *now*, as well as the archive of poetry, is more likely to be found on the web than in books. Modern reproduction technologies have also made available recordings of poets reading their work. These recordings, together with live performances, are a crucial part of any critical or scholarly approach to poetry over the past 100 years.

New poetry is being created and performed every day. All scholarship in poetry occurs against this backdrop. Poetry readings and poetry on the web are directly relevant to literary scholarship of any type and of all periods. In this sense, poetry and poetics, as I am imagining them here, are a core value of the literary academy. The ongoing creation of new poetics offers us a glimpse into how literature is made in response to ever-changing conditions. And it offers us a chance not to just observe the unfolding story but to change it.

In making this defense of poetics, I want to revisit the problem of innovation, since poetics and innovation are the Scylla and Charybdis, or possibly Mutt and Jeff, or then again dog and bone, or possibly singer and song or is it doctor and patient, or inner and outer or hook, line, and sinker, of the politics of poetic form.

Radical formal innovation in modernist and contemporary art has, at times, been seen as undermining the aesthetic, but it is more accurate to say that such work reinvents the aesthetic for new readers and new contexts. While modernist art remains a crucial site for any consideration of the aesthetics of poetic invention, I want to ground the discussion in the vicinities of the immediate present, where innovation, the new, ingenuity, and originality, perhaps even more than the aesthetic, are vexed terms, jinxed, perhaps ironically, by their own historical weight.

American Official Verse Culture operates on the premise that innovation and originality are not criteria of aesthetic value, and while not an absolute barrier to quality, are something to be held against a work, as if there were something unpleasantly immodest about any poetry that trades in the untried, something that smacks of elitism or arrogance or vulgarity. This attitude, while relatively easy to ridicule, has deeper roots than might be apparent on first blush (the blush that comes over the check after the first few slaps).

Innovation is not so much an aesthetic value as an aesthetic necessity. Nevertheless, I understand full well the great suspicion with which claims to innovation and originality are now held. Indeed, there is, at present, an enormous circumspection about the necessity of the new, even among many whose work is fresh and adventurous. Some of this suspicion a justified response to progressivist ideas in modernism (and modernization) that value the new over any other aesthetic quality, with the concomitant beliefs that the new replaces the old or that the new is better than the old. Too often claims for innovation seem to mime the marketing (and generational) imperative for "new and improved" (cultural) products. But such claims fail to recognize that poetic innovation is not necessarily related to improvement; at its most engaged, it is a means of keeping up with the present, grappling with the contemporary. We have to constantly reinvent our forms and vocabularies so that we don't lose touch with ourselves and the world we live in. The need for change in art is prompted by changes in the social and economic environment. The responses of the past are not always able to engage the present.

But such arguments for aesthetic innovation too often fall on deafened ears. For example, it is now fashionable to attack innovative poetry as frivolous, as the product of privileged individuals who do not have to face the harshest realities of poverty, war, or social injustice. This attitude, while often morally motivated, is aesthetically and ethically treacherous. For one thing, it risks denying the extraordinary innovations made by poets in the grip of just these harsh realities, without which the poetries of the Americas, for example, could not have developed as dynamically as they have. More accurate would be to say that innovation comes as response to the human crisis: innovation is the mark of rethinking, trying to break out of the obsessive repetition-compulsion that we see all around us, whether in an individual or a family, or politically (in the conflict between states or groups). The idea that innovation is a luxury for the privileged or those who remove themselves from struggle creates an, at best, Romantic, at worst, demagogic nostalgia for the greater authenticity of the experience of the imagined less well-off "other," as if only severe forms of oppression can create "relevant" poetry, as if we are so well off ourselves with so many things to keep us company.

You might say that severe forms of oppression rob a people of its right to poetry—and the crisis for poetry, for the aesthetic, is to create a space for poetry again and again.

For that, anything less than invention falters. Sometimes that faltering can be exquisitely beautiful and sometimes the fall away from faltering can seem crass or crude. But the human need to create anew is no less strong than our desire for lamentation. And even lamentation is not safe from the erosion of our consuming culture; even lamentation must be reinvented lest the dead be mocked and the living become ghost walkers, zombies of the tried and no longer true.

For well over a hundred years, we have been living through a period of aesthetic disruption, which is to say, shifting and readjusting to, reeling and spinning from, the social and technological changes of the long twentieth century. Of course the danger of invention is that your invention fails, it usually fails since most art produces failure no matter its successes. Of course, the risk for invention is that your invention fails; it usually fails, since most art produces failure, no matter its successes. The risk of not inventing is to succeed—at little or nothing.

According to Henry Petroski, in *The Evolution of Useful Things*, his great study of inventions, from paper clips to zippers, form follows not function but failure.[1] According to Petroski, it is the frustration with existing things that produces innovation. I am interested in thinking through how this applies to poetic invention and originality, where the motivation may be less to produce the new than a frustration with aspects of existing work, not just in terms of form or content, but also means of reproduction and distribution. Petroski states his "central idea" succinctly:

> [...] the form of made things is always subject to change in response to their real or perceived shortcomings, their failures to function properly. This principle governs all invention, innovation, and ingenuity; it is what drives all inventors, innovators, and engineers. And there follows a corollary: Since nothing is perfect, and indeed, since

even our ideas of perfection are not static, everything is subject to change over time. There can no such thing as a "perfected" artifact; the future perfect can only be a tense, not a thing (22).

Petroski's engineering perspective is remarkably free of the self-conscious unease that is the occupation hazard of the American poet working against accepted practices. Not surprising, Edgar Poe, in "The Philosophy of Composition" anticipates this peculiarly American struggle both for and against invention and originality along with Petroski's negation of the famous Bauhaus slogan, form follows function:

> My first object (as usual) was originality. The extent to which this has been neglected, in versification, is one of the most unaccountable things in the world. Admitting that there is possibility of variety in mere rhythm, it is still clear that the possible varieties of metre and stanza are absolutely infinite—and yet, for centuries, no man, in verse, has ever done, or ever seemed to think of doing, an original thing. The fact is, originality (unless in minds of very unusual force) is by no means a matter, as some suppose, of impulse or intuition. In general, to be found, it must be elaborately sought, and although a positive merit of the highest class, demands in its attainment less of invention than negation (180-81).

What's needed is a transvaluation of the concept of innovation, so that we can think of innovation in a modest and local way, as responses to historical and contemporary particulars—as situational not universal. More like the weather—and one's everyday adaptation to it—than like the forward march of scientific knowledge. Very often innovations comes in reaction to a sense of the perceived failure of the art work that precedes it (no matter how innovative it may appear to be). That sense of perceived failure creates a space for the new in the sense of the now. And it may often look like a swerve away from the innovations of the past, which, quicker than a wink, seem historical, fossilized. Innovation is a constant process of invention in the face of the given. From the outside, some of the innovations may seem very minor or technical, but in poetry the minor is the major and the major is often a bit tedious, like the windbag that keeps bellowing even after the air conditioning has been installed. Sometimes, the best thing you can do is stall, bunt, pass, loop, dodge, or just sit down and take a load off your feet.

I am particularly interested in the ways that inventive poetries can be disruptive not only to forms of poems but also to reading habits, audiences, and distribution systems. And how a poetics of invention can be seen in contrast to a poetics of refinement—not one better than the other, but one with radically different aesthetic and social concerns in a given point in time.

I am interested, that is, in what business theorist Clayton Christiansen calls "the innovator's dilemma." In literary terms (my own highly contentious translation of Christensen's theory), the dilemma has to do with the desire of some practitioners to produce refined and improved works based on the perceived expectation of the "best" readers, what Christensen calls the "sustaining" approach. The alternative model is to abandon the needs of these "best" readers and produce works that are disruptive of perceived ideas of quality, understood in terms of refinement (one might also speak of skillfulness, craft, fluency). That alternative may require finding new readers, as Whitman insists, or having no readers, as Dickinson found. In any case, if the art form changes, then that which was out of it, impossible to read, may end up somewhere quite else, though where this elsewhere is I have a hard time saying.

Poetic innovations are often noisy, messy, disruptive, disorienting. They do not form a neat line with the innovations of the past but often seem to swerve from a progressivist course. This may because they are reconceiving not only the nature of the poem but reconstituting the audience for the poem, reevaluating the contexts that gives the poem not only its meaning but its social force. On this model, you can contrast disruptive innovation with refinement. Very often the refined work that comes after disruptive innovations is "better" than the originals but may lack some of the initial energy. These movements toward refinement take place historically but you can also see it in a single poet's work, say the difference between early and late Eliot, or early and late Ginsberg for that matter. Still, it's important not to confuse the refinement of initially disruptive innovation as innovation while losing sight of actually existing innovation because it doesn't look like you think it "should."

After all my own motto is still, "should never say should," should you?

I realize I may appear to be valuing innovation over refinement, or at least registering my sense of how important inventiveness and indeed ingenuity has been for American poetry in the past century. But I want to suggest that the innovations of American poetry have not necessarily been toward improvement but, in contrast, have worked to disrupt the ascent of an American poetry of refinement and assimilation. At the same time, I want to flag the danger of morally coding either end of this spectrum of disruption or refinement. Great works certainly exist in both modalities, and bad ones too, nor can the modalities always be differentiated. I am talking relative direction not absolute qualities.

Inventive poetries, each in their own way, often very explicitly, abandon models for refining and improving poetry, of meeting the expectations of existing poetry audiences with more beautifully articulated poems that consolidate the innovations of the prior generations. They resist assimilation. Such poetries may be willing to discard the existing poetry audience by creating works—and imagining alternative poetic lineages—that call into being new kinds of language reproduction technologies, new constellations of readers, new methods of reading, and new methods of distribution: by reconstituting the field. As in the business model of innovation, inventive poetry is disruptive of existing values and indeed may appear to be—may actually be—messier, noisier, and cruder than other available poetic works.

Christensen's business model provides a uncomfortably accurate description, especially since discourse about the arts often goes to great lengths to distance itself from market models. Yet categories such as "mainstream" and "fringe" are familiar to both discourses, as is the underlying notion of received historical value. And aren't the poetry products of Official Verse Culture served up to customers expecting a certain kind of product performance that innovative poetries fails to provide, often because the work either doesn't register as poetry or because it lacks (or rejects) expected literary values. In any case, Christensen is a relief from tiresome clichés derived from Peter Bürger's and Renato Poggioli's theories of the avant-garde:

> What all sustaining technologies have in common is that they
> improve performance of established products, along the dimensions

of performance that mainstream customers in major markets have historically valued. [...] Occasionally, however, disruptive technologies emerge: technologies that result in worse product performance, at least in the near-term. Ironically, in each of the instances studied in this book, it was disruptive technology that precipitated the leading firm's failure. Disruptive technologies bring to a market a very different value proposition than had been available previously. Generally, disruptive technologies underperform established products in mainstream markets, But they have other features that a few fringe (and generally new) customers value (xv).

A good recent example of a disruptive and messy new technology is the digitalization of poetry, which is not just reproducing but producing new possibilities for both the art of poetry and the archive of poetry. There has been much fuss made in the press about copyright issues concerning the exchange over the web of digital sound files, but I am far more interested in the implications of mp3 files for poetry, since we are now witnessing a transvaluation in poetry from the printed book to the sound file of an individual poem.

Poetry doesn't improve nor do new modes of poetry replace existing modes; indeed, the new may bring back into play previous and even apparently outmoded styles, forms, contents, and dictions. In insisting on a poetics of invention—invention more than innovation—I am imagining a poetry that is not progressivist or developmental or even evolutionary, not about replacement, not us/them; one that is based more on dissatisfaction with previous inventions than any distinction between new/old, conventional/experimental, mainstream/outsider.

"What's new" can be an oppressive market constraint that stifles poetic work, but it can also be a form of human exchange as when we say to one another "What's new" meaning "What's up" or "What's happening?" What allows for a sense of opening, of a blank page that is not already completely inscribed? The problem here may be the evocation of Emerson, more than Michael Fried or Clement Greenberg or Ron Silliman; but the discourse of the avant-garde is too thick to cut through even with the new electric ideology weeder I bought last week at X-Mart.

The new is never new but we make it new in order to keep it from becoming dead to us. The motto shouldn't be make it new but make it live, but necrophilia surrounds us and we take its stench as the perfume of our hip indifference to art as something that changes in time, shifts against the tides, hollers out in anguish and exasperation at the suffocating banalities that seem to call our name out loud, as if we were written by them.

Are poetry and poetics at odds? Are poetics and scholarship opposing? Is innovation a matter of aesthetics or of applied research?

Several years ago, I went to a talk by Stanley Cavell at a bookstore in New York City, and what happened there may shed some light on this problem. A crowd of perhaps fifty people gathered into the upstairs space of the store to hear the distinguished philosopher talk about Hollywood melodramas of a bygone era. The question period that followed Cavell's initial presentation was characterized by a mix of erudition and over-the-top enthrallment in these films, both by Cavell and the audience members. While I had seen some of the films being discussed, I had only the haziest recall of any of the details being pored over by the group, as if they were a familiar part of a shared culture of those participating—a culture I also shared with them, but had fallen out of, at least to a degree. Toward the end, someone asked Cavell to talk about *Blond Venus* and in the course of his remarks he noted that in the film Marlene Dietrich sings in both a gorilla costume and in a white tuxedo; he said one of the questions the film raised is whether the Dietrich figure can appear in these ways and still be taken for a responsible mother. I heard this question as reflecting on what Cavell himself was doing: Can you do philosophy in a gorilla suit or a white tuxedo and still be responsible to the profession and to the activity of philosophy (not the same thing)?

Stanley Cavell is no guerrilla warrior in the trenches of the canon wars. And his suits, while appearing tailored, tend to be blue or gray. Nonetheless, what counts for him as an activity of philosophy, at least in this instance, is barely recognizable in terms of the ostensive subject matter of his talk. Because what is philosophical about his project is not the content but his mode of thinking, by which I don't mean a set of philosophical issues that he applies to a discussion of the subject, but rather an attitude of inquiry, a manner of listening, a mode of recognizing what is significant and proceeding from there to identifying networks of significance. So the answer to the question Can philosophy still be philosophy if it is performed in a guerrilla suit or a white tuxedo? is that philosophy can only be philosophy if it acknowledges the suits it is wearing and also that these suits are not (only) what are issued to us in central casting but (also) ones that we fashion and refashion ourselves. But is poetics the gorilla suit or the white tuxedo?

As a literary genre, poetics refers to works on the philosophy of composition, from Artistotle's *Poetics* to many contemporary works on the poetics of one thing or another, from scholarship to architecture. Poetics also is the term used for works about poetry written by poets. There is a long and storied history of both kinds of poetics, but this is not to be an account of the history of a literary form, but rather of the significance of poetics for literary scholarship. With that in mind, it is important to note a distinction between literary theory, philosophy, and poetics. Literary theory can be described as the application of philosophical, political, or psychoanalytical principles or methods to the study of literary or cultural works. Theory suggests a predilection for consistency and explanation, and like philosophy, may make take the form of stand-alone arguments. Poetics, in contrast, is provisional, context-dependent, and often contentious. Theory will commonly take a scientific tone, poetics will sometimes go out of its way to seem implausible, to exaggerate, or even to be self-deprecating (since this is a work of poetics, I won't note that poetics can also take a form directly opposite to what I am proposing; like politics, poetics is plural).

In some ways, literary theory, in its many forms, has displaced poetics as a model for scholarship and criticism. Anthologies of literary theory, while often including statements by poets from earlier centuries, largely turn their attention to literary theorists and related philosophers when they come to the 20th century. Perhaps this seems a more sensible choice as models for both scholarship and criticism. Poetics, in this system, becomes another form of poetry—something to be subjected to criticism and analysis, but not the model for the practice of criticism, scholarship, or interpretation that it, nonetheless, continues to be.

I am not trying to trump conservative criticism with special claims for innovative poetry; quite to the contrary. Indeed, any consideration of poetry and poetics needs to focus not just on the aesthetics of art making but also on aesthetics of criticism. For poems can't go it alone and never could, relying, as they so often do, not only on the kindness of strangers but the testimony of friends.

Maybe close reading would get a better rap if we called it *PSI: Poetry Scene Investigation*. Of course, that would mean treating the poem as a crime, but maybe it is: a crime against mass culture in the name of public culture.

Poetry is too important to be left to its own devices.

Interpretation is act, editing a form of writing, translation a condition of reading.

You remember the joke about the difference between the schlemiel and schlemazel: the schlemiel is the one spills the soup; the schlemazel is the one who it gets spilled on. You could say that this is just the difference between the poet and the critic, in my semiotic economy.

"Poetry is too important to be left to its own devices," means that poems can't do all the work of poetry by themselves. For poems to come into being, we need editors, publishers, designers, proofreaders, booksellers, web sites, teachers, critics, detractors, supporters, and of course, not to leave them out of the picture entirely, poets and readers. I think the phobia about explication comes from the fact that some of what calls itself that is obtuse, dishearteningly literal or thematic, in short, deadening. But bad teaching about poetry is a comparable problem to bad writing of poetry; poetry as an art may seem to suffocate under the blankets applied in a well-meaning effort to keep it warm (as if the body of the text was growing as cold as a corpse), but poems go their merry way irrespective and irregardless. Cut-'em up, mangle their meanings, weigh them down with unsupportable symbolism, reduce them to a sentiment, strip them to their empty cores... and they still keep coming back for more. Poems are remarkably resilient, and far less likely to be injured by incursions into their autonomy or excursions into their associations, than we have any reason to expect.

Yet if poems are uncannily resilient, poets, alas, are not.

That is, I don't mean to suggest that criticism is always, or even mostly, agonistic. Close reading is not a contest between poem and reading, but a dance, the two in tango. Moreover, without such external interventions, poetry would, indeed, be a dead art.

The poem is not finished even when it is completed. Completion or publication marks not the end of the poem but rather its entry into the world through the responses to it. For the poems we reread over time become cultural time capsules, linguistic dioramas in which each phrase is an imaginary hyperlink for our further exploration of—or reentry into—a particular time and place. In other words, crucial to any sense of the cultural details in a poem is the world they constitute; not only what the particulars are but also the economy of the particulars—how they are distributed and arranged. Inspiration is not what comes before the poet writes the poem but what happens when the poem is read (or heard).

A criticism is responsible to the degree it is able to respond.

Criticism engages and extends the work of the poem, but criticism is not the end of poetry. Nor is the poem the final destination of a process of analysis and research.

The poem is an initial point of embarkation on journeys yet to come, on earth as they are in the imaginary space between here and there, now and then, is and as.

Everybody talks about the fall of the humanities but few make the effort to get up. In other words, does the past have a future?

There are no core subjects, no core texts in the humanities, and this is the grand democratic vista of our mutual endeavor in arts and letters, the source of our greatest anxiety and our greatest possibilities. In literary studies, it is not enough to show what has been done but also what it is possible to do. Art works are not just monuments of the past but investments in the present, investments we squander with our penurious insistence on taking such works as cultural capital rather than capital expenditure. For the most part, our programs of Great Books amount to little more than lip service to an idea of Culture that is encapsulated into tokens and affixed to curricular charm bracelets to be taken out at parties for display—but never employed in the workings of our present culture. Ideas are dead except in use. And for use you don't need a preset list of ideas or Great Works: almost any will do if enactment not prescription is the aim.

Many of us write and teach works that raise, for many, some of the most basic questions about poetry: What is poetry? How can this work be a poem? How and what does it mean? These are not questions that I always want to talk about nor ones that the works at hand continue to raise for me. Whatever questions I may have of this sort, I have either resolved or put aside as I listen for quite different, much more particular, things. My own familiarity with the poetry I teach puts me at some distance from most students, who are coming to this work for the first time. And yet, when I overcome my resistance and engage in the discussion, which I often find becomes contentious and emotional, I am reminded that when a text is dressed in the costume of poetry, that, in and of itself, is a provocation to consider these basic questions of language, meaning, and art. Inevitably, raising such questions is one of the uses of the poetry to which I am committed; that is, poetry marked by its aversion to conformity, to received ideas, to the expected or mandated or regulated form. These aversions and resistances have their history, they are never entirely novel nor free of traditions, including the traditions of the new; that history is nothing less than literary history. But the point of literary history is not just that a selected sequence of works was created nor that they are enduring or great (or deplorable and hideous) nor that they form a part of a cultural fabric of that time or a tradition that extends to the present. All that is well and good, but aesthetically secondary. The point, that is, is not (*not just*) the transcendental or cultural or historical or ideological or psychoanalytic deduction of a work of art but how that works plays itself out: its performance not (just) its interpretation. But as history is written by the victors, so art (as a matter of professional imperatives) is taught by the explainers.

It needn't be so, for we are professors not deducers: our work is as much to promote as to dispel, to generate as much as document. I am not—I know it sounds like I am—professing the virtue of art over the deadness of criticism but rather the aversion of virtue that is a first principle of the arts and an inherent, if generally discredited, possibility for the humanities.

I suspect part of the problem may be in the way a certain idea of philosophy as critique, rather than art as practice, has been the model for the best defense of the university. I don't say critique as opposed to aesthetics but critique without aesthetics—that is, the sort of institutionalized critique that dominates the American university—is empty, a shell game of Great Books and Big Methods full of solutions and cultural capital, signifying nothing. That is, Professionalized Critique dogs every school of criticism when as a matter of routine (and perhaps against its most radical impulses), it turns art into artifact, asking not what it does but what it means; much as its own methods are, and quicker than a wink, turned from tools to artifacts. Like I told the man at the agency, if you want the guy to talk maybe you need to remove your hand from his throat, even if it looks to you like that's the only thing keeping him upright.

Poetry, and the arts, are living entities in our culture. It is not enough to know the work of a particular moment in history, removed from the context of our contemporary public culture; such knowledge risks being transmitted stillborn. Just as we now insist that literary works need to be read in their socio-historical context, so we must also insist that they be read into the present aesthetic context. So while I lament the lack of cultural and historical information on the part of students, I also lament the often proud illiteracy of contemporary culture on the part of the faculty.

I do not suggest that the (contemporary) practice of poetry should eclipse literary history (as, for a time, the contemporary practice of analytic philosophy eclipsed the history of philosophy). I do believe, however, that literary history or theory uninformed by the newly emerging forms of poetic practice is as problematic as literary criticism or literary history uninformed by contemporary theoretical or method-ological practices.

In a culture that too often derides learning, complexity, and nuance, and where the demand for intelligibility is consistently used as a weapon to suppress unwelcome or difficult ideas, there is no higher aspiration than scholarship. But students caught up in the "major," just as faculty caught up in the "profession," often act as if scholarship requires adherence to a set of norms, either in subject matter or style, that define the field. Consistency of tone, standardization of documen-tation formats, and shopworn modes of analysis are as likely to anaes-thetize a required paper as much as allow entry for the aesthetic. Rewriting may be admirable but not if it means stating a rote idea more clearly: rewriting should add reflection to a paragraph, not strip it of its unresolved thoughts. Felt inconsistency is preferable to mandat-ed rationalization.

To state the obvious: an unorganized (or "differently" organized) essay that suggests active thinking is often more useful in response to a literary work than a paper of impeccable logic that has little to say. I realize that I am setting up a false dichotomy; it is not a question of choosing logic versus thinking but rather understanding the value, and implications, of each. And yet, for the young scholar, the demands of expository normalcy may compete with the demands of poetics. Shall we demand all students be extravagant? No doubt, this would be rash. But shall we continue to demand that all students curb their writing, as if composition were a dog and not a god?

I prize the adventure of learning: scholarship, as much as poetics, not as a predetermined ride to selected port of calls, but an exploration by association, one perception leading to the next, a network of stoppages, detours, reconnaissance. Not double majors with extra requirements and ever more protocols, but multicentered *minors*, connected by peripheral routes, less-traveled passages, hunches.

Art students used to be told that the fundamental requirement for drawing or painting was to accurately render figures. But this confused one modality of representation with the entire process of visual aesthesis. It might have been better to say: *you can't draw if you can't perceive.* Correlatively, we might say, you can't write if you can't think. Scholarship requires poetics.

Paratactic writing, thinking by association, is no less cogent or persuasive than hypotactic exposition, with its demands that one thought be subordinated to the next. Poetics reminds us that the alternate logics of poetry are not suited just for emotion or irrational expression; poetics lies at the foundation of all writing.

Poetry is a name we use to discount what we fear to acknowledge.

The accurate documentation of information used in a work is a vital principle of scholarship. Similarly, scholarship requires a writer to consider challenges to her or his views: but this too often is assumed to mean considering challenges to the content of what is being said while ignoring challenges to the style and form. The importance of poetics for scholarship is not to decree that anything goes but rather to insist that exposition is an insufficient guarantor of reason. Poetics makes scholarly writing harder, not easier: it complicates scholarship with an insistence that the way we write is never neutral, never self-evident.

Clarity in writing is a rhetorical effect not a natural fact. One man's eloquence can be another's poison; one woman's stuttering may be the closest approximation of truth that we will ever know.

Read globally, write locally.

Narrowing down a "field" to one period or one genre or one

method inhibits one of the most important possibilities for scholarship: making connections across these divides. Lots of knowledge about a specific area of interest is admirable and sometimes invaluable, knowledge about lots of different areas is invaluable and sometimes admirable. It is not a question of being eclectic but developing your senses of association.

The greatest benefit of the university is not that it trains students for anything in particular, nor that it imbues in them a particular set of ideas, but that it is a place for open-ended research that can just as well lead nowhere as somewhere, that is wasteful and inefficient by short-term socioeconomic standards but is practically a steal as a long-term research and development investment in democracy, freedom, and creativity—without which we won't have much of an economic future or the one we have won't be worth flesh it's imprinted on.... We cannot make education more efficient without making it more deficient.

The university I envision is more imaginary than actual, for everywhere the tried and sometimes true pushes out the untried but possible.

What I value is not temperance but tolerance, for an insistence on temperance can mark an intolerance not only of the intemperate but also of unconventional—or unassimilated—forms of expression. We don't need to agree—or even converse—so long as we tolerate the possibility of radically different approaches, even to our most cherished ideas of decorum, methodology, rationality, subject matter. The university that I value leaves all of these matters open, undecided—and not just open for debate, but open for multiple practices. The point is not to replace one approach with another but to reorient ourselves toward a kind of inquiry in which there are no final solutions, no universally mandated protocols. The point is not to administer culture but to participate in it.

The arts and sciences of this century have shown that deductive methods of argument—narrow rationalizing—hardly exhaust the full capacity of reason. Induction and discontinuity are slighted only at the cost of slighting reason itself. There is no evidence that the conventional expository prose that is ubiquitous output of the academic profession produces more insights or better research than nonexpository modes. There is no evidence that a tone of austere probity rather than tones that are ironic or raucous furthers the value of teaching or inquiry. It may be true that standard academic prose permits dissident ideas, but ideas mean little if not embodied in material practices and, for those in the academic profession, writing is one of the most fundamental of such practices. Writing is never neutral, never an objective mechanism for the delivery of facts. Therefore the repression of writing practices is a form of suppressing dissidence—even if it is dissidence, I would add, for the sake of dissidence.

So while my attitude to the academic profession is highly critical, I want to insist that one of the primary values such a profession can have results from its constituents challenging authority, questioning conventional rhetorical forms, and remaining restless and quarrelsome and unsatisfied, especially with the bureaucratizing of knowledge that is the inertial force that pulls us together as a profession. Which is to say: *The profession is best when it professionalizes least.* As negative as I am about the rhetorical rigidity of the academic profession, comparison with journalism, corporate communications, or technical writing will show that these other professions police writing styles far more completely than the academic profession. That is why it is vital to raise these issues about rhetorical and pedagogic practices: because universities remain among the few cultural spaces in the North America. in which there is at least a potential for critical discourse, for violation of norms and standards and protocols, in which an horizon of poetics remains possible.

The sociologist C. Wright Mills got this just right when he wrote, "The aim of the college, for the individual student, is to eliminate the need in his life for the college; the task is to help him become a self-educating [person]. For only that will set him free."

My commitment is to public education: the education of the public at large and an education about the public, how it is constituted. What sort of investment are we willing to make in the intellectual and cultural development of our citizens so that we can remain, as a country, innovative, vibrant, socially responsible? How can we prepare ourselves for the unexpected, the difficult, the troubling events that are sure to lie ahead for all of us? Will we spend billions (in the U.S.) for defense while begrudging any money spent on what we are defending? The great experiment in mass education is not even a hundred years old: it has had virtually no downside. That we teeter on abandoning this commitment now is a testament to a smallness, to a lack of generosity, and to a contempt for noncommercial values that can only make us poorer—not only culturally, but economically.

Everybody talks about the crisis in the humanities but nobody takes responsibility for it.

It is often lamented that humanists make a poor case for their values in the face of the powerful claims by those who advocate, on the one hand, invariant, often religiously derived, principles; and those who advocate, on the other, technorationality—the idea that knowledge must be observer-independent and reproducible. I want to propose poetics as the foundation for a realm of values that is neither scientistic nor moralistic.

Poetics is an ethical engagement with the shifting conditions of everyday life. If it is poetic license to contrast ethics, as a dialogic practice of response in civil society, with morality, as a fixed code of conduct and belief, then poetic license I will happily claim.

Poetics is an activity, an informed response to emerging circumstances. As such, it cannot claim the high ground of morality or systematic theory. Poetics is tactical, not strategic. Indeed, it is poetics' lack of strategy, its aversion to the high ground, that often cause it to appear weak or confused or inconsistent or relativistic.

Yet, in the struggle between ethics and morality, ethics has the advantage even when it appears to be wandering in the wilderness. But this advantage is too rarely taken advantage of. What is needed is a *poetics of poetics*; that is, a defense of the ethical grounding of poetics. A poetics of poetics would allow for a greater self-awareness of the history and value of poetics. In that sense, my approach is closely related to what George Lakoff argues in *Moral Politics*: that we must be as strong in our advocacy of our values—what he calls the values of nurturing parents—as the moralists are for their values, what Lakoff calls the values of the strict father.

A poetics of poetics refutes the charge of relativism, just as a philosophy of aesthetic judgment refutes the idea that tastes are merely personal. Indeed, a poetics of poetics makes the cases that value judgments are better when they take into account multiple, and often competing, factors and refuse the simple solution of pre-existing rule.

It is not the poets born in North America that are native to our poetry, but the ones who came here, in exile, and made America their home; for exile is a native, indeed founding, experience for North American poetry.

Speak truth to truth.

I want a visceral poetics that articulates the value of the particular over and against the rule of the universal, that refuses to sacrifice the local in the name of the national or corporate, that is dialectical rather than monologic, situational rather than objective, and that prizes knowing and truthfulness more than knowledge and truth.

I want a social poetics that is embodied rather than neutral, that actively acknowledges context-dependence as a counter to the appearance of objectivity. Social poetics, like what Kenneth Burke calls "sociological criticism," begins with a conception of the poem as an action to be read in relation to its social motivation, not its intention. The motive or design is the underlying reason for a work to come into being in the world, its orientation or trajectory; in contrast, intention is the calculated effect of style and technique. Social poetics acknowledges the agency of a work of art, not simply its historicity, where agency is recognized in the works response to particular conditions.

How can such aesthetic or poetic readings be accomplished? So much literary training directs us toward the themes and content of a work, as if they are synonymous with the meaning, that we have almost come to believe, against ourselves, that all the rest is window dressing. Perhaps we've lost the hang for listening; perhaps we just don't hang in long enough. Perhaps we've lost the hankering.

But maybe it is just a matter of practice.

The aim of a course in poetics is not the memorization of facts but the engagement with works: and not so much the themes of work but their material emanations as sound and form.

The invention of which I speak underlies the practice of both poetry and poetics, scholarship and criticism. Such invention is not a matter of choice, not one among many possibilities, but a necessary probe of perception for grappling not only with things as they are but also things as they might be. For that task, words such as "innovation" and "invention" may be inadequate; perhaps better to invoke the aesthetic force of *no*: a resistance to the given state of things as not working or not working right or not working anymore. That doubt, that refusal—

a refusal especially of innovation—may be the mark of any such endeavor so conceived and so dedicated.

As blank may be its space.

Imagine poetry as a series of terraces, some vast, some no bigger than a pinprick, overlooking the city of language. The sound and light show begins in the dark: sentences dart by, one by one, forming wave after wave of the rag and boneshop of the quotidian, events passing before our eyes like the faint glimmer of consciousness in an alcoholic stupor. Facts, facts everywhere but not a drop to drink.

Now it is dawn, now night, now noon, now morning. It's as if the day never ends, it just keeps coming back for more.

Language is an event of the world, just as, for language users, the world is an event of language. Even the world is a word.

All the signs say no passage; still, there must be a way.

➤

Innovation and "Improbable Evidence"
Jed Rasula

> Now I'm talking about epic
> as Voice. and as
> disobedience. For
> example I have disobeyed his chart, or is it
> charter—Your, Yours, Yours.
> Your idea of how I'm supposed to write.
> (Alice Notley, *Disobedience* 224)

Innovation: a term I prefer to the more common application of "experimental" to any work that doesn't appear strictly conformist. Innovation is not altogether volitional; innovation in poetry can be circumstantial. But, in an American context suffused with a hunger for old world monuments, appreciating and even recognizing innovation has been difficult. The bounty of 1975—an auspicious year when the fruits of innovation were at a peak yet went unacknowledged—seems to have required a quarter century to meet with comparable abundance. The present profusion is evident in a short list of singular books published in 2001: *The Veil* and *The Pretext* by Rae Armantrout; *Lip Service* by Bruce Andrews; *The Downstream Extremity of the Isle of Swans* and *Louise in Love* by Mary Jo Bang; *With Strings* by Charles Bernstein; *Eunoia* by Christian Bök; *Radio, Radio* by Ben Doyle; *The Mercy Seat* by Norman Dubie; *Drafts 1-38, Toll* by Rachel Blau DuPlessis; *The Gauguin Answer Sheet* by Dennis Finnell; *Felt* by Alice Fulton; *Torn Awake* by Forrest Gander; *How to Do Things with Tears* by Allen Grossman; *A Border Comedy* by Lyn Hejinian; *Cascadia* by Brenda Hillman; *Notes on the Possibilities and Attractions of Existence* by Anselm Hollo; *Ring of Fire* by Lisa Jarnot; *Poasis* by Pierre Joris; *Again* by Joanne Kyger; *If in Time* by

Ann Lauterbach; *Seven Pages Missing* by Steve McCaffery; *Disobedience* by Alice Notley; *Airs, Waters, Places* by Bin Ramke; *Plot* by Claudia Rankine; *Fox* by Adrienne Rich; *The Weather* by Lisa Robertson; *Nova* by Standard Schaefer; *Earliest Worlds* by Eleni Sikelianos; *Fuck You— Aloha—I Love You* by Juliana Spahr; *Such Rich Hour* and *Oh* by Cole Swensen; *Self and Simulacra* by Liz Waldner; *To Repel Ghosts* by Kevin Young.[1] The alphabetic order accents the eclecticism, a reminder that traditional points of orientation and affinity have eroded dramatically in recent decades. Half of these authors are women, a fact requiring no special representational effort; many of these books are distinctly innovative, though their authors are not regarded as "experimental"; and as for the publishers—trade, university press, and alternative— there is no particular evident aesthetic disposition by which one might sort out the titles from conservative to radical as a way of determining publisher. Nor do they conform to standardized presentational models: six of the books are "selected poems," yet *Selected Poems* is not a title any of the authors have chosen. Twelve of the books are long poems or sequences, five of which are between two hundred and four hundred pages (and, I might add, making the most of their length). Of the remaining titles, the poems are so focally consistent that even some of them attain the feel of book length projects. Collectively, these works incarnate Lyn Hejinian's sense that "The daring statement unites us":

> A paradox
> A parody
> The paradise of comedy
> The imperative that permits
> It says that everything may make do
>   (Hejinian 211)

The originary scene of my ruminations, 1975, was another matter altogether. As background: the volatility of the sixties continued into the early seventies; within a short time the war in Vietnam was abandoned and Nixon driven from the White House; Allen Ginsberg's chronicle of the public debacle of the 1960s, *The Fall of America* was published in 1973; and the next year Gary Snyder's *Turtle Island* appeared, not only a book of poetry but a pledge of ecological and political allegiance which auspiciously won the Pulitzer Prize. 1975 was a momentous year in American poetry, consolidating the whole post-war period, it seemed, in the following publications: *The Collected Books of Jack Spicer*; the third volume of Charles Olson's *The Maximus Poems*; the final installment of Louis Zukofsky's lifework, *"A" 22-23* (*"A" 24* having previously appeared); George Oppen's *Collected Poems*; Edward Dorn's *Collected Poems 1956-1974* and his long poem *Gunslinger*; Robert Kelly's even longer poem *The Loom*; and John Ashbery's *Self-Portrait in a Convex Mirror*. The list should suggest that I had great respect for demanding books. There's not a bagatelle in sight. I was also attentive to a number of other books published the same year, like Anne Waldman's *Fast Speaking Woman*, and three book length projects: Charles Reznikoff's *Holocaust*; Nathaniel Tarn's *Lyrics for the Bride of God*; and Paul Blackburn's *The Journals*. The large Ethnopoetics conference in Milwaukee that spring helped consolidate a certain tribal aspiration: Tarn and Snyder were prominent; Rothenberg was at the center of it all (*Poland/1931* had appeared the previous year, and New Directions reprinted the Dial Press selected poems, *Poems for the Game of Silence*, in 1975); Antin's sharp intelligence was much in evidence, and his groundbreaking talk poems were being prepared for publication as *Talking at the Boundaries* (1976); Eshleman wasn't in attendance, but he was of the clan (*The Gull Wall* was another 1975 title), having provided a primary forum for alternative poetries in *Caterpillar* from 1967-1972. It was in *Caterpillar* that I first encountered Ron Silliman, Rae Armantrout, and Michael Palmer. (It would be a few years before I took note of *The Maintains* [1974] and *Polaroid* [1975] by Palmer's friend Clark Coolidge). There were scintillating books coming out of Canada, like Christopher Dewdney's *Fovea Centralis*, Steve McCaffery's *Ow's Waif*, and periodic installments of an immense poem by bp Nichol called *The Martyrology*. While I didn't see them at the time, by 1975 there were books or chapbooks out by Ron Silliman, Charles Bernstein, Bruce Andrews, Ray DiPalma, Bob Perelman, and Barrett Watten. There's more I could mention, but the point is that the achievement *and* the potential of adventurous poetry was conspicuous. These were bodies of work that said: Sit up and take stock, Proceed with caution (*and* Be bold and irreverent). The historical sense they imposed was considerable.

But apparently not enough. I can't say I was all that well informed about the poetry establishment in 1975, though I recognized the look of slick but inconsequential books that kept appearing on library and bookstore shelves, invariably published by East Coast trade houses that clearly had bigger fish to fry; their poetry books looked decorative, as if their proper element was a furniture showroom. I was in Indiana, having previously lived in Europe, so I hadn't developed distinct partisan coordinates. I remember reading Ammons, Lowell, Dorn and Duncan with equal enthusiasm. 1975 changed all that, as I naively expected some kind of public celebration of these eye-opening books by Spicer, Zukofsky and the others. It didn't happen. It was weirdly gratifying when Ashbery's book took the Pulitzer, the National Book Award, *and* the National Book Critics Circle Award. *But but but. . . .* didn't anyone notice the others, I wondered. "Notice" is too gentle a word: they were scorned with an air of implacable indifference. Nothing promotes theoretical reflection and self-examination like discovering the poetry you esteem is anathema to the rest of the world.

In hindsight, 1975 marks the decisive ascendancy of enfranchised writing programs, a world in which Columbia MFA graduate Gregory Orr was the latest *wunderkind*, *Burning the Empty Nests* having appeared when he was only 25, followed shortly by *Gathering the Bones Together* (1975). The Yale Younger Poets prizewinners of the time were Iowa MFA graduates Michael Ryan (*Threats Instead of Trees*, 1974) and Maura Stanton (*Snow on Snow*, 1975), followed by Carolyn Forché's *Gathering the Tribes* in 1976, a year that saw first books by other Iowa alumni Ellen Bryan Voigt (*Claiming Kin*) and David St. John (*Hush*). Another emerging reputation in the workshop world was Dave Smith, casting a wide net with *Mean Rufus Throw Down* (1973), *The Fisherman's Whore* (1974), and *Cumberland Station* (1977). Other 1975 publications include *The House on Marshland* by Louise Glück, *In the Dead of the Night* by Norman Dubie, *Bloodlines* by Charles Wright, and Robert Pinsky's *Sadness and Happiness*. Michael S. Harper was emerging as a black alternative to Don L. Lee and Amiri Baraka. His 1975 title *Nightmare Begins Responsibility* was flanked by *Debridement* (1973) and *Images of Kin: New and Selected Poems* (1977). Marilyn Hacker made an impact with *Presentation Piece* (1974, National Book Award 1975) and *Separations* (1976).

My 1996 book *The American Poetry Wax Museum* can be read as an attempt to make sense of how that perplexing moment came to pass. It's only in retrospect, of course, that these were harbingers of hegemonic forces to come. In general, the world of mid-seventies poetry was dominated by figures of long and secure standing in the establishment, a prizewinning cadre some of whom were gathering big heads of publishing steam. The septegenarian Robert Penn Warren was suddenly liberated into unprecedented productivity, while Robert Lowell famously published three books in 1973 (*The Dolphin, History*, and *For Lizzie and Harriet*), with a *Selected Poems* appearing the year before his untimely death in 1977. Anne Sexton's suicide was followed by nearly annual posthumous collections (four between 1974 and 1978). The closely set and continuously printed work of A. R. Ammons' *Collected Poems 1951-1971* (1972) filled nearly 400 pages; but hard on its heels came *Sphere* (1974), *Diversifications* (1975) and *The Snow Poems* (1977), doubling the total. James Merrill's ouija board epic *The Changing Light at Sandover* was furtively premiered in *Divine Comedies* (1976) before swelling to 560 pages by the end of the decade. And what would the seventies have been without the influential regionalism of Stafford, Hugo, James Wright? They all published regularly throughout the decade, along with Howard, Hollander, Feldman, Levine, Lorde, McPherson, Merwin, Moss, Rich, Strand, Simic, and Wagoner. Such abundance wasn't confined to the establishment. Creeley and Levertov published prodigiously; the Black Sparrow poets seemed to be laboring under a productivity quota (Kelly, Eshleman, Meltzer, Wakoski— though she had several trade publishers in hand as well); there were some very long poems by Frank Samperi and Theodore Enslin; and of course there was that human rival to the Los Angeles flood basin, Charles Bukowski.

The attention deficit disorder institutionalized in the poetry world is something I've addressed at length in *The American Poetry Wax Museum* and needn't reiterate here. My aspiration was to shame scholars (if not poets themselves) into a more informed approach to contemporary poetry. Even as I wrote it, however, I sensed that I was writing an epitaph. No doubt the inside moves of careerism are the same as ever— possibly more so—but the bifurcation of the poetry world into square versus hip, official versus renegade, metropolitan versus provincial, was rapidly eroding. In what follows I offer some reflections on the 1990s, a remarkably invigorating decade for American poetry.[2]

Remember the slogan that worked wonders for Bill Clinton's 1992 presidential campaign? "It's the economy, stupid." Substitute *women* for *economy* and you've got the new world of American poetry. This is far and away the most important transformation, and it's one that will continue to erode old protocols and refashion institutions in unforeseeable ways (the only thing that's predictable, I think, is that the changes will be for the better). A familiar air of elitist masculine privilege has long dominated institutions like the Academy of American Poets. The old boys network will, in time, subside to mortality; but even before then it faces certain demographic ravages, foremost of which is that publications by women are achieving statistical parity with those by men.[3] The big prizes remain in disequilibrium (it's as if the candidates are all on a rolodex established in 1975, which industry officials consult to make sure that Bill and Charles and Mark and Bob and John get equal share in the spoils), and if it weren't for Levertov, Rich and Josephine Jacobsen, the sum total of major awards to women would be even more paltry than it is. Where a welcome difference is evident is in awards for first and second books, the Walt Whitman and the Lamont (now James Laughlin) award. Seven of the Whitman, and six of the Lamont, awards in the 90s went to women.

The role of women poets in American culture has usually been symptomatic, meaning particularized and exceptional. Dickinson, H. D., Moore, Riding, Plath: each one of a kind, and chasteningly isolate, lost in a sea of men whose work collectively imposed a sense of poetry's tasks and possibilities. Women writers might be unique, but their singularity was rarely held up as exemplary. The postwar period imposed such a strictly masculine ethos on poetry that the careers of important figures like Rukeyser and Swenson become case studies in vanishing tracks. For a generation of women who were empowered by the women's liberation movement, as well as in the poetry workshops, the challenge of getting out from under masculine shadows was considerable, but it was not suffered individually. For all the negative consequences of the MFA programs (conformism, careerism, anti-intellectualism), the workshops did end up enfranchising women writers on a large scale. Women constituted 40 of the 104 poets in the omnibus workshop-oriented *Morrow Anthology of Younger American Poets* (1985), and more than half—21 of 37—of Nicholas Christopher's *Under 35: The New Generation of American Poets* (1989).[4] I don't mean to imply that a statistical ascendancy of women is automatically good for poetry; nor is there any reason to expect increased variety as a result, though I think that is now verifiably the case. More important is the singularity of invention. But there are two significant contributing factors to consider: age and heterodoxy. Heterodoxy is not programmatic, and may reflect nothing more than demographics. But, insofar as much of the postwar poetry map has been defined by alliances, groups, and movements, it's worth bearing in mind Alice Notley's claim about her own generation of women: "Our achievement has probably been to become ourselves in spite of the movements" (Foster 86).[5]

Age is important because it takes a generation (at least) to overcome a dominant paradigm. Pioneering figures in radical feminism are now seniors; and the baby boomers—first generation beneficiaries of institutionalized gains attributable to feminism—are middle aged. In terms of writing, not only are more women being published, but a considerable number of them are older, their work reflecting maturity and experience. Kathleen Fraser's career is a useful index, not only because of her own insightful testimony in *Translating the Unspeakable*, but on the evidence of her 1997 selected poems, *Il Cuore: The Heart*, which reflects the attending pressures of emancipation. She includes only fifteen pages published before she was forty, and the assurance and diversity of her work is most evident in the past two decades. A real diversity of styles and idioms among women writers has only recently become evident on a widespread scale, for particular historical reasons. Fraser recounts various institutions in which she taught from 1969 to 1974: "Women students constituted the majority of writers present, but they seldom spoke unless called upon and, in their writing practice, tended to follow a safe and limited model of prosody learned in earlier classes" (2). The figures who established and gave luster to this model—the low key personal free verse lyric of the 1960s—were largely male, and this was the dominant approved style in the workshops as they multiplied through the 70s. It took more than twenty years for women to work themselves free of this laconic idiom, going on to develop heterogeneous writing practices (a key moment along the way was Anne Waldman's performance text "Fast Speaking Woman," which was indebted to the breath-oriented poetics of Olson and Ginsberg while pursuing semantic liberation from the discursive and rhetorical protocols of Waldman's male models and peers). Women readily felt the need to divest themselves of a pre-gendered mode, while for male poets the beguiling sense of an agreeable manner easily adapted to masculine attitudes resulted in a dispiriting acquiescence to a moribund style, and the later books of many of the MFA heroes of 1975 are documents of a generational disaster.

In the polarized atmosphere that prevailed for about twenty-five years (1958-1983, say), certain acclaimed figures became moral-aesthetic icons. The reverence with which followers would refer the question of authenticity back to Roethke or James Wright, cultural authority back to Lowell or Olson, or elegance back to Auden and Merrill, now seems the mark of a vanished time. The dominant spirit of opposing camps marked such avowals with a devotional air. With Olson, Lowell and Ginsberg around (squirming under the shadows of Williams, Eliot, Pound), the figure of The Poet was at once glamorous and suffocating. The dominant poets today are less imposing—in part because they're less saddled with associated cultural baggage, but also because that baggage was deeply invested in specific forms of gender empowerment. Many of the most acclaimed *and* innovative poets now are women (the two facets are often combined), and there seems to be a more genial spirit of cohabitation. Little gladiatorial resolve is at stake, and even the ideological differences of personal background and poetic orientation are muted when one considers the success of Lyn Hejinian and Susan Howe as well as Alice Fulton and Jorie Graham, who now occupy the position of respected elders, having published regularly during the past two decades and built up reputations accordingly. Plenty of other names (from several generations) could be added—Guest, Waldrop, Lauterbach, (C. D.) Wright, Notley—but it's interesting that many of their peers only began publishing poetry near or after the age of forty (Fanny Howe, Susan Howe, Lyn Hejinian, Norma Cole, Beverly Dahlen, Rachel Blau DuPlessis, Joan Retallack, Hannah Weiner).

The phenomenon of the mature woman poet arriving fully achieved and as if out of nowhere dramatized the appearance of Amy Clampitt in 1983 with *The Kingfishers*—a phenomenon repeated with Anne Carson. Apart from a Canadian chapbook, Carson burst on the scene with two big books, *Plainwater* and *Glass, Irony and God* in 1995, at the age of forty-five. Three further volumes have confirmed that, unlike Clampitt, Carson's prodigality is matched by variety. In very short order she has slipped into place as a defining figure of the new millennium, one of the "wisdom writer[s]" for Harold Bloom, "in a less-than-fingers-on-one-hand group of writers" for Susan Sontag (Rehak 38). Such accolades have resulted in a lavish MacArthur fellowship and the lucrative Griffin Poetry Prize in Canada. The sudden lionization of Carson, along with the fact that her books are published by Knopf, would have been evidence of a set-up twenty years ago: a career manufactured for (and by) Manhattan literati.[6] But the terms of engagement and appraisal have changed. For one thing, *Glass, Irony and God* was published by New Directions, with a preface by Guy Davenport, whose previous attention to poets bore conspicuous marks of partisan affiliation (Pound, Zukofsky, Olson, Jonathan Williams, Ronald Johnson). But the Carson phenomenon is skewed in other ways as well, in that she is not (as would formerly have been the case) launching herself strictly as a poet; nor does she aspire to teach other writers, since she's a classics professor at McGill University in Montreal.

The sudden ascendancy of a middle-aged poet like Anne Carson is not unique—*Harmonium* was published when Wallace Stevens was 43; Frost was 39 when his first book appeared—but the modern prototypes for the figure of the poet as (virile) youth are pervasive: Pound, Crane, Eliot, cummings, (Langston) Hughes, and Riding gave modernism a youthful face, substantiated by the next generation (in England by Auden, George Barker, and Dylan Thomas, followed stateside by Rukeyser, Schwartz, Berryman and Lowell). In the postwar period reputations continued to be made by poets in their twenties: Wilbur, Merwin, Rich, Merrill, Hollander, Plath; and the Beats, too, embodied youth. At time of the Six Gallery reading in San Francisco in 1955, Ginsberg was still under thirty, Snyder was twenty-five, and McClure was a few weeks shy of twenty-three. (A month later, twenty year old Elvis Presley signed a contract with RCA). The phenomenon of flam-

ing youth was more or less institutionally imposed on the first genera-
tion of poets to go through the MFA programs, as published books
were necessary for career advancement. The meteor of youth, preter-
naturally gifted, continues to flare of course (Brenda Shaughnessy,
Larissa Szporluk, Jeff Clark, Lisa Lubasch, Tessa Rumsey), but more
and more of the "new" poets are actually older. Consider some recent
debut volumes: *Delirium* (1995) by Barbara Hamby (b. 1952); *Apology for
Want* (1997) by Mary Jo Bang (b. 1946); *The New Intimacy* (1997) by
Barbara Cully (b. 1955); *The Bounty* (1997) by Myung Mi Kim (b. 1957);
The Thicket Daybreak (1997) by Catherine Webster (b. 1944); *Bite Every
Sorrow* (1998) by Barbara Ras (b. 1949); *Of Flesh and Spirit* (1998) by
Wang Ping (b. 1957); *Hotel Imperium* (1999) by Rachel Loden (b. 1948);
A Taxi to the Flame (1999) by Vicki Karp (b. 1953)—all least forty.[7] Many
poets are now over forty by the time a second book appears: *The Dig*
(1992) by Lyn Emanuel (b. 1949); *Trace Elements* (1998) by Barbara
Jordan (b. 1949); *For* (2000) by Carol Snow (b. 1949); *Rough Cut* (1997)
by Thomas Swiss (b. 1952); *Smokes* by Susan Wheeler (b. 1955); *Transit
Authority* (2000) by Tony Sanders (b. 1957); *The Oval Hour* (1999) by
Kathleen Peirce (b. 1956); *After I Was Dead* (1999) by Laura Mullen (b.
1958). Even some of the so-called "young" poets are publishing first
books at an age formerly considered mid-career (the Rich of *Leaflets*,
Merwin of *The Moving Target*, Creeley of *For Love*): *Madonna anno domini*
(1997) by Joshua Clover (b. 1962); *And Her Soul Out of Nothing* (1997) by
Olena Katyiak Davis (b. 1963); *Polyverse* by Lee Ann Brown (b. 1963);
First Worlds (2001) by Eleni Sikelianos (b. 1965); *Point and Line* (2000) by
Thalia Field (b. 1966). Most striking, though, is the sharp surge of
accomplishment evident in a number of poets whose distinctiveness
became most evident in the 1990s (including Ann Lauterbach,
Marjorie Welish, Norma Cole, C. D. Wright, Forrest Gander, Mark
Doty, Brenda Hillman, Dean Young, Donald Revell, Bin Ramke,
Stephen Ratcliffe, Andrew Schelling).

All this is in striking contrast to career patterns a few decades ago. By
the time they were forty, poets like Jerome Rothenberg, Robert Kelly
and Clayton Eshleman were each listing a few dozen books (a number
augmented by their work as editors and translators). Mainstream poets
had lists less pumped up with chapbooks, but the numbers could still be
substantial (Merwin had thirteen titles by the age of forty). In addition,

those who rose to prominence in the postwar decade benefited from a relatively less prolific scene. By the time he was forty, Lowell had already appeared in eight major anthologies, as had Merrill by the same age. Others even more: Hecht (11), Wilbur (14), James Wright (10), and Snodgrass an astonishing 17 anthology appearances *before* his second book appeared at the age of forty-two. Some opposing poets also fared well, like Gary Snyder who, at forty, had been in at least 16 anthologies. The much discussed "anthology wars" of the 1960s benefited both sides, establishing various rosters which anthologists up to the present have felt obliged to duplicate or honorifically extend by rhetorical enframing. The prolonged *ideological* influence of the arrayed groupings lasted for decades. But to this point there has been only one comparably influential ideological bloc: Language poetry.

As with the Beat/Black Mountain predecessors, early publication— along with judicious anthologies of poetry *and* prose—meant that Language poetry had a reputation and growing influence well before most of the participants were forty. But because of the group identity, these *enfants terribles* were middle aged as they came to individual prominence. *As* a generation, the poets associated with Language writing have been publishing books regularly for several decades, so the body of work is now both extensive and documentary. But because of its procedural orientation, Language writing is not easily assessed in the normative terms of individual "growth and development." This has the effect of making early works by Bob Perelman and Bruce Andrews, say, look preternaturally "mature." But procedure is not all. By avoiding the alignment of the poem with a private voice and the vicissitudes of personal experience, Language writing was energized by its relationship to public discourse. Early critical references to blip culture—to the depthless surfaces of a postmodernism which Language poets purportedly reflected with corresponding depthlessness—gave the misleading impression of Language poetry as content with simple transcription. Twenty years later, a documentary propensity is far more evident. This hasn't by any means led to a wholesale acceptance of Language poetry, nor even absorption of its theories and principles. Anthologists venture only as far as Michael Palmer and Susan Howe; and Ron Silliman's appearance in the Oxford *Anthology of Modern American Poetry* (2000), edited by Cary Nelson, may have more to do with his past affiliation with *Socialist Review* than his role as Language poet and theorist. References to Language poetry abound, of course, but most remain references only.

Meanwhile, the mirage of an offending doctrine (or a disagreeable practice) persists. This can be jesting, as in David Lehman's *The Daily Mirror: A Journal in Poetry* (2000):

> I think I will write a one-line
> "Language" poem here it is
> it's called "Syntax" and the line
> is "Sin tax" .... (87)

As Lehman's poem indicates, Language poetry can now be assumed as a familiar reference, deserving a lighthearted roasting. A more pervasive assumption is that Language poetry is passé, or else something to surmount, as proclaimed on the cover of a 1996 book, *Vision of a Storm Cloud*:[8] "William Olsen's newest work is the harbinger of a new wave of American poetry. In moving beyond the 'new formalists' and the 'Language poet,' Olsen has crafted poems that are energetic, expansive, and romantic." Whether Language poetry is something to be lampooned or overcome, it has at least become habitually cited.

The most revealing response is a poem by Ronald Wallace from *The Uses of Adversity* (1998), which I take to be symptomatic of a widespread resentment usually not ventured in print.

L=A=N=G=U=A=G=E

The poet says that language is an absence,
and a *beautiful absence*, at that. Representation
is an illusion not worth pursuing, a limitation
on the imagination's plate. It makes no sense
to her, she says, mimesis and narration
are out of the question, boring, passé, old-fashioned.
She feels a rancor for the empirical. Abstraction,
disjunction, juxaposition, and all the other *shuns*

take her fancy. And all the friendly stories

of my childhood pack up and walk out the door,
taking with them their pungent oranges, melons, raspberries,
the sweet fruit salad of the juicy familiar,
leaving us with a mouthful of semiotics,
poststructuralism doing its after-dinner tricks (82).

A fugitive publication during its brief run (1978-1982), $L=A=N=G=U=A=G=E$ has long since come to signify something for a considerable number of people who never read it and have probably never even seen a copy. A selection of pieces from the magazine appeared in 1984 and had itself gone out of print by the time the phrase "Language poetry" had trickled down into the vocabulary of poets like Wallace, for whom it signifies a critical fashion, an obtuse scholastic ado about nothing. Given the considerable population of MFA graduates and poet-professors in the United States, many may have identified Language poetry as the probable cause of critical indifference to their own work. Foremost in Wallace's poem is the contention that Language writing abjures the tangible world, seeking solace in the boneyard of abstractions. Andrews and Bernstein, introducing *The L=A=N=G=U=A=G=E Book*, were worried by the persistence of such assumptions way back in 1984:

> [T]he idea that writing should (or could) be stripped of reference is as bothersome and confusing as the assumption that the primary function of words is to refer, one-on-one, to an already constructed world of "things." Rather, reference, like the body itself, is one of the horizons of language, whose value is to be found in the writing (the world) before which we find ourselves at any moment (ix).

The "bothersome" assumption that words should be compliantly referential clearly encompasses the position taken by Ronald Wallace.

Wallace's poem stakes a strikingly masculinist territorial claim, defending the integrity of personal identity and/as childhood memory, portraying the offending party as a woman—which is to say, an unnatural aggressor. In Wallace's world, there is clearly a place for women: as mothers, preparing "the sweet fruit salad of the juicy familiar" in the kitchen. What's most unusual about Wallace's poem is that it dates from 1998, twenty years after the magazine he names in his title was published. Regardless of one's own interest in (or some would say tolerance for) Language poetry, it is increasingly untenable to think of the Language writers themselves as merely executing further proofs or demonstrations of first principles, comporting, that is, within the boundaries of groupthink. The legacy of Language poetry has been disseminated into the environment of poetic innovation at large; and, as Wallace's worried poem suggests, there's something about this legacy of innovation and women that go together.

At least Wallace craves satiety, unlike William Logan, whose critical distemper thrives on disavowal. His 1989 review of *Sun* for *The New York Times Book Review* qualifies as some pinnacle of obtuseness: "Reading Michael Palmer's poetry is like listening to serial music or slamming your head against a streetlight stanchion—somewhere, you're sure, masochists are lining up to enjoy the very same thing; but for most people the only pleasure it can have is the pleasure of its being over" (46). "In Palmer's work, language is frequently reduced to its surface gestures, which is fine if you're a gesture and if not, not" (47).[9] In cavalier pronouncements like these, Logan substitutes grumpy posturing for critical discernment, repeating the time-honored gesture with which metropolitan sophisticates dismiss unwanted visitors: the clever rebuke, the archly casual put-down with which Rosencrantz and Guildenstern are sent from the court to their unwitting doom.

One exception to the intemperate rebuke and the offhand dismissal is Lyn Emanuel's cautionary essay, "Language Poets, New Formalists and the Techniquization of Poetry," in which she charges both camps with a dereliction of duty: "Beneath the rhetoric of innovation lies an investment in the status quo," she claims, as they fail to "renovate the ghetto of free verse" and "flee it," instead, "for the subdivisions of technique" (221). Emanuel does not take a populist view, exactly, but she is concerned with audience and access. "Language poets and new formalists must move from the issues of art—what is collected, withheld, made special—to considerations of audience, who will be walled out from these technologies, these new museums of language" (220). The precipitous rise of public poetry events like slams and contests has revealed a massive audience, to be sure, but I doubt this is what Emanuel has in mind. I think what she favors is a greater deliberation, when it comes to questions of form; what various formal choices signify to different constituencies; and, in the consideration of constituencies, whether one is content to preach to the converted. While her point is well taken, Emanuel's focus on formalism is out of touch with the abiding concerns of the Language poets. The blatant politicization of language evident in the work of Bob Perelman, Ron Silliman, or Bruce Andrews is hard to construe as driven by formalist criteria. Silliman's use of the Fibonacci series in *Ketjak* and *Tjanting* was no more formalist than another poet's decisions about line breaks. In both cases they are functional guides to the shaping and patterning of emergent material; but Silliman's books do not enact large scale rehearsals for the preservation of a fetishized form, whereas those poets who place a primary value on "writing in forms" are doing just that.

The issues that continue to emanate from Language poetry are not formal.[10] Formalism is a straw dog. The real dirty word in the American poetry clubhouse is *intellectual*. The fitful absorption of modernism into Anglo-American letters was prelude to a lurking and easily revived anti-intellectualism. Resentful accusations of "difficulty" in poetry, commonly associated with modernism, usually mean that the reader (critic) doesn't want poetry to think. This attitude consigns the poem to a kind of hotel bar cocktail hour pianism, a strictly decorative role. It doesn't proscribe thoughts from the poem, but asks that the thoughts be familiar enough so as not to disturb the atmosphere—that is, the idle chatter, the drinks, the flirting. Difficulty returned to poetry with a vengeance in the context of Black Mountain, but not always in the obvious terms of intellectualism. Creeley's work, for instance, is as accessible as that of Carl Sandburg on the level of diction and vocabulary; but it renders even the simplest declarations instances of a moral challenge. It is the singular pluralized in the simplest speech: "As soon as / I speak, I / speaks" (294). "There is / a silence / to fill" (344). "My face is my own, I thought" (152). Creeley's is a poetry difficult in its claims, and foremost among its claims is the thought of simplicity. The work of Olson or Duncan, on the other hand, is post-modernist: that is, it openly wears its learning, but doesn't pretend that its enigmas can be solved by tracking down references. The references have integrity; learning is invited, promoted, demanded, but as gymnastic prelude to a performance that doesn't end on the page but is an initiation to a life on call. You heed the calling (or not, as the case may be).

A fundamental cause of widespread misconceptions about Language poetry is ignorance of the poetics that gave rise to it, which is all the more alarming considering its availability. The "New American Poetry" convened by Donald Allen in 1960 was the immediate provocation. For those poets who ventured into *that* new world only as far as a dabble of Ginsberg, a taste of Snyder, a sidelong glance at O'Hara, the theoretical claims of Language poetry seem esoteric in the extreme. Another source behind the intellectualism of Language poetry was "theory" in the scholastic sense. In 1987 the Canadian critic Stephen Scobie asked, with deliberate provocation, "Wouldn't you agree that the two greatest poets of the last twenty years have been Roland Barthes and Jacques Derrida?" (240). Hyperbole aside, Scobie makes a legitimate point, one that takes us back to 1975. At that point I had read Derrida's *Speech and Phenomena* but knew nothing about him or the French intellectual scene; so my interest was piqued when, at the ethnopoetics conference in Milwaukee, I heard David Antin ask another poet if he'd read Derrida.[11] It was a time when poets were quick on the draw. Perhaps the first appearance of Foucault in English was in *Io*, Richard Grossinger's journal of poetics, esoterica, and bioregionalism. My own poetry magazine, *Wch Way*, devoted a substantial part of the first two issues (1975) to a discussion of Roland Barthes' *The Pleasure of the Text*.[12] The Canadian journal *Open Letter* was a trove of speculative riches, concentrated in the TRG reports of bp Nichol and Steve McCaffery. Coming into a life of poetry at that point, then, entailed a complex mix of work and play, esoteric and exoteric, body and mind. Above all, it meant that nothing could be taken for granted when it came to form *or* content. When Ed Sanders published his manifesto *Investigative Poetry*, the recognition of his claims felt immediate: what other kind was there?

Times change, of course, and the terms of investigation change too, at least in some respects. It's understandable if younger poets now feel that further investigation of the formal resources of language as ideological material feels dated; on the other hand, if you concede the ideological parasites language clearly supports, such investigations are always relevant. The ongoing trauma of vanguard innovation—what Paul Mann calls *The Theory-Death of the Avant-Garde*—is pertinent as well: that is, given the capitalist exhortation to constant revolution in the modes of production, how revolutionary is it for artists to replicate such a structure in their media? By the same token, complacent return to the anachronistic precedent of "tradition" is not a viable alternative. Above all, there's no excuse for not being informed, and this is tantamount to an intellectual avowal. The cultural outlook of Americans tends to vacillate between wide-eyed Euro-tourism and chest-thumping affirmations of a jar in Tennessee. This schizoid outlook filters down into stereotyped apparitions in poetry: "A Baroque Wall-Fountain in the Villa Sciarra" (Wilbur) versus "Autumn Begins in Martins Ferry, Ohio" (Wright); between the cosmopolitanism of Merrill and the poetry slam. Such effortless examples of contrariety have been mistaken for variety in surveys and anthologies, as if poets were types of animals to be led onto the ark, two by two.

The world's complexity contests the convenience of such an arrangement. Leslie Scalapino succinctly renders the challenge: "Poetry in this time and nation is doing the work of philosophy—it is writing that is conjecture" (19). The conjectural challenge was a vital concomitant to the New American Poetry: Allen's 1960 anthology had included a forty page section, "Statements on Poetics," and the impulse was extended to an entire volume in 1974, *The Poetics of the New American Poetry*.[13] By contrast, the establishment as well as the workshops maintained a superstitious hesitation to engage in the philosophical challenge of *poetics*, preferring to talk about "craft." Another (and maybe the most salutary) consequence of Language poetry is that poetics has become an increasingly vigorous feature across the denominational sockets of American poetry. Heather McHugh's *Broken English* (1993), Lyn Hejinian's *The Language of Inquiry* (2000) and Anne Waldman's *Vow to Poetry* (2001) are exemplary records of poetics as vitalizing accompaniment to the writing life. It's also encouraging to see how many compilations have appeared in recent years, including *By Herself: Women Reclaim Poetry* edited by Molly McQuade (2000), *After Confession: Poetry as Autobiography* edited by Kate Sontag and David Graham (2001), *We Who Love to be Astonished: Experimental Women's Writing and Performative Poetics* edited by Laura Hinton and Cynthia Hogue (2002), *American Women Poets in the Twenty-First Century* edited by Claudia Rankine and Juliana Spahr (2002).

A common mistake is to presume that poetics is afterthought, window-dressing, post-coital to the ontological drama of the poem itself. In the American context, there's a certain reverence for the posture of superstitious restraint in a poet when it comes to speaking about poetry. For some poets this may well be a psychologically creative necessity, but as cultural model it precipitates mystification about agency. A body of poetry, enshrined, may become paralyzing: aloof, authoritative, unapproachable, and mesmerizing. What I most admire in poetry is how it instructs me, and the provenance and methods of instruction are endlessly various. I take Thoreau's precedent seriously, and would abandon even the most beloved Walden of my imagination if I found myself cutting a steady track to the shore from the habit of dipping in its waters. So inebriating is the spell that Olson or Ginsberg, H. D. or Eliot cast over acolytes that some never recover (yet recovery needn't imply repudiation). My writing, admittedly, constitutes a kind of advocacy; but advocacy is not finality, any more than provisional recommendations for local acts of social justice are prescriptions for utopia. Emerson (sounding like a Situationist) entertained the bracing thought that we might ponder the disappearance of literature altogether.[14] He didn't mean that it might be crushed out, but that its own powers of transformation, if fully absorbed into the character of the culture, would erode the very institutions that form the context of literature, the background against which the figurations of literary activity are made legible.

A species of heckler's gloat is evident from time to time when pundits mention the academic success of mavericks (a.k.a. Language poets) like Charles Bernstein, Barrett Watten, Bob Perelman, and Steve McCaffery. (Oddly, the same charges were not made about Creeley or Snyder, even though their hipster patrimony was more substantive, with far greater risk of seeming co-opted). But changing circumstances demand more discernment, especially when it comes to the role of institutions. Poetry always has its institutions. A slam is no less *instituting* a scenario than a classroom: both fill up with expectations, and institutions reinforce expectations. Language poetry did not emerge as an oppositional enterprise, nor did it aspire to renegade or outsider status; so academic success does not necessarily imply betrayal. Language poetry is most important for backing up the determination of certain poets (by no means restricted to a group of insiders) to disentangle themselves from the prefiguring nets of less visible (but therefore even more dangerous) institutions than academe: the tyranny of the lyrical ego, the breath unit, the anecdote. Naturally, the institutional success of Language poetry means that its own procedural strictures, specific to the hegemonies of 1975, may now seem oppressive to younger poets. But before forgetfulness runs its course, it's imperative that younger poets realize that the very openness of the present milieu is significantly indebted to the Houdini routines of their predecessors, engineering an escape from the locked trunks (the noncommunicating vessels) of 1960—the Hall-Pack-Simpson "New Poets" and the Allen "New American Poetry"—as well as the weak détente represented by the workshops.

Language poetry emerged from (and to some degree perpetuated) the bipolar disorder of competing institutions in American poetry, but it seems to have nourished poetic practice in markedly non-denominational ways. This unintended enrichment, handled with care, has the potential to transcend sectarian vexations that have long seemed instinctive to readers: and, after all, the liberation of the *reader* was the guiding light of much that was published in $L=A=N=G=U=A=G=E$. Before the aura of theoretical intimidation began to emanate from Language poetry, there was an available assumption that you needn't *abashedly* point to "human interest" as the plausible rationale for reading a poem. By the same token, if your interest in others is genuine, a poem can be an effective vehicle for making acquaintances. There is a considerable body of poetry (e.g., Rodney Jones) that serves little purpose for me but this: it expresses views and sentiments, it negotiates pieces of fate and ponders the cost of inclination, in ways that offer me some access to all my kin with whom I have "nothing in common" but the fact of kinship. Who doesn't count such distance and dissimilarity as being in the family way? The poetry that enhances my understanding of those who don't think as I do may fall short of the demands I'd impose in the terms provided by theoretical sophistication, cultural complexity, or aesthetic gratification. But the measure of dynamics in a culture's poetry is that there *are* more satisfactions, and lessons, than any particular tradition or prospective practice can contain. That's why I admire Ron Silliman's pluck in listing a catalogue of alternates in his introduction to *In the American Tree* (xx-xxi)—a gesture he repeats in his afterword to *The Art of Practice*, edited by Dennis Barone and Peter

Ganick: "That more than 160 North American poets are actively and usefully involved in the avant-garde tradition of writing is in itself a stunning thought," he reflects, adding in boldface "**we in North America are living in a poetic renaissance unparalleled in our history**" (377). This may be the case, but I wouldn't attribute *all* the virtues to the avant-garde.

In the first issue of *Sulfur* (1981), Eliot Weinberger remarked, "One effect of the poetry pandemic has surely been the elimination of exogamous reading. It has become so hectic in one's own longhouse that one rarely has the time or stamina for visits to other clans. Twenty years ago, in the ardent days of the anthology battles, even diehard Beat or Black Mountain partisans could, at the least, recognize the insignia of the opposing troops" ("*Sunrise*" 221). The warning about parochialism in one's reading and associations is perennially relevant, though it shouldn't be taken to imply, as alternative, some vacuous universalism. I concur with Charles Bernstein's exhortation in *A Poetics* that "We have to get over, as in getting over a disease, the idea that we can 'all' speak to one another in the universal voice of poetry" (5). Much as I agree, I'm concerned that this can be construed as sanctioning a new parochialism within the heterodox pockets of American poetry. The division of labor is replicated in the disciplinary configuration of universities, and that division is mirrored increasingly in the special interest constituencies in the poetry world. Part of what these *special interests* compel is an assumption of prior consent. This quickly passes over into a covert regulation of taste. If you're keen on the avant-garde, your notice of Mary Jo Salter will be limited to the expected snicker or the rude aside. If *The Simple Truth* (Philip Levine) is your thing, the work of Leslie Scalapino will seem both creepy and beside the point. I'm not suggesting that "we all" must learn from one another or die (to vary Auden's infamously belabored line), but rather that there's a value in overcoming one's own presumptions, particularly presumptions of familiarity with what goes on across the way, in the enemy's camp, the neighbor's back yard, the other guy's poem.

This might sound like an ecumenical recommendation, urging a catholicity of taste it will prove impractical to sustain. After all, the sheer volume of published poetry now exceeds the grasp of even the most fanatical followers. Part of the survival value of a sectarian orientation is pragmatic: you learn to read signs of association (editorial boards of magazines, types of poetry published), you're attracted or repulsed by the names of the blurb writers, find certain presses reliably invigorating and others predictably bland, and so forth. For almost fifty years the poetry world as a whole constituted a varied but reliable system—so much so that I spent hundreds of pages in *The American Poetry Wax Museum* documenting how the system was established, and how inflexible it had become. In astonishingly short order the terms have changed. Traces of the old system will undoubtedly continue to have influence and even prevail in many sectors; but there is now some evidence of salutary transformations. There continues to be a plethora of published poetry (and the space devoted to poetry in bookstores seems to be mushrooming), but it's becoming more and more difficult to use place of publication (journal or book) as a reliable indicator of poetic orientation. Affinities are less binding, not so programmatic.

Small press, university press, and trade publishers no longer signify quite what they used to, and crossovers are more common. Alice Notley, whose work epitomized the range of small press formats for decades, is now a Penguin Poet, as is Anne Waldman. The variety of Cole Swensen's publishers can't be converted into a familiar record of "progress" from outsider to official status: *New Math* was published by Morrow in 1988 and *Try* by the University of Iowa Press in 1999; between these two, Swensen published three books with alternative presses (*Park* with Floating Island, 1991, *Numen* with Burning Deck, 1995, and *Noon* with Sun & Moon, 1996). Rosmarie Waldrop continues to traverse a similar terrain, as her New Directions titles (1987, 1994, 2000) are evenly interspersed amongst numerous books representing a veritable roll call of small presses (Tender Buttons, Kelsey Street, Station Hill, Paradigm, Burning Deck and others). Fanny Howe's books chronicle a smart catalogue of small presses (Telephone, Kelsey Street, The Figures, Alice James, Lost Roads, Littoral, O Books, Reality Street, and Spectacular Diseases), while her *Selected Poems* (2000) was one of the inaugural volumes in the New California Poetry series published by the University of California Press. Younger poets may be beneficiaries of this flexible mingling of alternative and mainstream publishing venues. Liz Waldner's first book, *Homing Devices*, was published by O Books in 1998, followed two years later by *A Point Is That*

Which Has No Part, a University of Iowa Press "Iowa Poetry Prize" recipient. Jena Osman's *The Character* was published by Beacon in 1999, awarded the Barnard New Women Poets Prize. A work like Stacy Doris's *Kildare*, published by Roof in 1994, might easily find a place with a trade publisher now. But lest the borders seem permanently blurred, I'd wager that another Roof book, *Free Space Comix* by Brian Kim Stefans (1998)—with its dense layering of typographic effects and inside references to vanguard poetry—is *not* crossover material.

The National Poetry Series is an interesting register of the gradual blurring of operational boundaries. Initiated by James Michener in 1978 (who declared it shameful that the publication of poetry in America was on such precarious footing), the Series publishes five titles with five different publishers annually. While some of the early books were promising, the judges were establishment choices, and an alarming number of the poets subsequently dropped out of sight. In 1989 Michael Palmer selected Cole Swensen's *New Math*, but it seemed an anomaly that Palmer was in such a position at all, his own work having been published exclusively by Black Sparrow and North Point. Regular involvement by judges with vanguard inclinations was slow in coming, but has been consistent since 1994 when Sun & Moon became one of the participating publishers. A few vanguard titles have appeared from other publishers now too—*The Human Abstract* by Elizabeth Willis (Penguin) and *Lost Wax* by Heather Ramsdell (Illinois)—and books like *The New Intimacy* by Barbara Cully and *Red Signature* by Mary Leader are more innovative and varied than their predecessors in the series. Even relatively conventional works like *Crash's Law* by Karen Volkman and *Placebo Effects* by Jeanne Marie Beaumont show signs of exposure to innovative writing.

The role of university presses in publishing poetry during the past thirty years has been extensive—and extensively lamented, with some justification, since the product was uniformly bland for so long, the poems seeming almost interchangeable from one title to another, and from one press to another. That has been changing. Books of unpredictable vintage (along with more readable instances of old vintage) are being published by the university presses of Wesleyan, Wisconsin, Iowa, Illinois, Louisiana, Massachusetts, Georgia, and even such diminutive presses as Colorado, North Texas, Notre Dame, NYU. The

Barnard New Women Poets series published by Beacon is admirably varied in its choices. The trade publishers tend to be more predictable. Knopf, having imported a whole contingent of the old Atheneum poets (Merrill, Merwin, Strand, Hollander), and benefited from Clampitt's ascension, favors the sleek aestheticism of Salter, Pankey, Sheck, Digges, Cole, Hirsch; but Knopf also publishes Sapphire, as well as those mavericks Anne Carson and Richard Kenney. Otherwise, it's hard to detect a specific house feel in the poetry issued from the eastern trade publishers, which manifest no particular distinguishing traits like those I associate with Graywolf, Copper Canyon, or Coffee House, let alone the more avowedly alternative presses like Sun & Moon, O Books, or Roof. But odd mutations are not unprecedented: North Point Press made a memorable debut twenty years ago with books by Ronald Johnson, Leslie Scalapino, and Michael Palmer; but since its transformation into Counterpoint, Alfred Corn is on the list.

The factors contributing to this ventilation of publishers' poetry options are hard to assess. That's one reason why I think a plausible contributing feature is the demographic bulge of new women writers. Increased familiarity with Language poetry has also played a chastening role. The MFA programs, being housed in universities, could only immunize themselves from intellectual life for so long. Something had to give; and it was conspicuous when academic champions of Language poetry began to proliferate throughout the nineties, and workshop poets had to make some accommodation to experimental challenges. The careers of Jorie Graham and Donald Revell exemplify the trend. The dominance of John Ashbery has probably also had some impact in convincing other poets that transparency and accessibility are not automatic virtues. In his wake, readerly tolerance for incomprehension has risen (and must account in part for the ascendancy of Irish poet Paul Muldoon). Finally, there has been a gradual accommodation of discursiveness (going back to O'Hara and Berrigan, Antin's talk poems, and C. K. Williams' work after he started using long lines).

Vindication for innovative poetry has also derived from a most unlikely source, David Lehman's Best American Poetry series, in which the following poets have appeared: Armantrout, Bernstein, Berssenbrugge, Coolidge, (Peter) Gizzi, Hejinian, Mackey, Mandel,

Moriarty, Mullen, Notley, Palmer, Owen, Perelman, Ping, Retallack, and Scalapino—many of them in several of the annual volumes. The timing helped, as the series was inaugurated in 1988, just when Language poetry was gaining visible scholarly acclaim. Ashbery and Graham were editors in the first and third year, and their choices were more consciously disposed to experiment than other early editors like Strand and Hall. But consider this: Bob Perelman and Michael Palmer each appeared in three of the first four volumes, and Coolidge twice, as well as single appearances by most of those named above. One should bear in mind that the series emphasizes poems, not poets as such; and even the most experimentally disposed writers produce poems assimilable to a context like The Best American Poetry. At the same time, editors appear not to have been under obligation to favor certain lengths, and the series has included some adventurous longer poems. Despite the emphasis on poems, editorial orientation and personal affiliations clearly emerge in the choices. Strand, Bly and Hollander are positively clanish in their conservatism, while Simic and Tate go out of their way to include work by unknown poets. Robert Hass's choices for 2001 field the most diverse array yet. Adrienne Rich proved that an entire volume could be programmatically commandeered (drawing the wrath of Harold Bloom who, editing a "Best of the Best" tenth anniversary publication, denounced Rich's volume and bypassed it altogether for his own selection).[15]

Inclusion in a Best American Poetry volume provides the poet with some exposure, of course, but the real benefit is brutally pragmatic, providing a juicy line item for a vita or an author's note.[16] The proliferation of prizes and honors is an increasingly pervasive (and invasive) element in the scene. Pushcart Prizes, National Poetry Series, Best American Poetry, Guggenheims, plus a half dozen (or more) prizes administered by each of several institutions (Academy of American Poets, the American Academy of Arts and Letters, *Poetry* magazine), not to mention the prizes associated with publishing series (Brittingham Prize, Piper Award, Sandeen Prize, APR/Honickman Prize, etc.): plenty of prizes, but also plenty of competition, so that even being in the running is a boost. Tory Dent's biographical note in *What Silence Equals* (1993) cites her as a finalist (not winner) in the Yale Younger Poet series, the National Poetry Series, and the Walt Whitman Award (Dent went on to win the James Laughlin Award, formerly the Lamont, for *HIV, Mon Amour* in 2000). The proliferation of awards has led to some (slight) diversification in recipients, though none so astonishing as the bestowal of the $100,000 Tanning Prize to Jackson Mac Low by the Academy of American Poets in 1999 (previously awarded to Merwin, Tate, Rich, Hecht, Ammons).

The fact is that virtually all poetry is now under some kind of institutional supervision. It's as if, a few decades back, poets said *Give us some money* and the NEA appeared, with Congress close behind asking for administrative (and eventually moral) accountability. And the universities said *Sure, come on in; we'll stake your share.* Then the poets said *Give us some notoriety* and the Academy of American Poets and other institutions got to work fetching lump sums from donors to beef up the stockpile of awards, and Bill Moyers and Helen Vendler televised it, while Miguel Algarín and Bob Holman took the soundwaves of the Nuyorican Cafe to the airwaves and "a bohemian rhapsody of rap swagger [spread] across the land" (cover copy, *Aloud*). By the end of the 1990s poetry was everywhere, showered with prizes, attention, and career opportunities. Even Hollywood personalities started trying to edge in on the glamour. But it was also full of contenders. Now the real challenge for younger poets is how to stake a claim, how to get some attention, without resorting to flamboyant self-abasement (shameless self-advertisement) or falling back on the consolations of the clique.

It's a dilemma made vivid in two recent anthologies of the thirtysomething generation: *The New Young American Poets* edited by Kevin Prufer (2000) and *An Anthology of New (American) Poets* edited by Lisa Jarnot, Leonard Schwartz, and Chris Stroffolino (1998). Both offer about three dozen poets, only one of whom appears in each anthology. Nearly all the poets in both anthologies are graduates of MFA programs, and many (possibly most) also hold other advanced degrees. Prufer's collection might be construed as mainstream, with an introduction by Richard Howard and publication by a university press. The other is published by Talisman, with editor Jarnot declaring that the poets share a "marginalization from mainstream literary culture" (1). Insofar as the Talisman poets think of themselves as outsiders, it's because they've been trained in those sites (like Brown, Naropa, Buffalo) where a romance of the outside has been institutionalized. But

Prufer's poets are only "mainstream" in a precarious sense: that is, with a mainstream swollen with contenders, their chances for success (a.k.a. national reputation) are very slim. In fact, at this point a pure outsider pedigree might prove more durable in terms of career advancement, and Jarnot's group may have an advantage that formerly belonged to the establishment: they went to the same schools together and have well developed networking skills. The differences between the two groups are not, in the end, very dramatic (and there's certainly no evidence of lifestyle distinctions like beats versus squares in the 1950s). The *look* of the poems is a bit more various in the avowedly vanguard volume, though hardly as eclectic and innovative as Walter Lew's *Premonitions: The Kaya Anthology of New Asian North American Poetry*. Whatever differences there may be, they are effaced by the format of the anthologies and by the presentational rhetoric that needlessly perpetuates the clannishness of the 1960s "anthology wars."

The real wild card now is the audience. For one thing, audience is no longer identical with readership. The boost in orality provided by the growth of poetry slams has certainly had some spillover effect, creating new readers; but American culture is being drained of literacy skills at a considerable rate. Curiously, this may result in a growing audience for published poetry as the very act of reading becomes more archaic, specialized, attaining a certain antiquarian glamour. There will be increased urgency on the part of readers to identify themselves to one another (and the poetry world may start to resemble gay subculture of the pre-Stonewall era; to say nothing of the fact that so much of American poetry culture always *has been* gay subculture: see *Word of Mouth: An Anthology of Gay American Poetry* edited by Timothy Liu). A clear symptom is evident on the internet, which has facilitated contact between special interests of every stripe, not just poetry. Far from promoting a demise of the book, it seems that the growth of the internet has precipitated a renewal of interest. The user-friendly marketing strategies of Amazon.com enables shoppers to track associative links based on purchasing patterns. If you like a given poet or a specific title, Amazon will prompt you with a series of covert advertisements by informing you that "other customers who bought X also bought Y." This is strictly demographic data uninflected by opinion or critical assessment, though that's available too, since Amazon provides review clippings from a variety of sources, and also encourages its users to write their own reviews.[17] The terms of appeal become more immediate, and more visceral. Consider the enticement on the back cover of *Selfwolf* by Mark Halliday, described as being "like reading e-mail from Whitman's unknown grandson to Pynchon's missing daughter, or vice versa. More readable than Hart Crane, more candid than Jorie Graham, and more up-to-date than Alexander Pope, Mark Halliday is either a new colossus on the scene of post-contemporary American poetry or an infinitesimal blip of male bourgeois anxiety."[18]

The terms of appraisal suggested in the blurb for *Selfwolf* provocatively situate poetry in its cultural moment. *Colossus* or *blip*. But the terms are prejudicially disposed to the *agora*, the marketplace, where the American attention span vacillates wildly between such extremes, and in doing so concede poetry to a permanently subordinate role in the mass media entertainment complex. But there is another order of poetry that goes about its business without the pretence of legislative intervention or cultural dictation; an order of poetry readily acknowledged elsewhere but hard to see in the United States where "esoteric" is a bad word, where cultural activity that doesn't suggest a desire for personal prominence is illegible. In the unitary endowment of national culture, merit is always confused with the politics of taste. But the claims staked so insistently by Olson, Duncan and Blaser, among others, are perpetual reminders of a continuum of language from private resonance to public law. While definitions of poetry may vary, poets do aspire to some finality and integrity of utterance. In the American context there's no more acute instance of the difference between the literary life versus a life in poetry than Emily Dickinson, who had no literary life at all, but whose life in poetry is as singular and exponentially imposing as a chunk of radium. This is what bedevils the thought of national culture in America, so much of which is comprised of the work of renegades and misfits. Even someone as eager as Whitman to be the national bard bore no resemblance to what his peers would accept in that role.

The presumption that centrality translates to significance where cultural politics are concerned invariably results in a warped perspective; but it's no less the case that the periphery precipitates its own idolatry (in terms of "avant-garde," "outsiders," "rebels," etc.). In a meticulously orchestrated class culture like that of France, such bipolarities might mean something; but the heterology of American culture has been oversimplified far too long by terms like Beat and Square, terms instantly absorbed by (if not invented by) Madison Avenue marketing. It's a common mistake for those in the vanguard to assume a comparable solidarity on the part of those who appear to be "mainstream": but heed the geographical implication here, which recognizes that exigencies of transport (like depth of water and width of channel) promote habits of attention. Corporate "culture" has long since colonized the roadways, and franchises along the interstate highways are symptomatic instances of national enterprise. There's no difficulty transposing this model onto poetry, where franchise operations also prevail along certain channels, places where the stream broadens, allowing a greater volume of traffic. But in our poetic archipelago there are lots of byways and wayside meanders which it's obtuse to think of as either mainstream or vanguard.

Distinguishing mainstream from avant-garde has some utility, of course; but its utility is limited to institutions. If such a distinction applies to particular works, those works are sadly no more than byproducts of the institutions to which they adhere. That's why I make a point of detaching the work of Bruce Andrews from the (institutional) phenomenon of Language poetry; its robust and impetuous character is "vanguard" at the level of somatic encounter, not adjudicated theory. A particularly poignant episode provides some insight into the *agon* suffered by younger poets in the 1990s as they confronted what seemed a bipolar disorder of literary options. A number of students in the Poetics Program at SUNY Buffalo (Lew Daly, Alan Gilbert, Kristin Prevallet, Pam Rehm) initiated a sort of palace revolt with their magazine *apex of the M*, the first three issues opening with lively editorials. The editors denounced the nihilistic mechanism of language-oriented poetry along with the self-help complacency of workshop verse, proposing instead "a radical transparency of language that is ultimately objectless" (*apex* #1, 5). The editors proposed as the goal of their magazine to explore "whether there can be a purely secular form of alterity" (6). Charged with mystical obscurantism, they ventured a political program in the second issue which retained spirituality by amalgamating it to extremity in every register, evidently following the precedent of Bataille's gnostic materialism: "Anguish and the ecstatic, not play and the ironic, are the tears in the fabric of ideology" (*apex* #2, 6). In the end, the editors offered up nothing less than a millennial utopian program, "a reintegration of poetry into the entire range of radical populist traditions, both 'secular' and 'religious': iconoclasm, apocalypse, democracy, tyrannicide, antinomianism, civil disobedience, prophecy, rioting, festival, unionization, communism, prison liberation, libertinism, work-action, ludditism, utopianism, exodus" (*apex* #3, 5). With this, the programmatic side of *apex of the M* became manifestly Rabelaisian. Its flamboyant contradictions and hectoring vivacity was salutary insofar as it reminded readers of the 'pataphysical ground of poetry in all places and times. As soon as poetry aspires to the social register and the political program, it loses touch with this groundless ground and becomes Literature. Poetry is fundamentally esoteric—in several senses: it is socially insignificant (although, as symbolical capital, poetry must exist the way gold bars exist in Fort Knox, in a precarious affiliation with currency standards) and therefore represents an uncommon or esoteric enterprise; but it has a long tradition of obscurity and obscurantism, and its legendary affiliations with the muse tradition suggest that poetry is esoteric with respect to mind or psyche as such.

As esoterica, poetry's value is at once inscrutable and beside the point. As public enterprise, on the other hand, poetry is now caught in a conspicuously widening culture gap (or series of gaps). Insofar as it is deeply invested in literacy and in the knowledge criteria of literate culture, poetry is bound to seem antiquated, esoteric, scholastic, and casually intimidating even when it purports a more populist orientation. As an active component in oral culture, poetry is periodically rekindled into prominence, even if only (or often) at the level of affective immediacy. There is a third zone, an interface between orality and literacy which is more emphatically visual, and that is the culture of electronic media. There is obvious potential here for the inauguration of new poetic enterprise, one in which poetry might conceivably rival film. Not a serious rival, maybe, since poetry's investment in the word will limit its semiotic appeal in the long run.

These different theatres of operation have already resulted in serious erosion of the model of a unitary tradition. The enticements of opening up the canon lead to the proverbial can of worms, as incommensurate practices sit side by side in the non-reciprocating terms of one medium or another. The first two volumes in The Library of America anthology of twentieth century poetry offer a case in point. The inclusion of lyrics by Cole Porter, Dorothy Fields and other Tin Pan Alley composers, as well as an assortment of blues lyrics, confronts the reader with an admirable model of poetic praxis even as it deprives these examples of their full register (*The Norton Anthology of African American Literature*, by contrast, includes a CD so that readers can be auditors). By the same token, even large scale efforts to transport orality into anthologies suffer an attenuation in the transfer: *Poetry Nation* edited by Cabico and Swift; *Aloud* edited by Algarín and Holman; and *The Outlaw Bible of American Poetry* edited by Kaufman are precarious monuments.[19] A positive side effect of this misplaced application of orality is that the poems in these anthologies disclose the poverty of so much other poetry intended primarily for the page. Also disclosed by the plenitude of anthologies (these and others) is the poverty of the anthology as a means of representing poetic activity. Anthologized certifications too easily submit to the old paterialist hypothesis of a master plan, divine providence applied to human enterprise from above, the canon of idealism (in both senses, as aspiration and as secret code). But poetry is nothing without matter and mutter, utterance and exigence. Its fetishism defines its utopian truth: "the fetish confronts us with the paradox of an unattainable object that satisfies a human need precisely through its being unattainable" (Agamben 33).[20]

Innovation does not mean change for the sake of change; experiment does not mean fiddling with a perfectly serviceable tool. Innovation is a necessary response to force of circumstance in which the apparent utility of the medium is insufficient. The myth of the self-sufficiency of the lyric occasion has been a dominant feature of late twentieth century American poetry, despite the abundance of long poems, sequences, and procedures of "disturbance" (in Jack Spicer's sense). The durability of lyric suggests it's a transcendent vehicle, something immune from historical change; yet current practice increasingly betrays a suspicion that there is no such immunity. From a broader perspective, (modern) lyric might be seen as a technical device specific to an historical formation: a means, within print culture, to yoke consciousness to certain subject positions amenable to the systems requirements of modernity. We don't have to blatantly refer this to Foucault's power/knowledge complex or outline some other hypothesis of coercion or self-induced entrapment by the wiles of capital or the byways of psychological sublimation. The point is to suggest that, in considering poetry, we at least acknowledge the potential of some viral disorder, a set of ascertainable pressures inflecting (and possibly initiating) the very impulse to *be a poet*, to assume a posture that signifies autonomous expression, exalted transport, rapt inwardness inexplicably concretized as utterance, the enigma of a *voice* in *print*.

Recognition of so imposing a circumstance does not entail unilateral response. It is possible to continue writing poetry just as one wears shoes, talks to strangers, or stops at traffic lights. The world compels our attentions in familiarly structured ways, so why develop a hyperbolic focus on just one of the structures and compel it to change? To put it this way, of course, reverts to the tool model: poem as utilitarian artifact, communication device or broadcast transmitter. As poets have commonly remarked (or complained), poetry makes nothing happen. Is the tool, then, dysfunctional? Might it not be the case that this says something, instead, about functionality, attesting to the scope of functional requirements permeating even the deepest levels of subjectivity? Adorno said of art as such that it's anarchic, since it harbors the dream in a functionalist society of having no function. Its function is to have no function, and this, he thought, preserved the image of utopia. The issue of innovation, I think, necessarily arises from this prospect. In the face of so many incitements to functionality—*serve and protect*—it takes a tremendous effort to detach the cognitive and affective powers from the instinct to belong; to divert these powers along non-remunerative channels; and to focus on the materiality of language as at once compromised yet happily received, in the precarious poetic labor of reconvening the world from scratch.

From scratch: the term evokes the "mark of distinction" in Spencer Brown's *Laws of Form*, from which Niklas Luhmann has elaborated a cogent theory of art. "The unity of art resides in that it creates for the sake of observation and observes for the sake of being observed, and the medium of art consists in the freedom to create medium/form relations" (Luhmann 117). The status of the *observer* here is important, for Luhmann regards art as a perceptual system distinct from a social system. *Communication* is specific to social systems, in his view, so artistic activity is undertaken primarily without reference to communication. This isn't to say it's antisocial. Even if a poet is pragmatically dedicated to transmitting a message, the temporal delay involved in preparing an artifact (poem as message) plunges the activity into a perceptual realm distinct from the intersubjective circuit of a communications environment. For poets deeply invested in the notion that poetry is vital to this communications environment, the means are plentifully available to sustain the illusion: the solace of formalism and the vanguard drama of dissidence are equally compliant. But artistic creation is not about living up to expectations or conforming to models of polite or impolite behavior. For Luhmann, following Spencer Brown, to create is to make a distinction. "The first step in the making of an artwork leads from the unmarked space into a marked space, and it creates a boundary by crossing that boundary" (117).

> Accordingly, for all genres the medium of art is the sum total of possible ways of crossing form boundaries (distinctions) from within toward the outside and of discovering fitting indications on the other side that stimulate further crossings by virtue of their own boundaries. The medium of art is present in every artwork, yet it is invisible, since it operates only on the other side—the one not indicated—as a kind of attractor for further observations. The process of discovery transforms the medium into form. Or else one fails. In working together, form and medium generate what characterizes successful artworks, namely, *improbable evidence* (118-119).

By means of the art work you find yourself on the other side of a boundary you didn't know you crossed until you found yourself on the far side of it. There is no name for that boundary except the name of the work ("Blood Count," "Le Déjeuner sur l'herbe," *A Border Comedy*), and the work itself is evidence of the crossing, but *improbable* evidence because there's no way of stipulating in advance where the work will take you. Or, if there is—if the poem simply gratifies your expectations—it's a commodity, a calculable deposit in a probabalistic environment.

Luhman's perception that "communication" is somehow alien to art is illuminated by French playwright Valère Novarina. Responding to an interviewer's question "What is the purpose of literature?" he responds:

> To make the ground less stable. We are surrounded by idols, with landmarks that are false because they are too solid, with wooden gods who do not speak. Literature is not an art of communication. Enough communication! Enough communicators! Before he communicates, man must frequently speak to himself. They want to give us a too uniquely social and utilitarian image of language; they try to reduce us to existing only as communicative beings, always under the other's gaze. But we are, above all, animals who attempt to be reborn by speaking (133).

For Novarina, "speaking" here doesn't mean rational discourse; but it's significant that he uses that verb rather than one more commonly associated with animal vocalization. Virginia Woolf (who pledged allegiance to the body as final resource of speech, yet whose writing is incessantly intellectual) wondered whether human articulation amounted to anything more than barking. Novarina touches on this double figuration—meaty mentation—in his remark that "language is not in my mind, like a tool that I would borrow in order to think. It is entirely within me: words are our true flesh, completely, much more so than our apparent body" (125). Contemporary violinist and composer Eyvind Kang also evokes the somatic integrity of art (in a passage in which the word "music" might be instructively replaced by "poetry"):

> Music isn't dead but held captive. They only allow a peep at music, which is kept prisoner within a parade of falsely glamourized forms. But like a corpse which has been overly made up, the forms are glamourized to the point where music is no longer recognizable.
>
> Why do we perceive the form of music, not its actual flesh? Music is flesh; it is molecules. Forms of music may be depraved or noble, fragile or strong—aren't the passages between them growing unfamiliar? In these ages music suffers like a body whose inner workings have been kept hidden away (167).

Much published poetry, viewed from the prospect afforded by Novarina and Kang, seems resolutely pitched in claims of reasonableness and self control, maintaining a polite distance from philosophical rumination as well as from bellowing. Very little may have changed since Whitman's lament that conformism was the measure of his day in the period following the Civil War. The image of Whitman as nurse situates the poet in an environment encompassing all utterance, groans of pain and desperation echoing in the halls of government buildings converted into makeshift hospitals and morgues; and amidst these helpless sounds emitted by bodies in torment Whitman goes from bed to bed, talking and listening, writing letters for wounded soldiers, transcribing last wishes: the poet as amanuensis of extremity—handling, with care, *improbable evidence.*

As I've elaborated here, the chances for improbable evidence are very good. Innovation in poetry is less contested (or ignored) now, and this is largely attributable to both the number and variety of women. If there is a danger ahead, it may be in the complacency with which we may come to *expect* singularity from women poets, and allow expectation to coerce experience. Routinized innovation is no better than routinized formalism. It's my hope that the auspiciousness of this moment won't be missed: 2001 should be more consequential than 1975, when institutionalized inattention held the field. The sounds that emanate from poetry should come from the stress of innovation, like the creak of rope in a ship's rigging as it attests to a nautical breeze and a breath of fresh air.

➤

Bruce Andrews' Venus:
Paying Lip Service to Écriture Féminine

Barbara Cole

There are some men (all too few) who aren't afraid of femininity.
—Hélène Cixous, "The Laugh of the Medusa"

Bruce Andrews has been compared to a veritable Who's Who of the twentieth-century avant-garde, beginning with Joyce and including everyone from Williams, Pound, Eliot, Céline, Bakhtin, and Beckett to Oppen, Burroughs, Barthes, Mac Low, Foucault, Olson, Creeley, Duncan, Ashbery, Jameson, and Susan Howe not to mention Abbie Hoffman, Robert Mapplethorpe, the Sex Pistols, Velvet Underground and The Clash, to name just a few.[1] And yet, despite how clear it is to any of us sitting here tonight that Bruce Andrews deservedly rises to such stature as an innovator, nonetheless, the work remains shockingly unrecognized.

I am not the first to notice. Hank Lazer begins his essay on the writing of Andrews by confessing: "I am puzzled by the fact that Bruce Andrews' poetry is not better known" (32). I want to echo the despair of this admission though I find it less of a puzzlement because, after all, it seems clear that Andrews' work resists the critic's routine of explication through close reading. Ben Friedlander writes that Andrews is "a revolutionist in poet's uniform [...] [using] pop culture the way a torturer uses cigarettes—to calm down, to inflict pain, to create an illusion of boredom, to show that what is most awful and strange is actually simple, easy as the flick of an ash" (62). The dilemma seems to come down to how to differentiate between the content—which we find problematic (even if we acknowledge that this is the nature of the project)—from the form, which we find brilliantly innovative. How to approach the work without a reductive separation of form and content? Even more, how do we as critics excerpt concise, illuminating quotations to efficiently prove our thesis when the work deliberately defies this desire for a 'clean' syntax or a single 'tidy' passage which screams: 'here's the point?'

And yet, I think there is still another reason why Bruce Andrews' work has been predominantly overlooked. As reductive as it may sound, it is my contention that this work is not better known because it is written by a man.

In the landmark essay, "The Laugh of the Medusa," first published in French in 1975 before being revised and translated into English in 1976, Hélène Cixous calls for a writing practice which proves politically subversive, deliberately transgressive and ambitiously complex. The first claim came in the directive to "write your self. Your body must be heard" (338). This call to 'write the body' was issued as an unmistakable alternative-call-to-arms:

> Write, let no one hold you back, let nothing stop you: not man; not the imbecilic capitalist machinery, in which publishing houses are the crafty, obsequious relayers of imperatives handed down by an economy that works against us and off our backs; and not yourself. Smug-faced readers, managing editors, and big bosses don't like the true texts of women—female-sexed texts. That kind scares them (335).

If *écriture féminine* is that which scares readers and publishers alike, then Andrews' poetry seems a prime example. From the beginning, Cixous employed the language of capitalism, of market values and assessed earnings, to speak of the need for a radical new writing which would explode from within.

> Because the 'economy' of her drives is prodigious, she cannot fail, in seizing the occasion to speak, to transform directly and indirectly all systems of exchange based on masculine thrift. Her libido will produce far more radical effects of political and social change than some might like to think. . . . (339).

Andrews spent the summer of 1968 in Paris; his "earliest poetry," as Craig Dworkin emphasizes, "significantly—dates from the moment immediately following the Situationist-inspired revolution of May '68"; and in 1975, when Cixous was birthing "The Laugh of the Medusa," he was finishing his dissertation comparing "French colonialism in Indo-China and American aggression in Vietnam" (Davies / Derksen 6). Why, then, is it not simply logical to imagine that Andrews, considering these alignments, wouldn't we see the connection with Cixous as nothing if not obvious?[2]

In the twenty-five years since Cixous offered her mandate, we seem all too often to have forgotten that this writing of the body was not merely a command to women, not solely about a gender war, but rather was directly connected to the larger sociopolitical and global sphere:

> she will bring about a mutation in human relation, in thought, *in all praxis*. . . . [she] must invent the impregnable language that will wreck partitions, classes, and rhetorics, regulations and codes, [she] must submerge, cut through, get beyond the ultimate reserve—discourse (340; 342; emphasis added).

For "she" here, I read "Andrews" for it is clear that Andrews' poetics is one which has accepted Cixous' challenge to "write a poetry of the body" which "will make the old single-grooved mother tongue reverberate with more than one language" (342). What remains unclear is why it has taken so long to recognize this aspect of Andrews' work.

If we are to step back from the current bastardization of French feminism and its incestuous North American cousin, indeed, any reader or critic truly interested in engaging the notion of *écriture féminine* would have to admit that Bruce Andrews' work is one of the most explicit and innovative enactments of Cixous' call. Indeed, to ignore *Lip Service* is to ignore feminine writing. To ignore Andrews' poetics of *écriture féminine* is to reinforce the marginalization, erasure, and silencing that feminism sought to stop. Despite all of the subtle analyses of the opacity and dissonance which other critics have offered, despite the endless wringing-of-hands over the 'difficulty' and 'offensive' language in Andrews' work, I wish to offer the much more cynical hypothesis that actually it is the gender of the writer himself which we find so difficult, so offensive, so impossible to swallow. What does it mean that perhaps the most challenging example of *écriture féminine* in contemporary poetry is written by a man? Even more troubling, what does it mean when we find all but inconceivable the very idea that feminism might have reached beyond the gals and dames? How successfully have we absorbed feminist politics if we continue to seek out a poetics of *écriture féminine* exclusively in works written by women? Does physiology really count more than praxis? In fairness, I should point out that Cixous herself is partially to blame for this essentialist thinking. In "The Laugh of the Medusa," Cixous first drew the dividing line by announcing: "I write woman: woman must write woman. And man, man" (335). But in 2002 we recognize quite easily that this separation is self-defeating. Andrews demonstrates that writing woman is no longer the burden of that outdated creature: the poetess. So, too, *Lip Service* demonstrates that male writers no longer need to be confined to the masculinist margins as patriarchal party-poopers who female readers (are supposed to) find alienating.

And aren't we glad? If the situation stayed women-writing-women and men-writing-men, what would have been the effect of feminism as a sociopolitical movement? Could there have been any 'progress?' The writers have caught up. The critics? Not so much. Discussing *Lip Service*, Andrews emphasized that the work he was doing as far back as 1986 specifically engaged "intimacy, the body, relationships, gender socialization, sex, & feminist theory" (*Paradise & Method* 251). But one would hope that we—close readers and careful critics that we are—would not require such a direct nudge. After all, the poem itself seems hint enough. With lines like

effigy bimbo-colored state-of-the-tart sandwich meat.

Adrienne Rich is quite an omission—(99)

how much more of a hint do we need that Andrews is directly addressing feminism? It is not surprising that the "Venus" section of *Lip Service* proves especially pregnant with provocations grappling with issues of feminine sexuality. "Venus 7," for example, which corresponds to the ninth canto of Dante's *Paradiso*, includes gems such as "c'mere let's squirt and ooze / the mercurochrome of pinch" or "penis dentato puffy when wet worker mouth / cheek bedecked fiend nympheta- mines" (121). It should be noted that one of the great joys (and ago- nies) of *Lip Service* is that one can find explosive sound bites like these on every page. The question is how we negotiate them. Do we con- clude that this is Andrews' voice, positioning these slightly misogynistic jabs, endlessly describing engorged orifices engaged in sexual acts? Are these merely the private fantasies of a lyric, penile "I"? Clearly not. Andrews' speaker explicitly states:

> I am but the loudspeaker
> of a symptom. (50)

And the symptom—or symptoms—never end, cataloging an incessant list of social ills and anxieties, including abortion and domestic abuse; poverty and homelessness; HIV and homophobia. The polyphonic voices of the poem remind us at every turn that all of these larger issues concern a pervasive discomfort with the body.

Andrews does not merely pay lip service to Cixous' call to write the body—he takes the directive literally, writing not just about lips and eyes—the cleaned-up pristine body we can appreciate with Ken Starr decorum—but the actualized, physical body complete with anus and hymen, enemas and pap smears, cocks as well as cleavages, real gen- uine fluidity including oozing, dribbling, and hemorrhaging. For all of our feminist-inspired theorizing of the body, why, then, do we find Andrews' writing the literal body—as opposed to some conceptual abstraction—so uncomfortable? Peter Quartermain writes:

> by and large, women in this poem [...] are, like women in advertise-
> ments, unreflective and largely uncritical creatures whose major
> interests and passions revolve around cosmetics, breast implants, sex-
> ual performance and social standing; vain, manipulative, inconstant,
> they seem by and large to participate more or less willingly in a life
> which is, by any standards, undesirable and indeed dehumanised—
> as the poem proceeds, its title comes among other things to suggest
> joyless oral sex. This paradise is a Hell in which women are more or
> less willingly complicit in their own damnation.

But I wish to extend Quartermain's claim to emphasize that it is not only women but also men who are complicit in this hell. Despite other readings of Andrews' poetics as inviting an autonomous relationship with the reader, it would be an over-polite oversight to ignore the fact that this is no genteel invitation. Marjorie Perloff describes his mode as "a searing critique of contemporary dislocation and fragmentation" in which "words are literally 'bombs,' thrown at the listener for effect" (160). In other words, Andrews, as the host and creator of paradise in *Lip Service*, is not invested in making us feel 'right at home' in the poem because it is this fallacy of feeling 'at ease' in language which he deliberately disrupts. Andrews makes us aware that we are already painfully comfortable in language—even as we may claim to be outside of its accusatory glare, far away in the safe prisons, er, confines of our offices. We are not supposed to construct hermeneutical interpretations of the poem, are not supposed to seek out the plot-driven narrative, are not supposed to feel comfortable with our knee-jerk 'recognitions' of specifically-gendered speakers.

> She invented writing
> > auditory abandon could get
> imperfectibly, swell overstuffed nightmare moisten
> syllable-less peek—*is it even remotely conceivable*
> *that a woman could have written this?*
>
> respond reverse detoothing at cruising altitude
> > (256; emphasis added).

Here, Andrews forces us to consider the essentialist fallacy of *écriture féminine*. Cixous' delineation of feminine writing referred to a mode that would be in counter-distinction to the then-prevailing-patriarchal model with its rigid syntax and normalized style. But, of course, if we read carefully, it is quite clear that the category of feminine writing is not restricted solely to women—especially considering that the specific writers Cixous identifies in "The Laugh of the Medusa" are Jean Genet and James Joyce. Cixous' emphasis on a fluid writing-of-the-body which would upend convention and allow for sexuality envisioned an attention to language previously silenced. Foolishly, we have reduced this notion to the most simplistic privileging of the writer before the work. Instead of changing how we write and how we read, we must admit that our application of *écriture féminine* has merely changed who we read and who we write about.

Fortunately, however, there is Mr. Bruce Andrews—exemplary practitioner of *écriture féminine*—doing what so many of his female contemporaries have not dared to do: to break syntactic convention and write without "that scission, that division made by the common man between the logic of oral speech and the logic of the text. [...] From which proceeds the niggardly lip service which engages only the tiniest part of the body, plus the mask" (Cixous 338-9). How appropriate that Andrews embraces this same notion of "lip service" as the title of his Dantean epic—an ironic homage to the oral beginnings of poetry and a simultaneous rejection of the notion of paying lip service, of using language as an artificial tool of social manipulation and control. Andrews echoes Cixous' rejection of paying lip service to the body and dares to truly compose a poetics of *écriture féminine*.

What we can't digest in Andrews' poetry is what the speakers themselves have trouble swallowing. These voices—or perhaps more aptly, these lip syncers—repeat what every hole has already absorbed. But what transforms these lip synced sound bites beyond mere ventriloquism is the genius of *Lip Service*'s fluid vibrations and stop-cut undulations. The sexuality—in content and form—is undeniable at every step of the way but, certainly, this is a cerebral sexuality. Indeed, Andrews gives new meaning to the notion of 'giving head.'

In the quarter century since Cixous first unfurled her French Feminist femifesto, *écriture féminine* has seemingly seeped into the different corners of writing. From Audre Lorde and bell hooks to Oprah's book club.... But before I get swept away in a facile french-fluid-fest, Virginia Slims-style "you've-come-a-long-way-baby" self-congratulatory romanticizing of feminism's successes, it is no doubt wise to pay careful attention to feminism's failures: that is, the regressive insistence that women writers must write fluidly, femininely, feministly, and that male writers must remain relegated to the bad-boy tsk-tsk territory of patriarchy, penises, and power. The speaker of *Lip Service* warns against becoming too complacent: "We have *not* come a long way & we are *not* babies" (168). The logic seems to be that, because we've had our fill of white heterosexual males in the canon for too long; there is room for no more. So pack it up boys! We've had enough of you! If a man acknowledged this, he'd be tarred and feathered. This has been the failure of feminism thus far: the regressive expectation that women critics should write on women writers and male critics on primarily male writers (with one or two ladies thrown in the mix as a nod to political correctness and professionalized pressures). I emphasize thus far because it is my hope that the poetics of writers such as Bruce Andrews and long poems such as *Lip Service* might demonstrate the blind-sighted omissions and self-defeating essentialism of looking only to poems written for-women-by-women as indicative of feminist politics. Going back almost as far as Cixous' first publications, Andrews' work demonstrates profoundly—even more profoundly than many of his woman-writer peers (especially within the community known as Language Poets)—one of the basic tenets of French feminism: that this subversive, avant-garde writing praxis works specifically to disrupt, disturb, and displace reductive simplifications of women=x and men=y.

Perhaps the most provocative aspect of Cixous' essay is her re-imagining the mythological figure of Medusa, the demon notoriously capable of killing those who looked at her. Cixous ponders:

> Wouldn't the worst be, isn't the worst, in truth, that women aren't castrated, that they have only to stop listening to the Sirens. [....] You only have to look at the medusa straight on to see her. And she's not deadly. She's beautiful and she's laughing (342).

Ironically, it seems to me that this image proves particularly relevant in considering *Lip Service*—a text which, in truth, is not problematic but which points out that which is problematic in our own tokenized lip service to feminist thinking. In the Venus section in particular, there are repeated allusions to cliché *Men are from Mars, Women are from Venus*-type assumptions: "M use intimacy to get sex, W use sex to get intimacy" (128) but it becomes obvious, as one speaker points out, that "when all disorders are taken into account, M and W / are about equally troubled" (129). The lesson of *écriture féminine* was to recognize a difference between masculine writing—that which upholds and adheres to strict conventions of syntactic regularity and linear narrative in order to preserve patriarchal power—and feminine writing, which revels in fluid discontinuities and alternative modes. The point was not to erect binaries or hierarchies but to appreciate difference, to focus on multiplicities and in-betweens. We have, for the most part, sadly missed this point, reading texts with predetermined expectations based on the sexual identity of the writer.

Andrews' poetics is indeed still phallic if we think in terms of a head like a battering ram, butting up against oppositional walls and spewing forth an oozing deluge of language; however, at the same time, this poetics is equally vaginal in its multiplicities, its folds of language, its fluid movements. But this notion of delineating clear categories of 'vaginal' and 'phallic,' 'feminine' and 'masculine,' is precisely what Andrews works to blur. In one of the last sections of *Lip Service*, the speaker poses the question:

the women's language seems to have
prevailed—true or false? (362)

To think in such simplistic terms is of course laughable. This is one of the brilliant aspects of the poem. In productively problematizing the sociopolitically-charged categories of 'male' and 'female' subjectivities as well as conventional lyric tropes such as 'he' and 'she' poetic speakers, Andrews forces readers and, perhaps more controversially, forces critics to consider in what ways we have sufficiently absorbed French feminist theorizings of *écriture féminine*. To begin assigning literal meanings to 'he' and 'she' voices, to read in terms of 'his' and 'hers' is to be made the fool. And, in this case, the laughing medusa is Mr. Bruce Andrews.

➤

Invitation to a Misreading:
Andrews' Lip Service

Gregg Biglieri

Rhetoric as a misreading in *the writing*
—Bruce Andrews

All truth is misreading, aren't my errors enough good?
—Bruce Andrews

Although no one's yet read it, Bruce Andrews' *Lip Service* is about to be misread by its critics-in-waiting. *Caveat Lecteur.* These readings will take familiar forms: celebration of its linguistic play, condemnation of its erotic politics, discrete analysis of its form, aloof dismissal of its structure. In the face of this future array of necessary distortions, another equally distortive approach suggests itself: relentless engagement.

I would prefer not to read it; I would prefer to misread it. To read him properly is to misread him. But we are not reading *him*; we are misreading him by reading the writing as his. The writing is the urged structure pencil-marked for lift off. The writer seeks readers. Andrews is Little Read (in his) Writinghood. I am getting red in my readership. And Andrews tells us that "Little Red Riding Hood/ does not escape the wolf" (*Lip* 74). The lean wolf of criticism?

A feast of his assumptions, his presumptions presciently presumptuous, gaudily displayed symptoms of the sumptuous. "Presumptions change to fit the innocent" (*Paradise* 250). A feast of consumption. Inundation is this nation. "Concreteness punctuated with defetishizing the ampler thoughts as phosphorescences papered over a sumptuousness in capitals" (*Paradise* 248). The appetite is tightly wedded to the words which speak the feast—even the teeth are wet with anticipation. The deferral against participation—words and words, not plastic fruit, that's 'real' color, carmine—syncopation depends on the negative enunciation.

But here we are never faced with what's not here: instead we hear *this* language at full-tilt, tilting the balance of empowerment. This empire of consumption is pre-edited for a betrayal of the feast. If Dante's Inferno is the name of a seedy rib joint, Andrews' version of the *Paradiso* is a place where things lick and are licked, abrade amazement, a series of "brocaded amplitude leaps" (*Paradise* 248)—no eating but friction: "absolutely tongue-tied—hand, I'm yours—not to act but to lick" (*Lip* 316).

Even as the text itself, or one of its voices, or language itself ventriloquizing Alice underground in NYC, exclaims, "Don't just sit there, eat me!" (*Lip* 280), we are reminded that "language is no diet" (*Paradise* 138). And even if at times we want to say to Andrews that "you're obviously trying to make an absolute idiot out of me" (*Lip* 173), we have to remember that "absolutes speak no equal" (*Lip* 172).

There is madness in this method. It's not an act; it's all transaction. As he addresses the attraction, he repulses and retracts his invitation to the addressee. The addressee is addressed and undressed in the encounter, "undress[ed] with address" (*Paradise* 262). That fruit, sure can't eat it, tree of knowledge licked and smelled, an ever increasing acceleration of temptation, tampering with heaven and hell. *Paradiso* built on a photogenic genetic code. Leaving genesis aside, since there is no actual penetration there is no need for penitents. But now that that's overt and the insight's out, can't we leave the mantra genre and blend to bliss or miss it? Quit crossing my sun! The clown pops out of the hourglass and sneers at what "the inkwell choreographs" (*Lip* 221), the father's figure against which night rubs those cows refusing nuance straight from his "polyurethral" Hegel.

PARODY, SO?

Paradise is re-entry into the womb. Let's not get physical. Or etymological. Biology is impossible. Let's get equivocal. *Let's Make a Deal.*

"Let's make ambiguity" (*Lip* 216). This is popcorn for the tormented. While others continue to get lost in regret, can't we stage our own commercial pause in this linguistic feeding frenzy to confect a few of our own readerly rumors rewritten as "THIS SIDE (FED) UP"? Amidst this barrage of language, can't we just say openly and without regret, alibi, or "lick-shaped excuses" (*Lip* 245) that language is not a thing, the thing itself, or the idea? Interrupt the voluptuous hiss to *say* this, or *write* this, or come clean as a new-born isotope? This is a misreading appropriate to a misstepped, mussed-up writing, but it's all words, for words and against words, across the clotted cream of the page. All this talk of fluidities is sonically extracted with surgical precision from the language tree and there is no stepping aside (*para*-), much less outside this text but in our own patently unstable missteps as readers writing and written producing our own social conjugations of this text. We write with white out. We lick with paper. We write over what we erase with liquid paper. Texting me softly with his sarong. We're in the language and we think we're protected in our smocks, but when we look down at our chests we see that we've been typed and typed on: "lanolined miracle smudge front/ makes the white-out look gray [...] blank verse playing black on my mind [...] furtive flashes curtailed boldface" (*Lip* 172).

And we have to, we must, in the face of, directly in the face of this onslaught (i.e., by means of 'facework'), DO something. Our minds are being tattooed by this language of address as if we were envelopes and this message or code is the fact of this address. What's inside the letter doesn't matter (content) because the inside's already outside and the letters themselves literally form the address. These letters are penned as tattoos to prick the envelope of our skin. And our needs are also on the surface, at cross-purposes, creating their own spider webs of intertextual, interlabial crosshatchings. And, needless to say, are *they* being addressed? You don't have to look inside this language; it's there, splayed on the page and you apply your own tourniquet to its flows, its spatter and machine gun spray, paintball epiphanic phantasms aimed at your eyes and splicing there. "Some scratch!: can words do *less*" (*Lip* 220). Print choreography, the words don't sit still and the *who* is *you*; i.e., a jury of your own appearances, a jury of another's forgery. "But enough about you,/ I collect liquid" (*Lip* 173).

So, in the "Jupiter" section of *Lip Service*, take your Lanolin, the words, the "pronominal wetting" (*Lip* 231), the grammar is too slick not to refer to its other in things. The things are already there because these things are words. Words sense and make sense just as the senses do; they are wet and grieve and chafe. Have not words big eyes? All the better to see you with my dear. Words do all these things at a distance of no distance—in your face—this is a language of in-your-face and not in other words. Writing is labial, lingual—as Andrews might write, but thus far hasn't, "parataxis ate my panties." Is it "paraphilic?" (*Lip* 214). "Stick to fact ate my mirror" (*Lip* 255). The critic eats its home-work/ vomit. Is this your homework, Larry? "Tongue teaches/ letters in the eyes" (*Lip* 233). There's enough fluidity here to simulate The Flood—this is a pro-diluvean, an unapologetically apoplectic poetics, yes, squeezed through "babyfood lips" (*Lip* 233).

How can we say there's no author here, sticking to the page and bugging us as if he were an electronic listening device (a bug) tapping the white noise of the social unconscious which breaches this text in the sonic surveillance of the overheard? He's biting a hole in time through the page, this cunnilingual word-forker, tonguing the hem of the unbe-gun, he who is that "voluptuary in teeth's clothes sliced same furry couch" (*Lip* 233). All the better to eat you with my dear. This isn't the language of the body, it's the body of language; equal parts velocity and equivocity, with "gelatinous patting pressure/ tenderly pent-up—the pen beguiles/ broad hips producing milk, looking for tonguing a lit-tle lie" (*Lip* 233). Andrews has done the Flaubert inkwell fuck; here are his own "quotable slaps" to the sap: "the erotic life of words & clusters of words & phrases [...] word-to-word fluidities [...] the secret of the ooze" (*Paradise* 259).

The 'real' history of L=A=N=G=U=A=G=E is this endless secre-tion of the equal sign—letter fucks letter, word fucks word and para-dise is a manifesto of manifestation. How many books of poetry do have to pucker up for? Andrews says, 'Me Puck,' and we concur. We say, 'Puck you.'

INVITATION TO A MISREADING OF *LIP SERVICE*
or Stand by Your Mons

You can't get any more "insider" ("DISABUSING sense to refuel the big insider," *Lip* 244) than in this discourse/ intercourse. Past the vagina and into the uterus—intra-uterine. Insider trading. Secret secretions. It's as if Andrews is a mole who has infiltrated the inner sanctum of the Society of the Speculum. "Exterior wants you back" (*Paradise* 270). He has a crush on the crushed velour interior, "a crush on the possible" (*Paradise* 268); that is, "the possible that cannibalizes the real" (*Lip* 54). Gatecrasher gazing at the Gates of Paradise. This is not art's official *Paradiso*. Nor is it Paradis Artificiel. An orificial parasite, Andrews sings the aria "La Donna è Primum Mobile."

Andrews adamantly refuses to cater to a reader's expectations. His address is not an invitation, rather it provides you in advance with all the reasons for neither coming or going. "Refuse the invitation to join what you are already a part of" (*Paradise* 139). If the poem is a vehicle, the reader is a hitchhiker; but the vehicle never slows down and if the reader wants to get a ride he needs to accelerate in his own terms to match the pace of the vehicle—more like the baton pass between relay runners. You must be up to speed.

SAPERE AUDIENCE

This is not an audience. No one is listening; *pace* Spicer, no one *ever* listened to poetry. The addresser and the addressee communicate across (*trans-*) the page, as language mediates mind by calling it forth and qualifying it in various visions and revisions of words. The audience, the sense of an audience is 'outside' of this relation (transaction). It is an historical construct, an abstraction of 'public,' or 'cultural' spheres, or a matter of the historical record. No one is listening to this recording. Poetry has always missed the Mass (*Missa Solemnis*) and the masses.

Whose sense is it that believes the audience to be a mass of consumers choosing products? HURRY UP PLEASE, IT'S LATE. "Last call for retorts!" (*Lip* 269). Late Capitalism, late Marxism, working late on the late work of an age past its bedtime. It is already too late: "the trouble is:/ antithesis, why always late" (*Lip* 265). Except that we know that there is no 'point of no return'—and this is Utopia, a reassertion of naïveté, a splinter of idealism. Who has marked this as a discourse of the market? Who markets what no one desires?

Poetry then embraces the failure of communication in terms of masses, but not between individual readers and writers, addressees and addressers. Advertising communicates to the masses by producing slogans which remain empty enough to be filled by anyone as if this emptiness were the very definition of fulfillment. But no one should be surprised when confronted by the language barrage that seems to bear no message, no product to buy, only endless aural dissonances as by-products. Perhaps it allows the reader to knock herself out—knock your 'self' out, stop dead in its tracks, and go in the opposite direction; i.e., infinitely minimize any potential audience. Speak only for those who still listen for ways of thinking about what they don't already know. The poem doesn't offer satisfaction; there is no money-back guarantee. You lose yourself and gain perspective on this loss, but you don't ever become an 'other.' You don't gain access to some superhero's closet where you can replace your vacuity by exchanging masks. If you accept the challenge of the work, then it's your responsibility to work on changing your own face. You have been slapped by Bruce Andrews. You can either turn the other cheek, or match the 'cheekiness' of the one who slapped you.

This strategy of offense is actionable in that it is meant to provoke you to action. You have been paralyzed by the way the world has been packaged for you. Your only option is to take a risk. JUST SAY KNOW. The poetry that faces you across the divide between the page and your eyes spits in your face the interstitial grumblings of the over-heard. This is not a gift: "the literally ecstatic—gliding on a plane alongside, outside, your 'self'. We're responding in fluid. Gift dishevels" (*Paradise* 266). Poetry is the ripped pages of the present—there is no reason to continue to look for what is past. Send this miscommunication to the next neo-human telephone you see. Perhaps they will pick up something from the static as they wait through the silence of the on-hold music.

He puts the "pop" back in apoplexy, the "lips" back in apocalypse.

If cosmetics are applied to the external body, the internal body is equally made up. At times, *Lip Service* seems to do for cosmetology what Dante attempted for cosmology. Fictionalized & frictionalized. Factionalized & fractionalized. Are we getting lyrical yet? Andrews is plucking out liars while the poem burns. He applies language to the social body as if it were a depilatory cream to remove unsightly rhetoric. The social body is made up of exchanges between subjectivities—the glue that holds these interiorities together is a bodily fluid, a florid fluidity. Andrews brings to surfaces the same attention usually reserved for 'depth.'

At the same time he shows that interiority, especially bodily interiors, are equally sites of decoration and ornamentation. His "scriptive depthcharges" (*Paradise* 250) recall the depths back to the surface. "The activity of defamiliarizing reference is caught up in a defamiliarizing or contesting of depth. It articulates and foregrounds a surface" (*Paradise* 259). The writing, writing itself, is a series of "chargings & rechargings & dischargings" (*Paradise* 259). How can you diss this honorable discharge? What do you think writing is? But enough about you.

"OBJECTIVE REALITY DETERMINES CONSCIOUSNESS"

'It is not the consciousness of men that determines their being, but, on the contrary, their social being that determines their consciousness'
'Bytie opredeliaet soznanie'
Bite me, O pre-delight sews anomie
'Bite! Bite!' (*Lip* 268)

'Language replaces consciousness' (*Lip* 226)

Social being determines word choice: where diction is impersonal and vocabulary is the lexicon's way of preventing identity theft. We read through damaged eyes the linguistic transactions that show how words shape what we see happening in the world. What is exchanged between speakers is not what 'you' think, but rather 'how' we assess the damage. Consciousness has webbed feet. Writing tattoos Y-O-U on your chest, which makes it difficult when you are trying to point to yourself and say ' 'I' think' because, therefore, I see only 'you.' But my objective reality must also be subjected to the same withering irony; the same dialectical vortex splitting extremes into what 'it' means. Do my eyes deceive me when I see 'you' tattooed on your chest? What's happening beneath the surface? What's eating you? Is my ability to read you up to me, or is it that "The Legibility is Enforced" (*Paradise* 250)? There must be some mistake. Or is some "Government practice-typing on the heart" (*Lip* 250)? "Do you copy?" (*Lip* 8). Can you read this "scripted dizziness" (*Paradise* 250)? A missive martyr of "stigmata kisses" (*Lip* 278), Andrews plies his trade at the Orifice of Dead Letters. And this particular postman always rings ideologically. I don't come without remembering where I came from. "I didn't come here to leave" (*Lip* 22). And neither do you. Reading is fungible because it's mental (let your eyes do the laughing). "It's not a criticism, it's funny!" (*Lip* 168). Reading is fun because it's funny—a quasi-tautology. "It's so funny/ because I was just thinking" (*Lip* 256). It promotes interchangeability; it promotes a translation of words for words. It's no longer about you and me, but about us. And the question is, as Zippy the Pinhead used to say, "are we having fun yet?" Language is a fungus. Molds, rusts, mildews and smuts. Smuts? Look it up. Reading is a re-learning experience. "Ah-hah! I hear you learning" (*Lip* 256). In response to one who writes "I think in trouble" (*Lip* 233), it is to be expected that "interpretation waits for troublemakers" (*Paradise* 249). If I'd known you were coming I wouldn't have been so opaque, but you should remember "to laugh is to ruffle clarity" (*Lip* 228).

THE ANECDOTE OF THE SWEATER
or "Don't do to my sweater what you did to my pants" (*Lip* 187)
or, "yo, bedwetters!" (*Lip* 160)

To make a stone feel wordy. To make a word feel stony. To make a stone feel stony—word.

> As far as objective reality is concerned, it certainly does determine consciousness.
> But in art it often runs counter to the consciousness. My brain is busy with the daily grind. The high point of the day is morning tea.
> And that is too bad: some artists shed their blood and semen. Others urinate.
> Net weight is all that matters to the buyer. (*Third Factory* 63)

Speaking of objective reality.... On a recent visit to cardiologist's office, I witnessed the following exchange between an elderly couple in the waiting room. The wife started picking at some stray crumbs on her husband's sweater and snapped, "Look at that sweater!" To which the husband retorted, "You look at it!" This kind of thing happens every day in 'objective reality.' Reading Andrews makes us realize that others are out there monitoring how such hectoring exchanges prove to be the Achilles' heel of language.

When Andrews writes, "I wet my pants—wet yours!" (*Lip* 86), it's funny; but there is an undercurrent of mischief in noting the structure of these exchanges. The artist can substitute any number of words for bodily fluids and still be witness to the wetness of all exchanges. I owe you. "Get wet=do it yourself" (*Lip* 148). Think of how of much our daily communication involves 'pissing' on each other. "Others urinate." Others wet their pants. And things are even more complicated when you think. Andrews writes, "I am but the loudspeaker/ of a symptom" (*Lip* 50). He marks with critical urgency the underlying aggressivity of our everyday language patterns and thus implicates 'us' in the very structure we often wish to deny—where "wishes are metaphors for words" (*Lip* 226).

Perhaps that's why it makes us feel so uncomfortable. He's hailing us as the 'I' hails the 'hey, you!' We breathe and breed and evacuate. Ideology as system of bodily fluids. Do we ever do anything but exchange? "Whenever I speak, I wet your pants" (*Lip* 50). Who's pissing on whose parade? In the first instance, the writer writes (wets) and cajoles or commands us (readers) to write (wet). Here, the writer tells us that whether or not we write (wet) our own (texts/ pants), he has already written (wet) us. And we are unavoidably implicated in this exchange: "we can stay dry, grammar pisses for us" (*Lip* 291). As a former president may have said, "I feel your irony." Because this 'funny' exchange about wetting one's pants is all too political. Whenever GW speaks, I feel that he has wet my pants.

Andrews' bark is worse than his *arbeit*. This is precisely the opposite of the arbitrary. I got your indeterminacy right here. Well, no, I guess I don't. Andrews works through ambiguity: "It's all over because we're not through" (*Lip* 162). His grasp exceeds his reading. His argument for absorption is that it's exorbitant: "exorbitantly—so ex-orbitally" (*Paradise* 269). Andrews is a poet who has been absorbed by language, by the discourse system, so that he has joined its flows. He has surrendered his authority as 'author' while absconding with the very identity we thought we had been left holding. When the writer reemerges in these words, he can only be seen in the traces of his tampering—the grin without the cat. And this Cheshire cat is definitely not in the bag.

Hypocrite Lecteur,—c'est moi! Say more...

Writing as action; reading as action, not a behavior observed by a text, sitting there, bored, looking at us.
 Binary, with the text as switchman
 Blurs, so fast=mesh

Texts read the reader (*Paradise* 12)

If the text isn't looking at us, we cannot become transfixed by it. Something is coming across, getting across. Smells a teeny bit like translation: "Each intimacy a translation, and a theory of translation. We do not have to listen. Text cannot expropriate the labor of reading" (*Paradise* 266). The text isn't motionless; it moves on and can switch tracks—shunting as an attitude toward risk. The text becomes a train that moves 'so fast' that it 'blurs'—mass becomes mesh. Fixed mass becomes mixed mediation. If the text is a train, it still doesn't train the reader. This doesn't require training. The text is a moving object (target); a verb that doesn't train, but texts the reader.

THE SUBLIME: I Hear You Quoting But You Can't Come In; or, The Sublime Object of Pornography: I Know It When I Don't See It;
 or, I Am a Little Dog Because I Know Myself

For, as if instinctively, our soul is uplifted by the true sublime; it takes a proud flight, and is filled with joy and vaunting, as though it had itself produced what it has heard (Longinus)

refining pleasure to resist/ in love by yourself; self-willing sublime/ ain't ashamed that "we" is a rare locution (*Lip* 61)

the silent language/ the visible languages misnamed sublime (*Lip* 239)

With this, purchase paradise/ helps it sublimer wish not want not/ so then give me my ring string attached/ releases the subjectivity of destroyed subjects (*Lip* 101)

Did I mishear you correctly? "Longinus describes the operation of sublimity as a kind of imprinting process which includes moments of expropriation and identification" (Guerlac 275). When I think about you I quote myself. For Andrews, the sense of quoting from overheard speech explicitly stakes out an aesthetics of expropriation rather than appropriation. Whereas to appropriate is "to make one's own, to take possession of or make use of exclusively for oneself," expropriation means fundamentally "to deprive of possession; to transfer (another's property) to oneself" (*American Heritage*). Andrews is engaged in the transfer, the exchange between speaker and hearer, addresser and addressee, writer and reader. He is not interested in the process of stabilizing subjectivities through the process of identification. He doesn't care what 'you' think—"You, scare quotes outside of the body" (*Lip* 137).

Let us quote now, you and I, now that we are outside our bodies and miming our minds. We are what we quote (eat, wet, teach, learn). Exchange changes 'us.' Exchange is based on a series of artificial equivalences and not on self-same identities. If the reader is meant to identify with anything, it is with 'language' itself, the mobile and motile 'scare' codes that course through a data stream that is never stabilized in a coherent union of personhoods (little red readinghood or writinghood) whether of writer or reader—"ain't ashamed that 'we' is a rare locution" (*Lip* 61). "The speaker vanishes into his text. The listener, on the other hand, undergoes a kind of traumatic inscription" (Guerlac 275).

In Andrews' case, a strange repositioning occurs. As writer, he inscribes the moments of overheard, quoted speech and in doing so places himself at the interface of listener/ reader and speaker/ writer. These moments inspire him to lose himself in others' words, to transport himself out of himself and into the discourse. "I cater your none soon pale exit words/ less than half absent Quotation Marks on the throne/ I don't like new" (*Lip* 97). Make it neutral. One should note the insistent literalization of the marks of writing as stigmata, print itself as imprinting or coding the reader before the reader can decipher the codes; simply to enter into language is already to be subjected to this imprinting process. The listener is 'voiceprinted' by the moment of the speaker's vanishing into the text, so any identification which takes place occurs between the listener/ reader and the text, and through the text to this now dispersed, imaginary speaker, this 'other' of the text as text. "The transport of the sublime, therefore, includes a slippage among the positions of enunciation, as the *destinateur* [speaker, addresser] gets 'transported' into the message and the *destinataire* [listener, addressee] achieves a fictive identification with the speaker" (Guerlac 275).

This 'slippage' between addresser and addressee is certainly one of Andrews' main topoi, but I should stress that any identification between listener and speaker can only be 'fictive,' precisely because the speaker has already disposed of and dispersed 'his' identity into the text—"Now as I other quote posed" (*Lip* 71). Thus, the subject becomes anonymous and "Anonymity transacts address" (*Paradise* 249). "This is not so different from what could be said to take place in the much milder, everyday occurrence of quoting. Indeed, the structure of citation appears to be embedded in the very operation of sublimity, while the sublime itself might be characterized in terms of the inevitability of repetition or citation" (Guerlac 275-6). In the case of quoted speech, there appears to be a significant inversion or reversal of the process inherent in 'sublime' citation. Andrews in no way as a writer imagines or feels that he himself has produced what he has only quoted, rather he 'loses' himself in the act of writing as overhearing (his writing is underwritten by the overheard as much as it has overheard the unwritten). Since he is repeating the words his agency is not attached to the source of the utterance, but instead it detaches itself from the cited speech's (i.e., the vanished speaker's) authority, and "releases the subjectivity of destroyed subjects" (*Lip* 101). In the very act of quotation, he is able to detach his own subjectivity and disperse it into the cross-connected historicity of language itself, displayed and splayed out across the panoply of social beings.

What does it mean to say that subjectivity has been transferred to the reader? First, the author's subjectivity is 'transported' to language itself where it enters the discourse stream in order to lose its 'self' there—to disperse, dematerialize, or mimetically camouflage itself; to disappear, or become invisible in the language itself only to rematerialize in the 'labor of reading.' What one has been able to decode is the fact that one has been encoded. Writing that employs quoted speech is an example of a practice of selection which manifests the concision of writing as reading as much as that reading must first have inspired the writing. The reader must then take up the baton, receive the message of this missive which has been addressed to her and thus respond to the invitation to have conjugal relations with the text. Self-reflexive, or grammatically aware, writing makes the writer's private monologue (*with* and *in* and *within* language) public and thus dialogical. It takes it to the streets, where the streets are paved with quotations rather than good intentions. Thinking is not a private affair. When he thinks about himself he quotes us. Andrews' marks of quoted or overheard speech are the stigmata which ground his external interiority, his euphoric pessimism, his infernal *Paradiso*, his deoxyribonucleic acid tongue.

STARVE A CODE, FEED A FETISH

One's gaze animates the inert thing—commodity fetish—but that thing then takes up residence in one's own vision as a pair of cement shoes say; or better, as the incipient germ that causes the slow infection which transforms one's own agency into an inert thing. The trick, if trick it is, would be to treat this infiltration as an inoculation against the full-blown, rampant spread of disease throughout the system. Or else to imitate the virus itself, to change one's own coloring to perform a counterinsurgency operation from within the enclave of the enemy, using its own codes and forms of discourse as camouflage. Thus, by making its own agency invisible it highlights by contrast one's inability to resist infection because by placing oneself at all in this discourse stream one is already infected by the toxicity of this system. "If you work within the system, the system works within you" (*Lip* 168). The residual medication (this will help me more than it helps you) of a capitalist reference system flattens people into things so that they can be more easily packaged and exchanged for the promise of a value (happiness?) that can only be realized by forfeiting one's agency, thus canceling out any chance that one could ever collect on this imaginary reflection of a real debt. Subjectivity is subjected to the pure products of American objectification. There is nothing to fear in the process of commodification but the fetish of fear itself.

Have you been listening to what is produced by this mill of slogans?

Sprite: "Image is everything—Obey your thirst." Virginia Slims: "You've come a long way, baby" (*Lip* 165). And just a few pages further, this rejoinder: "we have *not* come a long way & we are *not* babies" (*Lip* 168). Dow Chemical: "Without chemicals, life itself would be impossible" (*Lip* 263). Andrews' oxymorons become foxy morons. We live in a country where "too much makeup is our national bird" (*Lip* 56).

➢

from *Stuplimity: Shock and Boredom in Twentieth-Century Aesthetics*

Sianne Ngai

Less best. No. Naught best. Best worse. No. Not best worse.
Naught not best worse. Less best worse. No. Least. Least
best worse. Least never to be naught. Never to naught be
brought. Never by naught be nulled. Unnullable least. Say
that best worst. With leastening words say least best worse.
For want of worser worse.
—Samuel Beckett, *Worstward Ho* (1983)

There is stupid being in every one. There is stupid being in every one
in their living. Stupid being in one is often not stupid thinking or stu-
pid acting. It very often is hard to know it in knowing any one.
Sometimes one has to know of some one the whole history in them,
the whole history of their living to know the stupid being of them.
—Gertrude Stein, *The Making of Americans* (1906-08)

Sorry. Sorry. I'm sorry. I regret it. Please accept my apology. I'm
extremely sorry. I regret my mistake. Pardon me. Pardon me.
I hope you'll forgive me. I'm deeply apologetic. Do forgive me.
Pardon me. Accept my apology. Do forgive me. I'm
deeply apologetic. Excuse me. Excuse me. It was my own fault.
Do forgive me. I'm so sorry...
—Janet Zweig, *Her Recursive Apology* (sculpture), 1993

"Thick" Language

"Gertrude and I are just the contrary," writes Leo Stein in *Journey Into The Self* (1950). "She's basically stupid and I'm basically intelligent" (qtd. Schmitz, 100). What Leo finds "stupid" about Gertrude and her writing, which he abhorred, is perhaps analogous to what the character Tod finds "thick" about Homer Simpson's use of words in Nathanael West's *The Day of the Locust* (1939). When Tod coaxes the sluggish, almost comatose Homer to talk about the departure of Faye, Homer's speech is at first incomprehensible to him. "Language leaped out of Homer in a muddy, twisting torrent. [...] The lake behind the dam replenished itself too fast. The more he talked the greater the pressure grew because the flood was circular and ran back behind the dam again" (143-4). Yet Homer's "muddy, twisting torrent" has a logic of its own, eventually enabling Tod to understand his back-flowing discourse on its own terms:

> A lot of it wasn't jumbled so much as timeless. The words went behind each other instead of after. What he [*s.c.* Tod] had taken for long strings were really one thick word and not a sentence. In the same way sentences were simultaneous and not a paragraph. Using this key he was able to arrange a part of what he had heard so that it made the usual kind of sense (144).

Homer's dull stupor in the wake of unexpected loss produces its own "thick" language—one that initially suggests an inability to respond or speak at all—by eroding formal distinctions between word, sentence, and paragraph. To use terms Gilles Deleuze adapts from Duns Scotus, the thirteenth-century philosopher whose name gives rise to the word "dunce," these formal differences of quality or kind are exchanged for modal differences based on variations in intensity or degree.[1] Modal differences could thus be described as moody differences—unqualified, temperamental, and constantly shifting. Moreover, in West's novel the encounter with thick language, which is based on modal and as yet unqualified differences rather than on formal ones, produces a mimetic effect: Tod finds himself temporarily stupefied by the language generated by Homer's stupor. Which is to say that he discovers that it challenges his own capacity to interpret or respond to it in conventional ways.

Radically altering the temporal order dictated by normative syntax ("the words went behind each other instead of after"), and blurring the distinction between syntactic units (words, sentences, paragraphs), the thick or grammatically moody language that West describes can also encompass the signifying logic at work in Stein's dense *Making of Americans* (1906-8), where words are deliberately presented in "long strings" rather than conventional sentences and where the repetition of particular words or clauses produces a layered or "simultaneous" effect. As Stein puts it in "Poetry and Grammar,"

> Sentences and paragraphs. Sentences are not emotional but para-graphs are. [...] When I wrote the Making of Americans I tried to break down this essential combination by making enormously long sentences that would be as long as the longest paragraph and so to see if there was really and truly this essential difference between para-graphs and sentences, if one went far enough with this thing with making the sentences long enough to be as long as any paragraph and so producing in them the balance of a paragraph not a balance of a sentence, because of course the balance of a paragraph is not the same balance as the balance of a sentence (Stein, *Writings*, 142).

Stein's attempt to erode the formal difference—referred to above as "essential difference"—between sentences and paragraphs (a differ-ence in kind or quality) by bringing into play the modal difference between long and "enormously long" sentences (a difference in inten-sity or degree) poses a challenge to dominant systems of sense-making, a challenge that she would pursue throughout her career. In *The Making of Americans*, the strategy is also an agglutinative one, where the simple material build-up of language, turning already long sentences into longer ones, is invested with the potential for altering the "balance," or equilibrium, of normative syntax and prose structure.

The sense of urgency that inflects Stein's struggle to make sentences "simultaneous and not a paragraph" in *The Making of Americans* becomes amplified in *How to Write* (1928), whose opening piece, "Saving the Sentence," bears a title suggesting that language, like an occupied territory in time of war, is in need of rescue. In another sec-tion from *How to Write*, called "Sentences," Stein makes a similar effort to explore the relation between different units of sense: "*What* is the difference between words and a sentence and a sentence and sentences" (181, my emphasis). At first glance her statement seems to inquire about the element that enables us to distinguish one linguistic kind from another (words from sentences), as well as single instances from plural instances of a particular kind (sentence from sentence). It also seems to ask about the difference that lies *between* the two kinds of difference exemplified by two sets of paired terms: formal difference (words and a sentence) and modal difference (sentence and sentences). But, in addition, we can read it as a statement that names the term "what" as precisely this distinction. What is "what"? Several things at once. It is an interrogative adjective, as well as a relative pronoun equally applicable to single and plural objects. As a word capable of standing alone to form its own sentence, "what" can also function as a demand for repetition, or an expletive conveying a negative emotion such as disbelief, stupefaction, or incomprehension. Thus, in locating "the difference between words and a sentence and a sentence and sentences" in "what," Stein suggests that the difference is at once interrogative, relative, affective, and one that oddly compels or solicits repetition. Like the relationship between sentences and paragraphs in *The Making of Americans*, or between "one thick word" and a sentence in Homer's muddy discourse, difference as "what" could be described as a difference without determinate value or "difference without a concept"—which is one of the ways Deleuze defines repetition in *Difference and Repetition*.

The fact that "what" can become a demand for repetition also recalls Deleuze's counterintuitive thesis that repetition is what lies between two differences. If configured as "what," the "difference between words and sentences or a sentence and sentences" could be described as a demand for repetition that also poses a question: "What is a sentence. A sentence is something that is or is not followed" (Stein, *How* 213). As Stein notes here, the word "what" is a sentence, or becomes its own free-standing sentence ("What?") when it becomes a question that solicits but may or may not be followed by a reply. "Now the whole question of questions and not answer is very interesting" (Stein, *How* 32). Hence, the response that difference in the form of "what" solicits, as when encountered by Tod in Homer's thick speech, seems likely to take the form of a blocked or obstructed response—when the ability to "answer" the question posed by a specific kind of linguistic difference is frustrated or delayed. The negative experience of stupefaction arising from a relation to language founded on a not-yet-qualified or not-yet-conceptualized difference (as in Tod's relationship to Homer's "muddy" discourse) raises the significant question of how we might respond to what we recognize as "the different" before a value has been assigned to it or before it becomes qualified—as "sexual" or "racial" difference, for instance. We are used to encountering and recognizing differences assigned concepts or values; Stein's writing asks us to ask how we negotiate our encounters with difference when these qualifications have not yet been made. The explosion of modal differences in Beckett's *Worstward Ho* poses a similar question: we may have a concept for the difference between "best" and "worst"—but what about the difference that Beckett insists lies between "worst" and "worser worst," or between "Best worse" and "Least best worse"? (106).

Hence, in Stein's effort to "break down the essential combination" of sentences and paragraphs and suggest that "what" is the difference between "words and a sentence and a sentence and sentences," her agenda is not to be confused with an attempt to level or neutralize difference by repetition; rather, it is an effort to reconfigure one's relationship *to* difference through repetition and grammatical play. If a specific emotional quality emerges through this new relationship to difference, it seems important to understand how the former might organize and inform strategies of reading made possible by the latter. Throughout Stein's career—beginning around 1906, when she began developing what Marianne deKoven calls her "insistent" style based on repetition—fixed or "essential" distinctions are replaced with as yet unqualified ones to generate new frameworks of sense-making: standards of continuity, order, and "balance" alternative to the symbolic status quo (deKoven 50). What this requires from the writer, Stein suggests, as well as from her readers, is an experiment in both duration and endurance, testing whether one can go "far enough with this thing." As anyone who has read *The Making of Americans* in its entirety can attest, this astonishing 922-page narrative inevitably induces an exhaustion bound up with its taxonomic analysis and differentiation of human types. Stein's interest in how astonishment and fatigue, when activated in tandem, come to organize and inform a particular kind of relationship between subjects and language (or between subjects and difference, via language) can be further explored by examining how this peculiar amalgam of seemingly antithetical affects comes to bear on our contemporary engagements with radically "different" forms in American poetry.

Poetic Fatigue and Hermeneutic Stupor

In *Journey into the Self*, what Leo Stein implicitly defines as "stupid" language, in his characterization of his sister the writer, is language that threatens the limits of self by challenging its ability to respond—temporarily immobilizing the addressee as in situations of extreme shock or boredom. In the case of Homer's muddy and twisting torrent of words, the subject no longer seems to be the agent producing or controlling his speech; rather, language "leaps out" with its peculiar force and stupefies the listener. Yet as West's scene of interpretation demonstrates, Homer's emotional speech becomes intelligible once Tod recognizes that it constitutes its own system of sense-making and that it requires the addressee to readjust his sense of linguistic "balance." Like the affectively charged, insistent language that Gertrude Stein uses in *The Making of Americans* to *unbalance* conventional syntax and create a vast combinatory of "bottom natures," Homer's "thick" and "muddy" invites a critical journey not into the self, but into the more complex problem of the self's relationship to a particular kind of linguistic difference that does not yet have a concept assigned to it.

"The words went behind each other instead of after. What he had taken for long strings were really one thick word and not a sentence. In the same way sentences were simultaneous and not a paragraph" (West 14). Deviating from conventional syntax and its standard way of organizing signs, Homer's gush, like Stein's prose, produces a simultaneousness or thickness that recalls the cause of the cryptanalyst Legrand's stupefaction in Poe's tale "The Gold-Bug" (1843). Trying to analyze the image of a scarabaeus he has sketched on a piece of parchment, Legrand is surprised to discover a skull on the reverse side, superimposed immediately beneath his drawing:

I say the singularity of this coincidence absolutely stupefied me for a

time. This is the usual effect of such coincidences. The mind strug-
gles to establish a connection—a sequence of cause and effect—and,
being unable to do so, suffers a species of temporary paralysis. But,
when I recovered from the stupor, there dawned upon me gradually
a conviction which startled me even far more than the coincidence
(305).

In the scenes of analytical stupor staged by both West and Poe, the
obstacle posed to the interpreter involves a superimposition of forms.
Homer's words are placed "behind each other instead of after," and so
are Legrand's glyphs, creating a layered simultaneity of signs. In West's
narrative, the thickening of Homer's language is explicitly figured as an
effect of behindness—that of discursive flow "[running] back behind
the dam again" (144). The backward slippage dramatized in Tod's
description of Homer's language is likewise a feature of Stein's prose
in *The Making of Americans*, where narration is repeatedly forced to
"begin again," and it is an aspect of the style that dominates Beckett's
later prose and poetry. In "Stirrings Still" (1988), a prose poem that
deals specifically with a subject's experience of stupefying loss, the
overlapping accretion of phrases and clauses within the boundaries of
a severely limited diction results in a language that is paradoxically
both ascetic and congested, "thickening" even as it progresses into a
narrative of not-progressing:

> One night or day then as he sat at his table head on hands he saw
> himself rise and go. First rise and stand clinging to the table. Then
> sit again. Then rise again and stand clinging to the table. Then go.
> Start to go. On unseen feet start to go. So slow that only change of
> place to show he went. As when he disappeared only to reappear
> later at another place. Then disappeared again only to reappear
> again later at another place again. So again and again disappeared
> again only to reappear again later at another place again. Another
> place in the place where he sat at his table head on hands (259-260).

The theme of survival and endurance in the wake of a traumatic loss
is conveyed here through a drastic slowdown of language, a rhetorical
enactment of its fatigue—in which the duration of relatively simple

actions is uncomfortably prolonged through a proliferation of precise inexactitudes. This process occurs not only through repetition but through a series of constative exhaustions staged through the corrective dynamics of retraction and restatement, of statements partially undoing the completion of preceding statements by breaking the movements they describe into smaller intervals. The undoing paradoxically relies on a process of material build-up, where words are slowly added rather than subtracted. The finitude of a simple action such as "he saw himself rise and go" becomes disrupted by being rendered increasingly specific in degree. "He saw himself rise and go." Not exactly: first he rises and stands, then sits again, then rises again. Then he goes. Not exactly: then he *started* to go. No again: then *on unseen feet* he started to go. The intersitial *no*'s that are unstated but implied in "Stirrings Still" are actually filled in for us in *Worstward Ho*, which attempts to exhaust all combinations of the values we assign to difference: "Less best. No. Naught best. Best worse. No. Not best worse. Naught not best worse. Less best worse. No. Least. Least best worst" (106). In both cases, the logic of progression from statement to statement is paradoxically propelled by a series of implicit or explicit objections continually jerking us backwards, resulting in writing that continually calls attention to itself as lacking, even as it steadily accumulates. Because units of meaning are constantly shifting behind one another, Beckett's use of language performs a stacking of multiple temporalities, an overlapping of instantaneities and durations, rather than a linear progression in time.

Like Stein's style in the period of *Making of the Americans*, "Stirrings Still" becomes syntactically dense and complex while remaining minimalist in diction. As in the case of Homer's "simultaneous" or "timeless" language, its language is marked by the same absence of a "sequence of cause and effect" that stupefies Legrand, producing the effect of delay, fatigue, or "temporary paralysis" (Poe, 305). This discontinuity is generated within the speech or text itself, as well as experienced by its interpreter as an interruption of understanding. What Poe, West, and Beckett suggest in different ways is that when language thickens it suffers a "retardation by weak links," slowed down by the absence of causal connectives that would propel the work forward.[2] It is this change in temporal organization that in turn slows down the interpreter—as if the loss of strong links in the text or narrative para-doxically strengthens an affective link between it and the reader, trans-ferring the text's "stupor" to him or her.

To acknowledge and attempt to understand one's own experience of being stupefied by a "thick" or "muddy" text, as Legrand and Tod do—an effort which enables them to go on as interpreters in spite of "temporary paralysis"—is not the same as projecting stupidity onto the text that instigates the experience of stupefaction, as Leo Stein does when he displaces his emotional response to Gertrude Stein's writing onto the writing itself. Attempting to pinpoint the linguistic attributes that inform their stupefaction, rather than dismissing the stupefying text as senseless, Tod and Legrand perceive a breakdown of formal dif-ferences and a proliferation of modal ones, as well as a thick or "simul-taneous" layering of elements in place of linear sequencing. A similar logic prevails in Dan Farrell's prose poem *366, 1996*, which was pub-lished in 1997 and which bears some stylistic allegiance to the "thick" uses of language in Beckett and Stein:

> Monday, Tuesday, Wednesday, Thursday, Friday, Saturday, Sunday, Monday, Tuesday, Wednesday, Thursday, Friday, Saturday, going into the woods, Sunday, Monday, typical trees, Tuesday, typical grass traces, Wednesday, Thursday, typical excitations, Friday, typical regional sounds, Saturday, Sunday, why slow rather than slowest, Monday, clouded height, Tuesday, some same ground, Wednesday, Thursday, Friday, Saturday, left and possible, Sunday, right and pos-sible, Monday, Tuesday, could what there is not to be believed be asked, Wednesday, Thursday [...] (57).

Consider also this passage from Kenneth's Goldsmith *Fidget*, a poem and conceptual art piece transformed into a live performed at the Whitney Museum in 1997:

> [....] Tongue and saliva roll in mouth. Swallow. Tongue emerges through teeth and lips. Tongue lies on lower lip. Teeth click tongue. Lower jaw drops away from upper. Flesh folds beneath chin. Repeats. Upper lip sucks. Rubs against lower. Swallow. Saliva gath-ers under tongue. Teeth tuck inside jaw. Gather saliva. Swallow. Left

hand, grasping with three fingers, moves toward mouth. Swallow. Arm drops. Arm lifts. Swallow. Arm drops. Swallow. Arm lifts. Arm drops. Eyes move to left. Left hand hits. Arm lifts. Swallow. Arm drops. Right leg crosses left [...] (18-19).[3]

Just as Beckett's poem stylistically enacts a form of discursive exhaustion or fatigue, Farrell and Goldsmith's texts relentlessly focus on the tedium of the ordinary: the monotony of routines ("typical excitations") organized by calendar headings, the movements of a body not doing anything in particular. Simultaneously astonishing and boring, the experiment in "duration" is taken in each to a structural extreme: Farrell's poem incorporates every single day of the week of the year named in its title (366 days in all); Goldsmith's documents the writer's impossible project of recording every single bodily movement made in a twenty-four hour period (Bloomsday, June 16). Using a similar conceptual framework, Judith Goldman's poem "dictée" (2001), described by the author as "a study in the logic of paranoia" and its strategies of negation, is composed of every single word in Melville's *Moby-Dick* that begins with the prefix *un-*, in the exact order in which those words appear:

> under, unite, unless, unpleasant, universal, uncomfortable, unaccountable, under, unbiased, undeliverable, under, underneath, universe, unequal, understanding, unaccountable, unwarranted, unimaginable, unnatural, unoccupied, undress, unobserved, unknown, unwarrantable, unknown, unaccountable, understand, uncomfortable, unsay, unaccountable, uncommonly, undressed, unearthly, undressing, unnatural, unceremoniously, uncomfortableness, unmethodically, undressed, unendurable, unimaginable, unlock, unbecomingness, understand, under, unusual, unrecorded, unceasing, unhealing, unbidden, universal, unstirring, unspeakable, unnecessary, unseen, unassuming, unheeded, unknown, until, uncheered, unreluctantly, unto, unwelcome, unto, unearthly, uncouthness, unbiddenly, unite, unite [...] (50).

In a dramatization of the way in which modal differences usurp formal ones, the poet converts *Moby-Dick* into Moby-dictation, producing a hyperbolic version of the collage of quotations compiled by the Sub-Sub-Librarian in Melville's novel. If for Melville the Sub-Sub is always already a small subject encompassed, like Ishmael, by an enormous system, Goldman comically positions herself as an even smaller one. The exaggeration of language's iterability is similarly enacted in an encyclopedic work by Goldsmith entitled *No. 111 2.7.93-10.20.96*. Created in 1997, this is a collection of verbal materials that he compiled from February 7, 1993 to October 20, 1996—lists, phrases, conversations, found passages, and entire pieces of fiction, all ending on the sound of the letter *r* or schwa (his rhyme)—and that he laboriously ordered by syllable count, from a series of one-syllable entries to a piece containing precisely 7,228 (his meter).[4] Taking a more traditional versifier's attention to prosodic constraints to an extreme, and persistently subordinating content to the ruthless demands of its self-imposed rhyming pattern and metrical structure, Goldsmith's Sub-Subish work also results in what Raphael Rubinstein calls "a weirdly constructed Baedeker to late 20th Century American society." In "MDCLXXXVI" (the titles of Goldsmith's chapters reflect the number of syllables they contain, which in turn determine their order in the volume), constative fatigue is hilariously performed through an overdetermined self-referentiality and use of "literary devices" as clichés. That particular chapter, which self-referentially appropriates a text that could be described as prototypically postmodern in its own parody of postmodern appropriation and self-referentiality, seems designed to exhaust the parodying of these devices, as well as the devices themselves:

This is the first sentence of the story. This is the second sentence. This is the title of the story which is also found several times in the story itself. This sentence is questioning the intrinsic value of the first two sentences. This sentence is to inform you in case you haven't already realized it that this is a self-referential story containing sentences that refer to their own structure and function. This is a sentence that provides an ending to the first paragraph. This is the first sentence of a new paragraph in a self-referential story. This sentence comments on the awkward nature of the self-narrative form while recognizing the strange and playful detachment it affords the writer. Introduces in this paragraph the device of sentence fragments. A sentence fragment. Another. Good device. Will be used more later. This is actually the last sentence of the story but has been placed here by mistake. This sentence overrides the preceding sentence by informing the reader... that this piece of literature is actually the Declaration of Independence but that the author in a show of extreme negligence (if not malicious sabotage) has so far failed to include even ONE SINGLE SENTENCE from that stirring document although he has condescended to use a small sentence FRAG-MENT namely "When in the course of human events" embedded in quotation marks near the end of the sentence [...] (565-66).[5]

In extremely different ways, the conceptual work of Farrell, Goldsmith, and Goldman continues a tradition of poetic experimentalism ground-ed in the work of Stein, including her interest in affectively reorganiz-ing the subject's relationship to language through stylistic innovation. Though such diverse texts should not be reduced to a common equa-tion, each could be described as simultaneously astonishing and delib-erately fatiguing, much like Beckett's late fiction, or the experience of reading *The Making of Americans*. Through hyperbolic uses of repetition, reflexivity, citation, and clichés, the poems perform a doubling-over of language that actively interferes with the temporal organization dictat-ed by conventional syntax. When words or glyphs are placed "behind" each other, instead of after, "the mind struggles to establish a connec-tion—a sequence of cause and effect—and, being unable to do so, suf-fers a species of temporary paralysis" (Poe 305). Yet "temporary paral-ysis" is not merely a state of passivity; rather, it bears some resemblance to what Stein calls "open feeling," a condition of utter receptivity in which difference is perceived (and perhaps even "felt") prior to its qual-ification or conceptualization. In what ways do contemporary artists engender this affective dynamic through their work?

From Stupefaction to Stuplime Poetics

Modern art, according to Susan Sontag, "raises two complaints about language. Words are too crude. And words are also too busy—inviting a hyperactivity of consciousness that is not only dysfunctional, in terms of human capacities of feeling and acting, but actively deadens the mind and senses" (22).

Though Sontag's conjunction of "hyperactivity" with what "deadens" already hints otherwise, the excessive, if abrupt and fleeting excitation of shock, and the prolonged *lack* of excitement we associate with boredom, would seem to give rise to mutually exclusive aesthetics. As Silvan Tomkins might put it, the two affects have diametrically opposite "profile[s] of activation, maintenance, and decry" (88). Sudden in onset, brief in duration, and disappearing quickly, astonishment involves high levels and steep gradients of neural firing; whereas boredom, slow or gradual in onset and long in duration, involves low and continuous levels of neural firing. Yet even as the temporalities of shock and boredom are inarguably antithetical, both are responses that confront us with the limitations of our capacity for responding in general. As Ernst Bloch notes, in classic taxonomies of feeling both tend to be placed in the category of "asthenic" versus "sthenic" emotions, "i.e. those which paralyze [rather than strengthen] heart innervation" (73). Both "paralyzing" affects consequently inform aesthetic responses that tend to be written off as unsophisticated: from this point of view, only a philistine would be bored by the later Beckett's fatiguing repetitions; only a naïf would be shocked by Jeff Koons' pornographic sculptures. By pointing to what obstructs critical response, however, astonishment and boredom ask us to ask what ways of responding our culture makes available to us, and under what conditions. The shocking and the boring prompt us to look for new strategies of affective engagement and to extend the circumstances under which engagement becomes possible. Here we will explore the peculiar phenomenon of the *intersection* of these affects, in innovative artistic and literary production, as a way of expanding our concept of aesthetic experience in general.

As Stein acknowledges in *The Making of Americans*, "Listening to repeating is often irritating, listening to repeating can be dulling" (302). Yet in that book, which presents a taxonomy or system for the making of human "kinds" that is *The Making of Americans,* repeating is also the dynamic force by which new beginnings, histories, and genres are produced and organized. As Lacan similarly suggests, "repetition demands the new" (61), including new ways of understanding its dulling and irritating effects. It thus comes as no surprise that many of the most "shocking," innovative, and transformative cultural productions in history have also been deliberately tedious ones. In the twentieth century, systematically recursive works by Andy Warhol, Robert Ryman, Jasper Johns, John Cage and Philip Glass bear witness to the prominence of tedium as aesthetic strategy in avant-garde practices; one also thinks of the "fatiguing repetitiveness of Sade's books" (Sontag 22), and the permutative logics at work in the writings of Beckett, Raymond Roussel, George Perec, Alain Robbe-Grillet, Jackson Mac Low, and of course, Stein. This partnership between enervation and shock in the invention of new genres is not limited, however, to the avant-garde. It can likewise be found in the contemporary slasher film, which by continually using a limited number of trademark motifs replicates the serial logic of the serial killer (while also, of course, producing thrills), and in the pulsating, highly energized, yet exhaustively durational electronic music known as techno, which generated new musical subcultures in the 1980s.

Though repetition, permutation, and seriality figure prominently as devices in aesthetic uses of tedium, practitioners have achieved the same effect through a strategy of agglutination: the mass adhesion or coagulation of data particles or signifying units. Here tedium resides not so much in the syntactic overdetermination of a minimalist lexicon, as in Robert Ryman's white paintings, but in the stupendous proliferation of discrete quanta held together by a fairly simple syntax or organizing principle. This logic, less mosaic than congealaic, is frequently emphasized by sculptor Ann Hamilton in her installations, which have included 16,000 teeth arranged on an examination table, 750,000 pennies immobilized in honey, 800 men's shirts pressed into a wedge, and floors covered by vast spreads of linotype pieces and animal hair (Wakefield 10). A similar effect is achieved by Gerhard Richter's *Atlas* (1997), which confronts the spectator with 643 sheets displaying more than 7,000 items—snapshots, newspaper cuttings, sketches and color fields—arranged on white rectangular panels. While here the organization of material is primarily taxonomic rather than compressive, like Hamilton's, the accumulation of visual "data" induces a similar strain on the observer's capacities for conceptually synthesizing or metabolizing information. The fatigue of the viewer's responsivity approaches the kind of exhaustion involved in the attempt to read a dictionary.

This mode of tedium is specifically foregrounded in Janet Zweig's computer printer installations, where rhetorical bits and scraps are automatically produced in enormous quantities, then stacked, piled, enumerated, weighed on scales, or otherwise 'quantified.' To make *Her Recursive Apology* (1993), for example, four computers, each hooked to a dot-matrix printer, were programmed to randomly generate apologies "in the smallest possible type" on continuously-fed paper. As Zweig notes, "The printer apologized for two weeks, day and night. Whenever a box of paper ran out, the computer displayed the number of times it had apologized. Because the apologies were randomly chosen by the computer, no two sheets of paper are alike. I arranged the pages in a recursive spiral structure, each stack one sheet larger than the next" (248-9). Pushing the boundary between the emotive and the mechanical, and ironically commenting on the feminization of apologetic speech acts, *Her Recursive Apology* stages the convergence of gendered subject and machine not via a fashionable cyborg, but through a surprisingly "flat" or boring display of text, its materiality and iterability foregrounded by the piles of its consolidation. Zweig's work calls attention to language as the site where subject and system intersect, as Stein similarly demonstrates through her own vast combinatory of human types—a text in which new "kinds" or models of humans are made through the rhetorically staged acts of enumerating, "grouping," "mixing," and above all repeating. For both Stein and Zweig, where system and subject converge is more specifically where language piles up and becomes "dense."

Like the massive *Making of Americans*, the large-scale installations of Zweig, Hamilton, and Richter register as at once exciting and enervating, astonishing yet tedious. Inviting further comparison with Stein's human taxonomy is the fact that each of these installations functions as an information-processing system—a way of classifying and ordering seemingly banal bits of stuff: newspaper clippings, snapshots, teeth, words and phrases, repetitions. To encounter the vastness of Stein's system is to encounter the vast combinatory of language, where particulars "thicken" to produce new individualities. As an ordering of visual data on a similar scale, what Richter's *Atlas* suggests through its staggering agglomeration of material is not so much the sublimity of information, but the sublimity of its ability to thicken and heap up.

But sublimity does not really seem the right concept to use here, despite its early role in making emotion—negative emotion, in particular—central to aesthetic experience. The sublime might be thought of as the first "ugly feeling," in the sense of being explicitly contrasted with the feelings or qualities associated with the beautiful. It thus comes as no surprise that the sublime, conscripted to theorize an observer's response to things in nature of great or infinite magnitude (what Kant calls the mathematically sublime) or of terrifying might (Kant's dynamical sublime), has had a revitalized cachet in what Arthur C. Danto describes as the twentieth-century avant-garde's attempt to separate the concepts of art and beauty. Though the dynamical sublime is characterized in particular by "astonishment that borders upon terror" or by a kind of "holy awe" coupled with "dread" (Kant 109), both sublimes involve an initial experience of being overwhelmed in a confrontation with totality that makes the observer painfully aware of her limitations—or at least at first. There is a sense in which astonishingly massive and totalizing works like Goldsmith's *No. 111 2.7.93-10.20.96* and Richter's *Atlas*, which reveal the limited reach of our perceptual and cognitive faculties, would seem to do the same. But Kantian sublimity remains the wrong aesthetic concept, as well as the wrong concept of feeling, to appeal to in describing the effects of works like *No. 111*, *Atlas*, and *The Making of Americans* on the reader or viewer. And its *interesting* failure to account for the affects summoned by works like these stems from reasons more complex than the ones detailed explicitly within the *Critique of Judgment* (1790), such as the fact that Kant limits his concept of the sublime to "rude nature," and explicitly bars it from being applied to products of art "where human purpose determines the form and the size" (91). [....] Our encounters with astonishing but also fatiguing works like *Americans* call for a different way of thinking what it means to be aesthetically overpowered—a new way of characterizing an affective relationship to enormous, stupefying objects that may seem similar to, but ultimately does not fall within the scope of, either the Kantian or popular sublime. Our strategy for calling attention to the difference between the mixture of shock and exhaustion produced and sustained by a text like *Americans*, and the "dread" and "holy awe" eventually superseded by disinterested pleasure that are particular to the sublime, is to refer to the aesthetic experience in which astonishment is paradoxically united with boredom as *stuplimity*.

This term allows us to invoke the sublime—albeit negatively, since we infuse it with thickness or even stupidity—while detaching it from its spiritual and transcendent connotations and its close affiliation with Romanticism. [....]

While stuplimity offers no transcendence, it does provide small subjects with what Stein calls "a little resistance" in their confrontations with larger systems. The fatigues generated by the system which is *The Making of Americans* may be "nervous and driving and unhappy," but such fatigues can also be darkly funny, as Beckett's Molloy, Buster Keaton, Harpo Marx, and Pee Wee Herman remind us by their exhausting routines: running endless laps around a battleship, trying to enter a door, falling down and getting up again, collapsing in heaps. Significantly, the humor of these local situations usually occurs in the context of a confrontation staged between the small subject and powerful institutions or machines: thus we have Chaplin versus the assembly line; Keaton versus military engines such as *The Navigator* (a supply ship) and *The General* (a locomotive); Lucille Ball versus domesticity. Here we might add: Stein versus her own vast human taxonomy. Critics have suggested that Stein's refusal of linear for cyclical time signals a rejection of official history for an alternative temporality grounded in the body. Yet this preference for the cycle, an endless round of driving excitations and fatigues, could equally well suggest the temporality of slapstick, or Stein in Chaplin drag.

Just as in Kierkegaard's *Repetition,* where Constantin describes himself, while consumed by laughter at Beckmann's stuplimity, as a pile of discarded clothes, the "kinds" of subjects produced in *The Making of Americans* function like garments without bodies—heaplike outlines, as it were, waiting to be "filled up" with the repeating that makes them "whole ones." Whole yes—but mushy as opposed to firm. In *The Autobiography of Alice B. Toklas,* Stein similarly calls attention to Charlie Chaplin's use of misshapen that "were all the delight of Picasso and all his friends" (qtd. in Wagner-Martin 75)—and this is an allusion to Stein herself, well known for her loose and flapping garments. We see here again the role of limpnesses or "flabby masses" in counteracting an oppressive system's fantasies of phallic virility: the clothes worn by Chaplin so admired by Stein are, of course, always falling down. Hence slackness becomes underscored by slacklessness. As if in anticipation of

Claes Oldenburg's soft and puffy typewriters and other machines, or Yayoi Kusama's squishy penis-shaped pillows covered with polka-dots, Stein's love of the wobbling heap or mushy mass similarly recalls the fascination with flabby substances in Chaplin's *Dough and Dynamite* (1914), where he shapes dough into handcuffs and missiles. Perhaps he is asking us to imagine: what might happen to a machine when the exaggeratedly obedient cog within it, while continuing to maintain its function, goes limp? As when the characters played by Chaplin or Keaton, continually in confrontation with the larger systems enclosing them, repeatedly fall into heaps? Here we might also imagine Beckett's incontinent Molloy, collapsed under his bicycle, or Murphy, overcome by the "total permutability" of his assortment of five biscuits when no preference for a particular flavor limits the order in which they might be eaten—"a hundred and twenty ways!" (97). This astonishing figure, of course, leads Murphy to collapse in exhaustion: "Overcome by these perspectives Murphy fell forward with his face in the grass, besides those biscuits of which it could be said as truly of the stars, that one differed from another, but of which he could not partake in their fullness until he had learned not to prefer any one to any other" (97).

In the tradition of Beckett's and Stein's reliance on "exhaustive series" of objects which lack a privileged term or referent, formulating a materialist poetic response to the "total permutability" of language is perhaps what is most at stake for poets like Farrell, Goldman, and Goldsmith, as well as visual artists like Zweig (Deleuze, "Exhausted," 154). For these contemporary practitioners, the staging of "accidental concretions" (Constantin Constantius' term for the way comic characters are built in farce [Kierkegaard 163]) strategically enables us to find new forms of "coherence" in an incoherent world—such as the form we see in Alice Notley's feminist epic *The Descent of Alette* (1996):

> "When the train" "goes under water" "the close tunnel" "is transparent" "Murky water" "full of papery" "full of shapelessness" "Some fish" "but also things" "Are they made by humans?" "Have no shape," "like rags" "like soggy papers" "like frayed thrown-away wash cloths" [...].[6]

Each phrase, presented as a citation becomes "thick" and carries with it

a contextual behindness—creating a series of halts or delays in the narrative pro-
duced through their accumulation. There's clearly nothing accidental about this
concretion of language, yet the poem nevertheless seeks to look accidental. Like
the massive accumulations of hair or type pieces in Ann Hamilton's installations,
Stein's mushy masses, and the lumps formed by comic actors in their continual col-
lapses and falls, such concretions challenge existing notions of form and aesthetic
order. We can see how unsightly "heaping" offers a strategy of what Stein might
call a "little resistance" for the postmodern subject, always already a linguistic
being, hence always a small subject caught in large systems. As Deleuze suggests,

> There are two known ways to overturn moral law. One is by ascending towards the
> principles: challenging the law as secondary, derived, borrowed, or 'general';
> denouncing it as involving a second-hand principle which diverts an original force
> or usurps an original power. The other way, by contrast, is to overturn the law by
> descending towards the consequences, *to which one submits with a too-perfect attention to*
> *detail.* By adopting the law, a falsely submissive soul manages to evade it and to taste
> pleasures it was supposed to forbid. We can see this in demonstration by absurdity
> and working to rule, but also in some forms of masochistic behaviour which mock
> by submission (Deleuze, "Exhausted," emphasis added).

This "too-perfect attention to detail" is the main strategy utilized by Notley,
Goldsmith, and Farrell, all of whom exaggeratedly submit to structural laws in
their work: Farrell, to the days of the calendar ("Monday, Tuesday, Wednesday...");
Goldsmith, to the mechanisms of the body ("Swallow. Arm lifts. Arm drops... ").
Exhausting as well as astonishing, this "too-perfect attention" is also the main
strategy used by Stein's endlessly classifying and subdividing narrator in *Making of*
Americans, and by nearly all of Beckett's "combiners" or "exhausted persons
[exhausting] the whole of the possible" (Deleuze, "Exhausted" 152): Pim, Molloy,
Murphy, Watt. For as Deleuze also notes, though one can oppose the law by try-
ing to ascend above it, one can also do so by means of humor, "which is an art of
consequences and *descents,* of suspensions and falls" (*Difference* 5, emphasis added).
Like other "falsely submissive souls" before them, a significant group of contem-
porary American poets have followed this stuplime path in their confrontations
with the systems encompassing them, formulating a resistant stance by going limp
or falling down, among the bits and scraps of linguistic matter.

➢

A Week of Blogs for the Poetry Foundation

Kenneth Goldsmith

Conceptual Poetics

> . . . i had always had mixed feelings
> about being considered a poet   "if robert lowell is a
> poet i dont want to be a poet   if robert frost was a
> poet i dont want to be a poet   if socrates was a poet
> ill consider it"
> > —David Antin

A poet finds a grammar book from the late 19th century and, inspired by Gertrude Stein's confession, "I really do not know that anything has ever been more exciting than diagramming sentences," proceeds to parse the entire 185 page book—every word and letter, from the table of contents to the index—by its own system of analysis.

Another poet teams up with a scientist to create an example of living poetry by infusing a chemical alphabet into a sequence of DNA, which is then implanted into a bacterium. Thousand of research dollars later, they are in the process of creating an organism embedded with this poem, strong enough to survive a nuclear holocaust, thereby creating a poem which will outlast humanity and perhaps even the lifespan of the planet earth.

Yet another poet decides to retype an entire edition of a day's copy of the *New York Times*. Everywhere there is a letter or numeral, it is transcribed onto a page. Like a medieval scribe, the poet sequesters himself for over a year until he is finished. The resulting text is published as a 900 page book.

Sounds like something out of a Borgesian fantasy? No. These works are key examples of conceptual poetry, a broad movement that has been receiving a fair amount of attention lately. Conceptual writing or uncreative writing is a poetics of the moment, fusing the avant-garde impulses of the last century with the technologies of the present, one that proposes an expanded field for 21st century poetry. Not satisfied to exclusively be bound between the pages of a book, this new writing continually morphs from the printed page to the webpage, from the gallery space to the science lab, from the social space of the poetry reading to social space of the blog. It's a poetics of flux, one that celebrates instability and uncertainty. And although its practitioners often come from disciplines outside of literature, the work is framed through the discourse and economy of poetry: these works are received by, written about, and studied by readers of poetry. Freed from the market constraints of the art world or the commercial constraints of the computing & science worlds, the non-economics of poetry create a perfectly valueless space in which these valueless works can flourish.

Conceptual writing's concerns are generally two-pronged, as manifested in the tensions between materiality and concept. On the materiality side, traditional notions of a poem's meaning, emotion, metaphor, image, and song are subservient to the raw physicality of language. On the conceptual side, what matters is the machine that drives the poem's construction. The conceptual writer assumes that the mere trace of any language in a work—be it morphemes, words, or sentences—will carry enough semantic and emotional weight on its own without any further subjective meddling from the poet, known as *non-interventionalist* tactic. To work with a machine that is preset is one way of avoiding subjectivity. It obviates the necessity of designing each work in turn; thus, it is the plan that designs the work.

In his introduction to the *UbuWeb Anthology of Conceptual Writing*, Craig Dworkin posits:

What would a non-expressive poetry look like? A poetry of intellect rather than emotion? One in which the substitutions at the heart of metaphor and image were replaced by the direct presentation of language itself, with 'spontaneous overflow' supplanted by meticulous procedure and exhaustively logical process? In which the self-regard of the poet's ego were turned back onto the self-reflexive language of the poem itself? So that the test of poetry were no longer whether it could have been done better (the question of the workshop), but whether it could conceivably have been done otherwise."[1]

If it all sounds familiar, it is. Conceptual writing obstinately makes no claims on originality. On the contrary, it employs intentionally self and ego effacing tactics using uncreativity, unoriginality, illegibility, appropriation, plagiarism, fraud, theft, and falsification as its precepts; information management, word processing, databasing, and extreme process as its methodologies; and boredom, valuelessness, and nutritionlessness as its ethos. Language as material, language as process, language as something to be shoveled into a machine and spread across pages, only to be discarded and recycled once again.

Language as junk, language as detritus. Nutritionless language, meaningless language, unloved language, *entartete sprache*, everyday speech, illegibility, unreadability, machinistic repetition. Obsessive archiving & cataloging, the debased language of media & advertising; language more concerned with quantity than quality. How much did you say that paragraph weighed?

Conceptual writing's primary influences are Gertrude Stein's densely unreadable texts, John Cage & Jackson Mac Low's procedural compositions, and Andy Warhol's epically unwatchable films. Conceptual writing adds a 21st century-prong to a constellation of certain 20th century avant-garde movements that were concerned with the materiality of language and sound: Mallarmé's spatialist concerns, the Futurist page, Zaum's invented languages, concrete & sound poetry, Musique concrète, plunderphonics, sampling, and rap. On the conceptual side, it claims allegiance to the works of 'pataphysics, Marcel Duchamp, James Joyce, process & conceptual art, as well as aspects of 1980s consumerist-based appropriation in the fine arts.

In their self-reflexive use of appropriated language, conceptual writers embrace the inherent and inherited politics of the borrowed words: far be it from conceptual writers to morally or politically dictate words that aren't theirs. The choice or machine that makes the poem sets the political agenda in motion, which is often times morally or politically reprehensible to the author (in retyping the every word of a day's copy of the *New York Times*, am I to exclude an unsavory editorial?). While John Cage claimed that any sound could be music, his moral filter was on too high to accept certain sounds of pop music, agitation, politics, or violence. To Cage, not all sounds were music. Andy Warhol, on the other hand, was a model of permeability, transparency, and sliver reflectivity; everything was fodder Warhol's art, regardless of its often unsavory content. Our world turned out to be Andy's world. Conceptual writing celebrates this circumstance.

With the rise of appropriation-based literary practices, the familiar or quotidian is made unfamiliar or strange when left semantically intact. No need to blast apart syntax. The New Sentence? The Old Sentence, reframed, is enough.[2] How to proceed after the deconstruction and pulverization of language that is the 20th century's legacy. Should we continue to pound language into ever smaller bits or should we take some other approach? The need to view language again as a whole—as syntactically and grammatically intact—but to acknowledge the cracks in the surface of the reconstructed linguistic vessel. Therefore, in order to proceed, we need to employ a strategy of opposites: unboring boring, uncreative writing, valueless speech—any method of disorientation used in order to re-imagine our normative relationship to language.

David Antin's sentiments in the epigraph are correct: conceptual writing is more interested in a *thinkership* rather than a readership. Readability is the last thing on this poetry's mind. Conceptual writing is good only when the idea is good; often, the idea is much more interesting than the resultant texts.

And yet ... there are moments of unanticipated beauty, sometimes grammatical, some structural, many philosophical: the wonderful rhythms of repetition, the spectacle of the mundane reframed as literature, a reorientation to the poetics of time, and fresh perspectives on readerliness, but to name a few. For an ethos claiming so much valuelessness, there's a shocking amount of beauty and experience to be siphoned from these texts.

Uncreative Writing

I teach a class at the University of Pennsylvania called "Uncreative Writing," which is a pedagogical extension of my own poetics. In it, students are penalized for showing any shred of originality and creativity. Instead, they are rewarded for plagiarism, identity theft, repurposing papers, patchwriting, sampling, plundering, and stealing. Not surprisingly, they thrive. Suddenly, what they've surreptitiously become expert at is brought out into the open and explored in a safe environment, reframed in terms of responsibility instead of recklessness.

Well, you might ask, what's wrong with creativity? "I mean, we can always use more creativity."[3] "The world needs to become a more creative place."[4] "If only individuals could express themselves creatively, they'd be freer, happier."[5] "I'm a strong believer in the therapeutic value of creative pursuits."[6] "To be creative, relax and let your mind go to work, otherwise the result is either a copy of something you did before or reads like an army manual."[7] "I don't follow any system. All the laws you can lay down are only so many props to be cast aside when the hour of creation arrives."[8] "An original writer is not one who imitates nobody, but one whom nobody can imitate."[9]

When our notions of what is considered creative became this hackneyed, this scripted, this sentimental, this debased, this romanticized... this *uncreative*, it's time to run in the opposite direction. Do we really need another "creative" poem about the way the sunlight is hitting your writing table? No. Or another "creative" work of fiction that tracks the magnificent rise and the even more spectacular fall? Absolutely not.

One exercise I do with my students is to give them the simple instructions to retype five pages of their choice. Their responses are varied and full of revelations: some find it enlightening to become a machine (without ever having known Warhol's famous dictum "I want to be a machine"). Others say that it was the most intense *reading* experience they ever had, with many actually embodying the characters they were retyping. Several students become aware that the act of typing or writing is actually an act of performance, involving their whole body in a physically durational act (even down to noticing the cramps in their hands). Some of the students become intensely aware of the text's formal properties and for the first time in their lives began to think of texts not only as transparent, but as opaque objects to be moved around a white space. Others find the task zen-like and amnesia-inducing (without ever having known Satie's "Memoirs of an Amnesiac" or Duchamp's desire to live without memory), alternately having the text lose and then regain meaning.

In the act of retyping, what differentiates each student is their choice of *what* to retype. One student retyped a story about a man's inability to complete the sexual act, finding the perfect metaphor for this assignment. Another student retyped her favorite high school short story, only to discover during the act of retyping it, just how poorly written it was. Yet another was a waitress who took it upon herself to retype her restaurant's menu in order to learn it better for work. She ended up hating the task and even hating her job more. The spell was broken when purposefulness and goal-orientation entered into the process.

The trick in uncreative writing is airtight accountability. If you can defend your choices from every angle, then the writing is a success. On the other hand, if your methodology and justification is sloppy, the work is doomed to fail. You can no longer have a workshop where people worry about adjusting a comma here or a word there. You must insist that the procedure was well articulated and accurately executed.

We proceed through a rigorous examination of the circumstances that are normally considered outside of the scope of writing but, in fact, have everything to do with writing. Question arise, among them:

> What kind of paper did you use? Why is it on generic white computer paper when the original edition was on thick, yellowed, pulpy stock? What does it say about you: your aesthetic, economic, social, and political circumstances?

> Do you reproduce exactly the original text's layout page by page or do you simply flow the words from one page to another, the way your word processing program does? Will the texts be received differently if it is in Times Roman or Verdana?

For a task so seemingly simple, the questions never end.

A few years ago I was lecturing to a class at Princeton. After the class, a small group of students came up to me to tell me about a workshop that they were taking with one of the most well-known fiction writers in America. They were complaining about her lack of imagination. For example, she had them pick their favorite writer and come in next week with an "original" work in the style of that author. I asked one of the students which author they chose. She answered Jack Kerouac. She then added that the assignment felt meaningless to her because the night before she tried to "get into Kerouac's head" and scribbled a piece in "his style" to fulfill the assignment. It occurred to me that for this student to actually write in the style of Kerouac, she would have been better off taking a road trip across the country in a '48 Buick with the convertible roof down, gulping Benzedrine by the fistful, washing 'em down with bourbon, all the while typing furiously away on a manual typewriter, going 85 miles per hour down a ribbon of desert highway. And even then, it would've been a completely different experience, not to mention a very different piece of writing, than Kerouac's.

Instead, my mind drifted to those aspiring painters who fill up the Metropolitan Museum of Art every day, spending hours learning by copying the Old Masters. If it's good enough for them, why isn't it good enough for us? I would think that should this student have retyped a chunk—or if she was ambitious, the entirety—of *On The Road*. Wouldn't she have really understood Kerouac's style in a profound way that was bound to stick with her? I think she really would have learned something had she retyped Kerouac. But no. She had to bring in an "original" piece of writing.

At the start of each semester, I ask my students to simply suspend their disbelief for the duration of the class and to fully buy into uncreative writing. I tell them that one good thing that can come out of the class is that they completely reject this way of working. At least their own conservative positions becomes fortified and accountable; they are able to claim that they have spent time with these attitudes for a prolonged period of time and quite frankly, they've found them to be a load of crap. Another fine result is that the uncreative writing exercises become yet another tool in their writing toolbox, upon which they will draw from for the rest of their careers. Of course, the very best result—and the unlikeliest one—is that they dedicate their life to uncreative writing.

Information Management

I am a word processor. I sympathize with the protagonist of a cartoon claiming to have transferred x amount of megabytes, physically exhausted after a day of downloading. The simple act of moving information from one place to another today constitutes a significant cultural act in and of itself. I think it's fair to say that most of us spend hours each day shifting content into different containers. Some of us call this writing.

In 1969, the conceptual artist Douglas Huebler wrote, "The world is full of objects, more or less interesting; I do not wish to add any more."[10] I've come to embrace Huebler's ideas, though it might be retooled as: "The world is full of texts, more or less interesting; I do not wish to add any more." It seems an appropriate response to a new condition in writing today: faced with an unprecedented amount of available text, the problem is not needing to write more of it; instead, we must learn to negotiate the vast quantity that exists.

Contemporary writing requires the expertise of a secretary crossed with the attitude of a pirate: replicating, organizing, mirroring, archiving, and reprinting, along with a more clandestine proclivity for bootlegging, plundering, hoarding, and file-sharing. We've needed to acquire a whole new skill set: we've become master typists, exacting cut-and-pasters, and OCR demons. There's nothing we love more than transcription; we find few things more satisfying than collation.

There is no museum or bookstore in the world better than our local Staples.

The writer's solitary lair is transformed into a networked alchemical laboratory, dedicated to the brute physicality of textual transference. The sensuality of copying gigabytes from one drive to another: the whirr of the drive, intellectual matter manifested as sound. The carnal excitement from supercomputing heat generated in the service of poetry.

The weight of holding a book's worth of language in the clipboard waiting to be dumped: the magic is in the suspension.

The grind of the scanner as it peels language off the page, thawing it, liberating it. The endless cycle of textual fluidity: from imprisonment to emancipation, back to imprisonment, then freed once more. The balance between dormant text warehoused locally and active text in play on the Web. Language in play. Language out of play. Language frozen. Language melted.

The text of a newspaper is released from its paper prison of fonts and columns, its thousands of designs, its corporate and political decisions—all now flattened into a nonhierarchical expanse of sheer potentiality as a generic text document begging to be repurposed, dumped into a reconditioning machine and cast into a new form.

A radio broadcast is captured and materialized, rendered into text. The ephemeral made permanent; every utterance made by the broadcaster—every um and uh—goes onto the ever-increasing textual record. The gradual accumulation of words; a blizzard of the evanescent.

Cruising the Web for new language. The sexiness of the cursor as it sucks up words from anonymous Web pages, like a stealth encounter. The dumping of those words, sticky with residual junk, back into the local environment; scrubbed with text soap, returned to their virginal state, filed away, ready to be reemployed.

Sculpting with text.
Data mining.
Sucking on words.
Our task is to simply mind the machines.

Andy Warhol: I think everybody should be a machine. I think everybody should like everybody.
Interviewer: Is that what Pop Art is all about?
Warhol: Yes. It's liking things.
Interviewer: And liking things is like being a machine?
Warhol: Yes, because you do the same thing every time. You do it over and over again.
Interviewer: And you approve of that?
Warhol: Yes, because it's all fantasy.[11]

Writing is finally catching up to Warhol. And it's just the beginning. Soon we will not have to be bothered minding the machines for they will mind themselves. As poet Christian Bök states:

We are probably the first generation of poets who can reasonably expect to write literature for a machinic audience of artificially intellectual peers. Is it not already evident by our presence at conferences on digital poetics that the poets of tomorrow are likely to resemble programmers, exalted, not because they can write great poems, but because they can build a small drone out of words to write great poems for us? If poetry already lacks any meaningful readership among our own anthropoid population, what have we to lose by writing poetry for a robotic culture that must inevitably succeed our own? If we want to commit an act of poetic innovation in an era of formal exhaustion, we may have to consider this heretofore unimagined, but nevertheless prohibited, option: writing poetry for inhuman readers, who do not yet exist, because such aliens, clones, or robots have not yet evolved to read it.[12]

Boredom

I am the most boring writer that has ever lived. If there were an Olympic sport for extreme boredom, I would get a gold medal. My books are impossible to read straight through. In fact, every time I have to proofread them before sending them off to the publisher, I fall asleep repeatedly. You really don't need to read my books to get the idea of what they're like; you just need to know the general concept.

Over the past ten years, my practice today has boiled down to simply retyping existing texts. I've thought about my practice in relation to Borges's Pierre Menard, but even Menard was more original than I am: he, independent of any knowledge of *Don Quixote*, reinvented Cervantes' masterpiece word for word.[13] By contrast, I don't invent anything. I just keep rewriting the same book.

John Cage said, "If something is boring after two minutes, try it for four. If still boring, then eight. Then sixteen. Then thirty-two. Eventually one discovers that it is not boring at all."[14] He's right: there's a certain kind of unboring boredom that's fascinating, engrossing, transcendent, and downright sexy. And then there's the other kind of boring: let's call it boring boring. *Boring boring* is a client meeting; *boring boring* is having to endure someone's self-indulgent poetry reading; *boring boring* is watching a toddler for an afternoon; *boring boring* is the seder at Aunt Fanny's. *Boring boring* is being somewhere we don't want to be; *boring boring* is doing something we don't want to do. Unboring boring is a voluntary state; boring boring is a forced one. Unboring boring is the sort of boredom that we surrender ourselves to when, say, we go to see a piece of minimalist music. I recall once having seen a restaging of an early Robert Wilson piece from the 1970s. It took four hours for two people to cross the stage; when they met in the middle, one of them raised their arm and stabbed the other. The actual stabbing itself took a good hour to complete. Because I volunteered to be bored, it was the most exciting thing I've ever seen.

The 20th century avant-garde liked to embrace boredom as a way of getting around what it considered to be the vapid "excitement" of popular culture. A powerful way to combat such crap was to do the opposite of it, to be purposely boring. By the '60s and '70s this type of boredom—boring boring—was often the norm in art circles. I'm glad I wasn't around to have to sit through all of that stuff. Boredom, it seems, became a forced condition, be it in theatre, music, art, or literature. It's no wonder people bailed out of boredom in the late '70s and early '80s to go into punk rock or expressionistic painting. After a while, boredom got boring. And then, a few decades later, things changed again: excitement became dull and boring started to look good again. So here we are, ready to be bored once more. But this time, boredom has changed. We've embraced unboring boring, modified boredom, boredom with all the boring parts cut out of it. Reality TV, for example, is a new kind of boredom. *An American Family*, broadcast in the early '70s—strutting its ennui—was the old boredom; *The Osbournes*—action-packed boredom—is the new. There's no one more tedious than Ozzy Osbourne, but his television presence is the most engagingly constructed tedium that has ever existed. We can't take our eyes off the guy, stumbling through the dullness of his own life. Our taste for the unboring boring won't last forever. I assume that someday soon it'll go back to boring boring once again, though for reasons and conditions I can't predict at this time.

I don't expect you to even read my books cover to cover. It's for that reason I like the idea that you can know each of my books in one sentence. For instance, there's the book of every word I spoke for a week unedited. Or the book of every move my body made over the course of a day, a process so dry and tedious that I had to get drunk halfway though the day in order to make it to the end. Or a book in which I retyped a day's copy of the *New York Times* and published it as a 900 page book. I've transcribed a year's worth of weather reports and a 24-hour cycle of one-minute traffic reports as broadcast every ten minutes, resulting in textual gridlock.

Now you know what I do without ever having to have read a word of it.

I think that there were a handful of artists in the 20th century who intentionally made boring work, but didn't expect their audiences to fully engage with it in a durational sense. It's these artists, I feel, who predicted the sort of unboring boredom that we're so fond of today. Andy Warhol, for instance, said of his films that the real action wasn't on the screen. He's right. Nothing happened in the early Warhol films: a static image of the Empire State Building for eight hours, a man sleeping for six. It is nearly impossible to watch them straight through. Warhol often claimed that his films were better thought about than seen. He also said that the films were catalysts for other types of actions: conversation that took place in the theatre during the screening, the audience walking in and out, and thoughts that happened in the heads of the moviegoers. Warhol conceived of his films as a staging for a performance, in which the audience members were the Superstars, not the actors or objects on the screen. Gertrude Stein, too, often set up a situation of skimming, knowing that few were going to be reading her epic works straight through (how many people have linearly read every word of *The Making of Americans?*). The scholar Ulla Dydo, in her magnificent compilation of the writings of Gertrude Stein, remarked that much of Stein's work was never meant to be read closely at all, rather she was deploying visual means of reading. What appeared to be densely unreadable and repetitive was, in fact, designed to be skimmed, and to delight the eye (in a visual sense) while holding the book.[15] Stein, as usual, was prescient in predicting our reading habits. John Cage proved to be the avant-garde's Evelyn Wood, boiling down dense modernist works into deconstructed, remixed Cliff Notes; in his *Writing Through Finnegans Wake* he reduced a 628-page tome to a slim 39 pages, and in *Writing Through The Cantos* he reduced Ezra Pound's 824-page life's work to a mere handful of words.

At a reading I gave recently, the other reader came up to me and said incredulously, "You didn't write a word of what you read." I thought for a moment and, sure, in one sense—the traditional sense—he was right; but in the expanded field of appropriation, uncreativity, sampling, and language management in which we all habit today, he couldn't have been more wrong. Each and every word was "written" by me: sometimes mediated by a machine, sometimes transcribed, and sometimes copied; but without my intervention, slight as it may be, these works would never have found their way into the world. When retyping a book, I often stop and ask myself if what I am doing is really writing. As I sit there, in front of the computer screen, punching keys, the answer is invariably yes.

➤

Stops and Rebels:
a critique of hypertext [remix]

Brian Kim Stefans

1. Though the computer-poem (hereafter known as CP) is, by its nature, not centered on "themes" in the way that narrative or lyric poetry is, it is nonetheless a textual experience that will be limned based on the source files and the algorithms used for accessing them. In this way, the CP is an image, or final description, of an algorithm's interaction with a database, the fossilization of an activity performed within the space of no locatable "time" except the time from prior to the reader's engagement with it. "All the broken letters of the alphabet / the crustaceous husks of invertebrates" writes Christian Bök in his book of poems *Crystallography*, an exhaustive evocation of the many ways in which language, with its recombinant qualities, takes on crystalline form when the elements of its structure acquire a certain integrity, a complete adherence to language's self-constructive properties. When crystalline, language "defies" time, or at least gains access to geological scales of time that extend beyond years, hence providing a record for some unimaginably distant future of this pre-"historic"—which is to say pre-readerly—engaged moment of activity called "writing." Likewise, the "well-tempered" CP—a CP that induces in the reader, who might otherwise be called a user, the desire to read and interpret—is both an excavation of the sediment of language and a revelation of hitherto-unknown properties of the language. The making of a CP becomes an act of research in this fashion. The successful CP, the true fossil, defies the dispersive properties of time (boredom, changing cultural paradigms) and adopts the properties of a "poem," including some of the cultural capital that this form obtains. Aesthetically, the CP attempts to dissimulate an aesthetics of becoming, of organically devel-

oping through a self-reflexive process like "writing," but this is a concession on the part of the artist to some of the conventions of reading. Even should the database consist of the entirety of the contents of the web, the data will not be "infinite" because web spiders (small programs that search the web scouring for text, as in a search engine) are only able to access data that is in a format it can recognize (text spiders will not find images, for example) and does not have "firewalls" (security programs) blocking them. Of course, spiders will not be able to access data not on the web, and they are limited by what the parameters of the program (a parodic double for the "paradigm" in which an artist works, a mirror of the dominant cultural paradigm) accepts as useful data. (For the duration of this essay, the program will be called the "demon" and the term "program" will refer to the source files and the demon together. This is because of my belief—and personal experience—that the creator of CPs can spend as much, if not more, time working on the source files as he will on the poem itself, understanding them to have a symbiotic relationship to each other that corrupts normal cultural valuations of what "code" is and what "language" is. That is, certain demons, especially if they are not intended to be passed on to other poets, only become "utile" in art-making with a particular type of source, though interesting effects can be created when a demon is applied to a set of texts for which it was not intended; a greater politics of "chance" obtains here. A robust demon will, of course, work with a variety of input—that would be its quotability, of sorts). Without "human" intervention nothing can get into a CP that is not in the database or is acceptable to the program. This might seem obvious, but because there is always a limit to the range of data, there will always be some sort of thematic, or matrix of meanings, operating in a CP. This thematic will contribute to the "affect" of the CP, which is its particular insistence as a singular textual artifact (these themes will become clearer in later parts of the footnotes). The shape of the source data is one of the many variables that have to be conceptualized prior to instigating the creation of a CP, which will always be "conceptual" due to its distance from "organic" or anthropocentric modes of artistic creation.

3. The CP sets up hermeneutic expectations—the promise of being "interpretable"—that can neither ever be satisfied or ignored. It is this promise of interpretability that makes the language of a CP navigable information, something more than a data field or a "constellation" (as named by Concrete poet Eugen Gomringer), and thus turns the reader into a "data cowboy" in quest of uncovering its matrix of meanings. These plays of readability and resistance can be clarified using Veronica Forrest-Thomson's vocabulary in her book *Poetic Artifice*, in which she describes a component of conventional reading strategies she calls "Naturalization" as

> an attempt to reduce the strangeness of poetic language and poetic organization by making it intelligible, by translating it into a statement about the non-verbal external world, by making the Artifice appear natural. Critical reading cannot, of course, avoid Naturalization altogether. Criticism is committed, after all, to helping us to understand both poetry as an institution and individual poems as significant utterances. But it must ensure that in its desire to produce ultimate meaning it does not purchase intelligibility at the cost of blindness: blindness to the complexity of those non-meaningful features which differentiate poetry from everyday language and make it something other than an external thematic statement about an already-known world (xi).

Those "non-meaningful" aspects of poetry include the punctuation, line breaks, gaps between the words and sentences, sound and visual impression—basically anything about a poem that stands apart from common ways of communicating sense. One could call these "non-meaningful" elements those parts that don't contribute to the syntagmatic understanding of a sentence—its quality as a linear sequence of words that form a meaningful utterance—but rather to the paradigmatic understanding, in which the elements of a sentence become isolated, outlined, objectified, and point back toward their grammatical subsets as "nouns," "verbs," etc. Collage poems, such as those collected in John Ashbery's *The Tennis Court Oath*, could be said to emphasize this quality: "Night hunger/ of berry ... stick" presents something more closely related to a literary shape, or gestalt, than a sentence or meaningful utterance. The CP, because of its looping functions, introduces new elements of "non-meaning" in the form of, for example, repetitions that are not based on rhetorical strategies (such as chiasmus or the refrain) but are simply redundant information coughed up by the demon. These repetitions may point to the "meaningful" aspects of the program, which are those parts that contribute to the affect of the dissimulated subjectivity, the loop perhaps suggesting obsessive human behaviors. In general, however, the demon itself must be considered "non-meaningful" simply because it is not part of language, and it certainly, in Forrest-Thomson's view of things, would separate the CP from "everyday language." The early permutational poems of Brion Gysin, for example, were merely the exhaustion of combinations of a limited number of words—"I am that I am" is one example—the same word being stored once in a computer's memory but accessed several times by the demon. A performance of these poems turned the reader into a cyborg by introducing to the human body the looping structures of programming, an experience that might be "naturalized" by the auditor as a form of "obsessiveness." A good non-CP digital work that explores methods of digital repetition, in both its text and visual imagery, is the innovative hypertext essay by Charles Bernstein and Dante Piombino called "An Mosaic for Convergence." It operates both in terms of spatial collage, as in a picture, and in temporal montage, as in a poem, and exploits the excesses that digital repetition makes available in its strategically tasteless use of wallpapers, loud fonts, dissonant colors and, in the text itself, irreverent tweaking of common communicative codes. Repetition in "An Mosaic" also serves to exaggerate the difference in scale between digital cut-and-paste methods and repetition in organic, crafted literary works—by Gertrude Stein or John Taggart, for example—or in visual works that require repetitive action—the grids of Agnes Martin or the toothpicks and -paste of Tom Friedman. This is not so much to mock the limits of human endeavor but to demystify the quality of the "infinite" that is often touted as inherent to circuit boards and memory chips, not to mention hypertext itself. For Forrest-Thomson, a critic trying to make a total statement about a poem will be involved in a push-and-pull with these nonmeaningful elements, and no interpretation is adequate if it does not bear the marks of this struggle. She is against an overdetermined, monologic reading of a poem, one that has closed all gaps, permits no dialogue, and does not recognize the poem's dependent place in the world of texts or its status in textuality—as shards of grammar arrayed on a page. Although she doesn't write this, naturalizing interpretations can also be seen as pursued in the quest for a "cathartic" experience for the reader, a personal epiphany that acts as a form of socialization and forces the reader to reproduce societal values in perfect, and not "illegitimate," form. This transference, which the CP troubles, is described in Donna Haraway's "Cyborg Manifesto" [see footnote 19]. Forrest-Thomson continues:

> There would be no point in writing poetry unless poetry were different from everyday language, and any attempt to analyze poetry should cherish that difference and seek to remain within its bounds for as long as possible rather than ignore the difference in an unseemly rush from word to world. Good naturalization dwells on the non-meaningful levels of poetic language, such as phonetic and prosodic patterns and spatial organization, and tries to state their relation to other levels of organization rather than set them aside in an attempt to produce a statement about the world.

The CP, like Dada (which Forrest-Thomson recognizes as much concerned with Artifice and as not merely disruptive), values its materials over and against determinant meaning structures, whether narrative or philosophical, thus focusing the attention on the microscopic, concrete levels of the poetic organization—one might call this its architecture. The CP, as a form of "civilized Dada," foregrounds a new element: that of a structure that is not transcendent (this is not the world of infinite connections or a form that aspires to Platonic perfection) but is yet illustrative of a possible, if counter-intuitive, organization of knowledge. This would be its "non-meaningful" frame, its crystalline qualities, that can itself be the object of study. John Wilkinson, an English poet who, like Forrest-Thomson, is often associated with the circle of writers often called (inaccurately) the "Cambridge" school, richly describes such a principle of organization, which he calls "metastatic," in his poems (not themselves CPs):

What gives the poems such coherence as they exhibit is not a development, but a set of linked and transforming entities, which can be syntactical gestures, vowel and consonant patterning, imagistic or discursive modes. "Metastasis" is a term in rhetoric, but my use derives from a brief experience of nursing in a cancer hospice, the way metastatic tumours echo about the body and these nodes define the shape of the body subjectively, through pain. Of course, the location of the primary tumour is outside the poem's realm; the poem develops around the metastatic nodes, and these gestures come to evoke its physical lineaments. The reticence of the primary helps guard against a reductive essentialism in approaching the poem, that it is about such-and-such—in fact, there will be a number of extrinsic primaries. Too many indeed for amenability (54).

He later writes that metastases are the "scattered receptor sites of a primary memory process, retrievable only in faint traces," which is to say they point to each other, and perhaps to an external structure, but more as hints than determinants. These "cosmologies may be the lyric traces of a primary event, a Big Bang," but Wilkinson spurns the "cosmological eschatology which returns the basic creation in the Big Shrink," an "encapsulation of the poem." Metastasis is an organizing principle that operates, in a systematic way, as a hold against final interpretations, but it instigates this challenge to interpret in the reader by teasing her with the recurrence of thematic conglomerations—after all, nodes of "pain" must be addressed, even if the "primary tumour" will never be discovered. The metastases, in a CP, are what conveys to the reader the sense that narrative is being constructed out of the materials from a database; they are the channels to the wholeness of the invisible source files. Consequently, "Cambridge poetry" of the sort that Wilkinson, Drew Milne and J. H. Prynne write often resembles Language poetry to the uninitiated, especially when it approaches a full atomization of language as in Prynne's sequence "Red D Gypsum": "Flow / flow my phloem dear ones, fibre life thickens limpid / blue aglets to mind your step or stop to look notable / avernus lee-side of a post." But Language poetry—due, perhaps, to its closer ties to classic Dada—struggles for a clean break with traditional interpretive strategies, sometimes even mocking the reader in his or her attempt to enact anything resembling "deep reading." The CP, because of its high overhead of non-meaningful elements, will also engage in this cycle of transparency and resistance by challenging conventional reading— even the conventions of reading a Language poem. It will avoid fetishizing the "clean break" because it is starting from a point that is already outside the continuum of organic, human artistic activity—it starts from noise and algorithm and moves toward convention. There are few enough reasons for reading a cyborgian text unless it be that the metastases that the non-meaningful, "deictic" [see footnote 41] demon plants in the stream take on some engagement with the "human." It is fortuitous that, in Wilkinson's description of metastasis, "pain" becomes the node that limns the "body" of the textual stream, as it is "pain" that, for Wittgenstein in the *Philosophical Investigations*, was the channel or link between "reality" and the language game, the latter of which was threatened with solipsism. Touch, our one sense that can be experienced in a "non-linear" fashion, as several different inputs from a sheet of skin which combine into a feeling of "pain" or "comfort," is a useful analogy to the way the thematic of a CP can exist as a "harmonic" overtone, as indebted to no particular part but as the composite of its affects. But because the CP has no organic component—either in the form of a creation narrative or the direct link to human labor (there is labor, but it can be equated more with building the factory than working in it) its engagements will hardly be to reaffirm humanism as a philosophical framework. Nonetheless, it creates an uncomfortable contract with humanism to inaugurate this cycle of reading and resistance.

4. One of the key features of the CP is the high-speed switches in modalities that it exhibits, shocking changes-of-gears that impress the reader as having no grounding in intuitional poetic artistry. The result of these ruptures, which occur with a frequency determined by the demon, but also based on the informational temperature [see footnote 22] of the source texts, is a liberation of meanings that can range from the erotic to the political, the parodic to the morose—a carnival of loosed emotions and competing "egos," not to mention words. In CPs that utilize source texts which themselves possess carnivalesque characteristics, the outcome can appear to be a sort of bawdy social comedy,

one without reference to a specific object, though perhaps to a genre or set of themes. That is, the singular attitude of the CP toward another linguistic system—a conventional "poem," an essay, the vocabulary of social critique—grants it the quality of parody or satire. Of course, "carnival" has been a central theme of the writings of Mikhail Bakhtin—he devotes an entire book to it, *Rabelais and His World*—and his understanding of this concept points to another aspect of the CP, which is its relation to the social sphere and how it operates as an engine for recycling, reshuffling and leveling values. John Lechte provides a useful summary of the carnival theme in *Fifty Key Contemporary Thinkers*, first writing on the theme of laughter:

> Carnival laughter cannot be equated with the specific forms it takes in modern consciousness. It is not simply parodic, ironical or satirical. Carnival laughter has no object. It is ambivalent. Ambivalence is the key to the structure of carnival. The logic of carnival is, as Kristeva has shown, not the true or false, quantitative and causal logic of science and seriousness, but the qualitative logic of ambivalence, where the actor is also the spectator, destruction gives rise to creativity, and death is equivalent to rebirth (8).

The cyclical nature of carnival and its property of symbolic reversals—in which the grave becomes the womb, for example—is readily apparent in the CP, in which looping routines and their indifference to human "meanings" make all words, and even punctuation, objects of exchange and refiguration. The algorithms seek, through destruction of prior literary "wholes," to create new stable forms in their own image, and hence the impression of infinite reinvention—technology's power play. What is more important is the nature of "laughter" in the CP, a laughter that is not the effect of an authorial gesture—the Wildean twist, the Twainian irony—but requires some creativity from the reader herself. That is, because the CP partly operates on the principle of the interpreted gestalt—there is no narrative, so each word event takes on the quality of an incomplete image, like an inkblot in a Rorschach test—whatever humor that occurs operates in contrast to some system of values that exist outside of the poem. One could say that all humor operates this way, but in a CP there is no set-up, and hence no punch-line. Rather, the CP is a pointer to another set of values it is perversely mirroring, as if a linguistic Photoshop filter had been run over a set of terms from a recognizable field of knowledge or another literary work. The reader "completes the joke" not through wit but because the "joke" is on the reader herself and on the expectations and predispositions of the reader as configured by experience and society. Of course, the creator of a CP—the human who edits the output, if there is editing—also partakes in this readerly activity, tightening up here and there based on her reactions to the "inkblots." All objects are put into the position of being mocked because of their vulnerability to the demon's philistine banality. The demon, likewise, implicates the reader, who is vulnerable to participation in the poem by being (one assumes) a text-creating being. Thus, though there is often a satiric aspect to a CP, there is no "object" to the laughter, unless that object be the conventions of poetry itself—the whole myth of "inspiration," for example—which is always going to be put in a denigrated light by the cyborg author. The incorporation of all people within the space of the CP is most realized in those demons that operate on the live data of the internet. The most relevant one here, perhaps, is called the "pornolizer" [www.pornolize.com] which takes any submitted web page and replaces its words with exaggeratedly obscene substitutes. This "pornolization" renders any text, from stock market reports to literary masterworks, to the operations of the demon—which is to say, the cycle of carnival. Another example of this is Darren Wershler-Henry's rewrite of Kenneth Goldsmith's work *Fidget*, in which Goldsmith schematically described every action that he made for an entire day into a tape recorder, resulting in text such as: "Left hand tucks at pubic area. Extracts testicles and penis using thumb and forefinger. Left hand grasps penis. Pelvis pushes on bladder, releasing urine," etc. Goldsmith's book is a literary response to some of the fascination with privacy and the panopticon whose best known symptoms are web cams and reality shows. Consequently, it is also a commentary on the phenomenon of data transference that is endemic in cultural activity—digitizing photographs, scanning texts—in this case, making the body the original "medium," like a floppy disk. Wershler-Henry's "filter," a very basic algorithm, puts the word "tiny" before each of the nouns. His rewrite of *Fidget*, called *Midget*, runs partly: "Tiny left hand tucks at tiny pubic area. Extracts tiny testicles and tiny penis using tiny thumb and tiny forefinger. Tiny left hand grasps tiny penis. Tiny pelvis pushes on tiny bladder, releasing urine," etc. This teleactive action—turning the persona of Goldsmith into a midget—illustrates the power of the CP to recreate reality, to shuffle meanings, with a total indifference to the particulars of its actions. As Lechte writes later: "Carnival [...] embraces lowness. Degradation, debasement, the body and all its functions—but particularly defecation, urination, and copulation—are part and parcel of the ambivalent carnival experience" (9). In this way, carnival seeks to incorporate everything into its cycle of exchanges: the sanctity of the Church brought down to the level of the marketplace, the lowness of the bodily functions brought into the eternal cycle of death and fecundity. Carnival was opposed to the artificial temporal measures—the hour, the day, the week—that organized the life of "economic man," and it brought the bourgeois as well as the peasant into a public space of laughter. In some CPs, this "low" dimension is not so prevalent, but as often occurs with randomized juxtaposition of words, sexual innuendo often sprouts from the most innocent phrase. When the indifference of the demon to human taboos is left to govern, minor slips are transformed into grotesque explosions, and the nuance is exchanged for the obvious. Of course, these can all be modified by the creator of the CP in the editing stage, but it is likely that they will not be entirely deleted as these accidents help integrate the machinery of the CP into humanistic concerns, at least as humorous commentary. One aspect of carnival on which Bakhtin focuses is the carnival mask, which he sees as a site of negotiation that is both contradictory and ambivalent, that both hides and reveals. It is the agent of dissimulation, pointing to the "human" but not revealing it; yet in folk culture (as opposed to Romantic culture) it is valued as being the transitory space between selves. As he writes in *Rabelais*:

> The mask is connected with the joy of change and reincarnation, with gay relativity and with the merry negation of uniformity and similarity; it rejects conformity to oneself. The mask is related to transition, metamorphoses, the violation of natural boundaries, to mockery and familiar nicknames. It contains the playful element of life; it is based on a peculiar interrelation of reality and image, char-

acteristic of the most ancient rituals and spectacles. Of course it would be impossible to exhaust the intricate multiform symbolism of the mask. Let us point out that such manifestations as parodies, caricatures, grimaces, eccentric postures, and comic gestures are per se derived from the mask. It reveals the essence of the grotesque (40).

Likewise, the well-tempered CP—a cyborgian construct operating in a cultural sphere that prizes individual achievement—is the mask of the artist, or simply the mask of the "poem" as social construct. It rarely reveals much about the "author" other than a congeries of preferences, a topography of strategies, that are peculiar to the creator of the CP—a singular attitude or affect not traceable to any source. The mask of the CP satisfies the need for familiarity in the supposedly "public" sphere of digital communication; it is the ghostly representation of non-individualized personhood which organizes the indifferent flows of information that is text. It also suggests the cyberpoet to be a version of the "digital flaneur," the anonymous stroller of arcades who, by interactions too quick for subsumption into a narrative, subtly re-orchestrates the internal dynamics of the crowd. Consequently, it is the interface for the reader (or "user") through which she might hope to engage with the poetic entity. It's not incidental that Pound's use of "personae" coincided with his early investigations into the uses of different vocabularies—Provençal, Anglo-Saxon, Chinese—as if he were relying on the mask to invite the reader into an engagements with new forms of information. Robert Browning's information-laden poems do a similar thing. *The Ring and the Book* is probably the apotheosis of this method of channeling information through both personae and architectural structure, each of its twelve sections describing the same murder scene as a merry-go-round whodunit. The mask, with its spirit of play, also suggests an element in the contract that would be formed between a CP and reader: that the "grotesque"—or the "monstrous" in both scale and content—is an acceptable value in the poem. Without such a contract, the CP might be frightening, threatening the ontological security of the individual by the formation, out of pure information and noise, of this simulated personhood. Readers of poetry appreciate brevity; the demon shuns it, but the competence of the mask helps forge a promise that the text is nonetheless a distillation of intense aesthetic activity. It is for this reason that cyberpoetry that seeks only to reveal the machinations of "data"—that fetishizes the streaming and not the "fashionability" of language—falls short in the digital realm which is already reducing human linguistic constructions, or subjective expression of the "self," to the level of indifferent exchange.

16. The connection of Artificial Intelligence (or AI) with certain CPs, in which the semantic values of the source text are not engaged by the demon, is distant, though less so as experimental branches of literature such as Language poetry have become influential and have established, unwittingly perhaps, new conventions of reading—the "reader-activated" text, for example. Artists such as David Rokeby, creator of a machine that emits poetry based on the input of an electronic eye, and Darren Wershler-Henry and Bill Kennedy, whose *The Apostrophe Engine* takes a source text and reproduces its basic syntactic features with different content based on matching rhetorical patternings on the web, are attempting to create semantically coherent output based on some interaction with the "physical" world—the former through an eye, the latter through the collections of numberless human text agents. "The Impermanence Agent," created by the team of Noah Wardrip-Fruin, A. C. Chapman and Brion Moss, constructs narratives based on a user's browsing patterns, utilizing the texts on the visited web pages and, taking it another level, also creating collaged composites of the images contained on these same pages. The products of these machines—which are not "final descriptions" so much as running commentary—can be considered subsets of the CP aesthetic, but are upping the ante by being products of recursive structures that actively interact with the "limitless" database of the world. Some ideas on the relationship of structure to intelligence expressed by Norbert Wiener in *The Human Use of Human Beings,* the popular version of his seminal *Cybernetics,* help pull some of the dimensions of "computer intelligence" out of inchoate metaphysical thinking, painting a porous border between AI and the CP. Wiener expostulates on the difference between the circulatory structures of ants and of humans, noting that the difference in complexity of each (ants don't actually "breathe" but let empty chambers fill up with oxygen) is an analog to the difference between the ventilation system of a cottage and a skyscraper. He writes

that "*The physical straitjacket in which an insect grows up is directly responsible for the mental straitjacket which regulates its pattern of behavior*" (italicized in the original), a correspondence which has great implications for the CP. He continues:

> Here the reader may say: "Well, we already know that the ant as an individual is not very intelligent, so why all this fuss about explaining why it cannot be intelligent?" The answer is that *Cybernetics takes the view that the structure of the machine or of the organism is an index of the performance that may be expected from it.* The fact that the mechanical rigidity of the insect is such as to limit its intelligence while the mechanical fluidity of the human being provides for his almost indefinite intellectual expansion is highly relevant to the point of view of this book (80).

In terms of the CP, however, there is a twist, which is that structural efficiency—the goal of any good programmer (the "elegant solution")—stands apart from structural complexity, and indeed structural redundancy may lead to greater "intelligence" than a streamlined model. Superfluous loops, dead ends, and memory-draining ways of doing things, may lead to greater "intelligence" if only for the opportune moments of chance associations and digressions this may provide, while efficiency might just lead to greater predictability of output: less resonance, less interest as reading. For the makers of CPs, this implies that the more the demon is introspective, self-reflexive, maybe even cobbled-together and modular—that is, the more prone to unpredictable feedback—the more "intelligent" its output might appear. Object-oriented languages, which is to say nonlinear, modular, and reusable, such as C++ thus become enticing, ever-expanding landscapes of possibility, with modules conceived for completely different functions—the "gaussian blur" algorithm from Photoshop, for example, or the diagnostic routines for car mechanics—serviceable for language production. This modular aspect of programming points to another aspect of the CP, which is its relationship to procedural art that utilizes only one or two processes. My sense is that, with the ease of modularity—the reusability of code, even "found" code, and its reassembling in different structures with minimum programming skill—manual conceptual literary projects will be recognized as much for their rejection of modularity as for their rejection of normal writing procedures. That is, whereas processual art was almost always a matter of doing one or two things over and over again as a diagram of "obsessive behavior"—such as photographing oneself once an hour for a year while confined to a cell (Teching Hsieh's project in "Art/Life One Year Performance 1983-1984"), or collecting all the phrases that end in the "r" sound and alphabetizing them, as in Kenneth Goldsmith's *No. 111*—digital art, which has no creation narrative outside of the banal activities of the demon, will tend to be more modular, utilizing a variety of tactics, even reusing old ones from the analog world, in larger interrelated structures. One could compare these modules to the circulatory, respiratory and nervous systems operating in concord in a human body; they each end up handling some of the same molecules, but for entirely different purposes and with different output. Wiener provides a convincing argument for increased complexity and even inefficiency, thus addressing, in a roundabout way, how certain analog aesthetics—such as the "dirty" concrete poem based on repeated photocopying—can be achieved in digital poetry, in which there are more than enough tools for cleaning up noise. Another side note: noise and sense are more closely related in the digital realm, as they are both dependent on the same general binary principles. "Sense" in one system, say the bit-sequence that produces an image of the *Mona Lisa*, would be "noise" in another, in an ASCII readout for example. Despite the peculiar closeness of this relationship between "noise" and "sense," some poets view this transference of data across mediums as a version of "translation," such as John Cayley, an idea he has elaborated in various programmatic works, equating it further with cultural translation—between Chinese and English orthography, for example. This is a poeticization of the structure of the bit-sequence, making it some version of the Rosetta Stone that has only to find its proper medium to be fully decoded. (As Lev Manovich claims frequently in *The Language of New Media*, all new media art is abstract art, as all digital films are abstract until they are arranged to approach some convention of "realism"—which is to say, are translated). Translation across media could add a unique quotient of 'intelligence" in the structure of a demon, subjecting bits to sets of rules that "replicate" completely different forms of human cultural activity—painting and music, for example. The next step to "intelligent" computer programs—and an exponential increase in the complexity of the source files—would be to hook them up to the internet, such that the computer could be engaged in its own sort of response to the "infinite memory" of the world's media. Noam Chomsky criticizes in an interview in *The Generative Enterprise* certain approaches to AI that attempt to create intelligence out of finite automata:

> It is the wrong approach because even though we have a finite brain, that brain is really more like the control system for an infinite computer. That is, a finite automaton is limited strictly to its own memory capacity, and we are not. We are like a Turing machine in the sense that although we have a finite control unit for a brain, nevertheless we can use indefinite amounts of memory that are given to us externally to perform more and more complicated computations. A finite automaton cannot do that. So the concept of the finite automaton is OK, as long as we understand it to be organized in the manner of a control unit for a much bigger, unbounded system (14).

This was written long before the internet, with its seemingly infinite number of contributors, "took off," yet one supposes that even the huge store of information on the internet would not satisfy Chomsky. For Chomsky, the program would have to be an entity that constructed its own ways of gathering new information, either from its human users (via statistical surveys, for example) or through other input devices (such as satellite dishes, weather balloons, or video cams). Furthermore, self-interest, and not a set of predetermined, hardwired goals, has to be included in any AI structure, otherwise it would have no more reason for spontaneous creation, for transforming its own information-gathering potentialities, than any mathematical equation would have for proving itself to itself. This makes true AI nearly impossible for a CP, since, were a truly intelligent automaton to create artworks, they would only have to be satisfactory for itself—and those like itself—to count as "art." There would be a good possibility that human onlookers would just not appreciate its "value," just as early explorers to Africa and Asia may have been unaware of how the art of these cultures were valued in their respective contexts. We would be asking too much to request that these works for machinic consumption also be satisfactory for us; it's possible they might be, but it could not be held as a criterion for determining a machine's artistic skills, especially as the art-historical continuum of computers will be very different from that of humans. Machines won't have, for instance, anything called "Dada" with which to conceptualize their creations, or anything like "bourgeois mores" to scandalize with them, though we often accept literary creations by machines as partaking in these social and artistic paradigms. Christian Bök may be the most passionate proselyte, and suggestive interlocutor, for this future culture of robots, as when he writes, in an essay on "Robopoetics," of an "obscure passion in the machine—an ironic reflex, perhaps, not unlike the apostasy of mischief." It would take a good deal of informed speculation to imagine how a series of "discrete glitches," in his phrase, could generate an entire culture of pleasure-seeking robots, but Bök offers a stimulating, if anthropocentric, vision of what they might be doing—and reading—once they arrive.

18. Susan Sontag, in her famous essay "The Pornographic Imagination" from *Styles of Radical Will*, describes the inner operations of literary pornography in a fashion that resonates with much of the CP aesthetic. She writes:

> The universe proposed by the pornographic imagination is a total universe. It has the power to ingest and metamorphose and translate all concerns that are fed into it, reducing everything into one nego-tiable currency of the erotic imperative. All action is conceived of as a set of sexual exchanges. Thus, the reason why pornography refus-es to make fixed distinctions between the sexes or allow any kind of sexual preference or sexual taboo to endure can be explained "struc-turally." The bisexuality, the disregard for the incest taboo, and other similar features common to pornographic narratives function to mul-tiply the possibilities of exchange. Ideally, it should be possible for everyone to have a sexual connection with everyone else (66-67).

There is an irony in Sontag's phrasing in her last sentence, written in a time before the existence of chat room pedophiles and cyberporn, not to mention online shopping and "spam." That is, one could become convinced that the "ideal" of the pornographic imagination forms the very foundational paradigm for new media apologists, thus adding a dubious ethical component to the argument that "information wants to be free." Even web site "personalization"—touted as a way to configure a website to provide content specific to the user's interests—can be seen as the internet's way of obtaining a snapshot of your "self" in order to "[reduce it] into one negotiable currency of the erotic imperative." The argument that industrial capitalism relies on conformity, and post-industrial on individuality, is tripped up by the limitations of "options" available on, say, a website or in the Mac's color options, but also by the exploitation of one's personal data—age, race, economic status—to increase the agility of capital's ability to focus on more aspects of a consumer's preferences to the neglect of those inimical to capitalism—not just conformity, but cyborgian hegemony. The CP's ties to the pornographic imagination are in the output's resemblance to works constructed along the lines of the "libidinal economy," which banks on the erotic pleasures released in semantic breakages and slippages and has ties to gestural poetics—projective verse, for example. In a CP, a semi-colon existing within close proximity of an em-dash becomes a microtonal incident of digital frottage, the demon resembling an obsessive, and seemingly tireless, recycler of once recalcitrant data. When it has ties to the everyday, it approaches the level of the "Rabelaisian" [see footnote 4] in its robotic, exploitative, and often total leveling of the source files to one cybernetic system of rhetoric and affect. Since there is no true narrative possibility in a CP beyond that of the demon's interaction with a database, the names—of people, of things—become completely objectified, breaking down the distance between personhood and objecthood. There is an analogy to the dolls of Hans Bellmer in that the operations of the demon provide warped (in this case "reedited") versions of common figuration, treating the mannequin factory as a form of database itself. The human body—in the form of the name, like "Brad Pitt," or in the referencing of body parts—becomes rendered plastic and mute like any sex toy. It is for this reason that the "fashioned noise" of a CP is more effective when it permits narrative elements, however atomized, since mere juxtaposition would not provide an animating mechanism substantial enough to instigate interpretation. The narrative drive of a CP turns a word's repetition later in the textual stream into the recurrence of a figure: a metastatic node [see footnote 3]. This becomes a resurrection of continuity, of linearity, in a textual world predicated on digression and material discontinuities. The variety of personages in a CP may not engage in sexual activities, and yet the CP, ignorant of human taboos, is so intoxicated with the limitlessness of possible linguistic constructions that it makes the determined nature of human taboo systems (such as the incest taboo) appear arbitrary. For this reason, it is not surprising that certain proto-CP works, like Goldsmith's *No. 111* and *Fidget*, Bök's *Eunoia*, and Caroline Bergvall's *Goan Atom* have strong taboo or pornographic elements, since the effort to regroup negotiable linguistic clusters from "noise" starts at an associative, pre-adolescent and pre-socialized, level and works upwards toward convention. Of course, a true CP is never able—due to the demon's opposition to syllogistic argumentation—to attain platforms of moral perspective, which is why these works can seem mute in the ethical sphere. Sontag continues:

> Indeed, one might speculate that the fatiguing repetitiveness of Sade's books is the consequence of his imaginative failure to confront the inevitable goal or haven of a truly systematic venture of the pornographic imagination. Death is the only end to the odyssey of the pornographic imagination when it becomes systematic; that is, when it becomes focused on the pleasures of transgression rather than mere pleasure itself (62).

The CP, predicated on the validity of plagiarism, also becomes a map of minor transgressions. It systematically violates the sanctity of the "whole," though it never, itself, confronts death, since it has no tone, no narrative arc, no cadence, no "end" beyond the final control element in a loop—the satisfactory completion of an "if... then...." As Tan Lin suggests in his "Notes Towards an Ambient Stylistics," there is no teleology in long, formless poems, such as Silliman's "Sunset Debris," composed entirely of questions, or even Pound's *Cantos*, which ends in fragments. An "ambient" poem would be one that uses each moment of reading as little more than a celebration of the activity of reading itself, as if the word were just a placeholder, a minor diversion in real-time,

intended to let reading continue but not to the exclusion of other activ-
ities—walking down the street, for example, or watching TV. A last
remark by Sontag is suggestive of the aesthetic, even spiritual, power
that CPs possess, when she writes that pornography points

> to something more general than even sexual damage. I mean the
> traumatic failure of modern capitalist society to provide authentic
> outlets for the perennial human flair for high-temperature visionary
> obsessions, to satisfy the appetite for exalted self-transcending modes
> of concentration and seriousness (70).

One immediately thinks of poets like Blake and Rimbaud (who were
open to sexual investigation in their work) or to Carlyle and Pound
(who weren't) and their "visionary," perhaps paranoiac [see footnote
35], obsessions that often resulted in enormous, detailed creations.
None of these works could be considered "programmatic," but they
were all premised, in different ways, on rhetorical structures involving
feedback and variation—the recurring figures in Blake's prophetic
works, for example, which never settle into stable physical properties—
a poetic method that seems peculiar to information-saturated sensibil-
ities on the verge of engulfment. The CP's demon can thus be seen as
the virtual embodiment of the medicine man, the half-cracked partner
in aesthetics who makes a visionary of even the most bureaucratically-
minded programming artist. Consequently, since coding is the most
marginal of literary activities—if it is literature at all—it shares with
pornography the distinction of being an over-productive textual indus-
try that is nearly entirely unserviceable for personal edification or,
indeed, socialization.

19. In the context of the world system which has absorbed individual-
ity into the logic of "personalization"—sets of personal stats such as
age or race that websites gather in order to better market to them—the
trace of the artistic gesture is pressured to expand exponentially, per-
haps to attain the proportions of the "monstrous." One way the CP
does this is to draw deeply on the available stock of cultural informa-
tion, which is to create texts that rely on comprehensive acts of plagia-
rism. In this way, the CP can be conceptualized as an immaterial rip-

ple against the stability of static, available knowledge, like the trace of wind on a still lake—a strike against entropy [see footnote 22]. The demon of a CP, because it extends the powers of the individual into the power of machines, can be said to share some of the qualities of the factory; and the writer, similarly, can be said to share the aspect of the producer in a virtual, and highly individual, cycle of production that has its own quarterly rates, stock markets, forecasts and manner of bookkeeping. This cycle, of course, runs in contrast to normative economic cycles; for example, this economy doesn't respect copyright laws (obviously) and its products lack the packaging that is usually required for the literary market (human authorship, obviously). It is rampant with puns, word play, and linguistic raw matter [see footnote 41], and subverts the normal relationship of labor expended in "writing" to the size and quality of the final product—huge, aesthetically coherent CPs can be constructed quite quickly. The CP thus becomes part of a larger tradition of cultural détournement—the modification of "found" materials to express divergent viewpoints—exploited most famously by the Situationists in the time leading toward the May '68 uprising in Paris. A more systematic example of détournement is the practice by the lesbian creators of K/S "slash" comics described in "Brownian Motion: Women, Tactics and Technology" by Constance Penley. K/S slash comics are fictions based entirely on the 79 episodes of the original *Star Trek* series—their source texts, or database—reedited and dubbed to draw out socially suppressed contents, most importantly the homosexual relationship between Kirk and Spock. K/S comics, like pornography in Sontag's description [see footnote 18], utilize a permutational methodology for erotic creations. Nothing, presumably, enters a slash comic that was not in fact in the original narratives, but like those scientists who isolate the beta cells of pancreases to inject them into diabetics, the creators of slash comics isolate and magnify those moments in the narrative that, when still fitting in the whole, reify their own sense of social displacement, and when mischievously rearranged serve to critique and obliterate it. Penley writes:

Michel de Certeau uses the term "Brownian motion" to describe the tactical maneuvers of the relatively powerless when attempting to resist, negotiate, or transform the system and products of the relatively powerful. He defines tactics as guerrilla actions involving hit-and-run acts of apparent randomness. Tactics are not designed primarily to help users take over the system but to seize every opportunity to turn to their own ends forces that systematically exclude or marginalize them. These tactics are also a way of thinking and "show the extent to which intelligence is inseparable from the everyday struggles and pleasures that it articulates." The only "product" of such tactics is one that takes the results from "making do" (*bricolage*)—the process of combining already-existing heterogeneous elements. It is not a synthesis that takes the form of an intellectual discourse about an object; the form of its making is its intelligence (139).

De Certeau is suggesting that détournement does not create a discourse of social critique but turns the existing discourse back onto itself in a warped fashion, a form of feedback that is contrarian yet productive of a new field in which a new cyborgian discourse in which identity is understood as socially constituted, more virtual than essential, can occur. His suggestive last line—"the form of its making is the intelligence itself"—points to one important element of the CP, which is that it is not an "art object" in the normal sense. When it draws on sources available to the public domain, it makes a refusal to be silent, to retreat into a position of interpretability by the dominant art-historical paradigms, even when it is quite opaque or has the "aura" of objecthood. Since it is operating in "Brownian motion" to articulate the terms of engagement via plagiarized texts, it retains a residue of the old terms—the rhetorical gestures, the vocabulary, the information density [see footnote 22]—and thus always bears some relationship to discourse, never serving an entirely "ritualistic" or aesthetic function. Whereas a lyric poem that would want to deceive one with an illusion of deep meanings can only be derived via biographical and historical studies, the CP never makes the promise of depth, or if it does, it is a dissimulation, a projection of authorial presence. If there is a way to get "into" a CP, it is only by going to sources, by considering the tensions that exist between them, and from there to move upward into the poem's form and its social conventions. This is an idea of "depth" as a moving horizontally, into the contemporary, rather than vertically into the past or the subjective interior. Penley continues:

The K/S fans, however, seem to go Certeau's "ordinary man" one better. They are not just reading, viewing, or consuming in tactical ways that offer fleeting moments of resistance or pleasure while watching TV, scanning the tabloids, or selecting from the supermarket shelves (to use some of his examples). They are producing not just intermittent, cobbled-together acts, but real products (albeit ones taking off from already-existing heterogeneous elements)—'zines, novels, artwork, videos—that (admiringly) mimic and mock those of the industry they are borrowing from while offering pleasures found lacking in the original products. K/S fandom more than illustrates Certeau's claim that consumption is itself a form of production (139).

Since the CP is not a "real product" of the industriousness of human activity (but, indeed, seems to admire it), what invariably occurs upon reading a CP is a form of "ontological anarchy" (to borrow Hakim Bey's phrase in *T.A.Z.*), a textual product that dissimulates human intellectual activity but which in fact is a form of "admiring mimicry" and "mockery." It questions one's sense of authorness by playing the games of society that writers themselves play—publication, cultural capital—but by a different set of creative rules. The CP, even more than the "poem," attains the status of producthood not only by having been created by an automated process, but by illustrating (though perhaps not demystifying) both the banality and wonders of its demon—by flaunting its machinism. No CP can be read without consciousness of this automation, and any reader of a CP is invariably pulled into the ethical discourse on automation in the creation of art—the use of assistants following templates to create large sculptures for sale, for example. This ethical dimension is rendered even more complex as the CP is able to achieve admirable aesthetic effects beyond the possibilities of an individual. Because of its factory-like nature—which operates as fast as the CPU will allow—one could construct a "life-work" on the scale of Zukofksy's *"A"* or Silliman's *The Alphabet* in an afternoon, just as Brian Eno composed *Thursday Afternoon*, a 61-minute recording (the most a CD would hold then), on a Thursday afternoon with algorithms and sound files. This might be pretty common practice these days—DJs using sequencers do it all the time—but it hasn't been explored with great success in literature. Though there is not yet a wide readership of CPs, as evinced by no noticeable set of aesthetic and critical mores by which to judge them, the activity of reusing CPs for other CPs, or of using the same source texts for a cycle of CPs written by several individuals—hence turning the social circuit of friendship and shared marginality into a demon of its own—is a phenomenon of the future. It is worth noting that the playwright Richard Foreman, who constructs his often highly repetitive plays based on jottings that he collects, with a calculated indifference to their dominant themes, over the course of several years, has put pages of these notes online in HTML format for reuse by other writers. This leaves the option open for an entire culture—or at least a writing contest—centered entirely around the unused writings of an important living artist.

22. CPs present the image of a foreign language: some alien but consistent discourse that, with some practice, could be mastered. At the same time, one is presented with the image of information barely being held together by form, as if the poem would split apart were some aspect of its sound and sense combination to prove flawed. The prospect of complex, semantically sensitive algorithmic activity makes room for the existence, in a virtual "literature," of every possible combination of phrases, any sort of style—this would be a distant foretaste of the "entropy" of text itself, the maximum amount of information possible in a system. Individual lyric expression seems to stall in the face of this possibility, hence the appearance of such works as *Eunoia* and *The Inkblot Record*, which seek alternative systems for keeping information whole, and for creating new gaps—new eddies in the stasis of entropic progression— outside of its own provisional organizing principles. These works take on the aura of being "monstrous" not just in their diversion of fluid expressivity into intricate, often recursive, literary forms, but due to the exhorbitant amount of systemized work that goes into their production. Because the CP does not aim to satisfy any of the Aristotelian poetic criteria—plot, mimesis, catharsis, etc.—and because the foreign language of a CP—those new consistencies the demon introduces—can never, in fact, be learned, reading a CP invariably sinks into certain modes of data analysis: which figures are reappearing and which not, which phrases carry more weight in the context of other phrases, what consistencies and inconsistencies exist in rhythm, stanza and meter, etc. That

this is a viable, if unusual, method of "reading" is supported by a form of literary analysis known as "information density," which hopes to discover how many words are present in a text in relation to the number of concepts and aesthetic effects. "Information density" has been a concern of Haroldo de Campos, one of the primary theorists, along with Decio Pignatari, of the Concrete poetry movement in Brazil. Critics hostile to Concrete poetry, which was premised on using the least amount of words necessary for a poem, usually expressed with graphically expressive methods (such as colored typefaces that suggest industrial icons), claimed that it was "impoverishing language." One supposes this is because they were using few words and adorning them with shape and color, rather than using a great number of words and adorning them with punctuation. De Campos refutes this claim in his essay "The Informational Temperature of the Text," with a detailed, unique consideration of how the statistical sciences and poetics interrelate:

> If we take 1 as the highest limit of a text's informational temperature, that temperature, in a given text, will be higher the nearer it is to 1. In such cases, for Mandelbrot "the available words are 'well employed,' even rare words being utilized with appreciable frequencies. Low temperature, on the other hand, means that words are 'badly employed,' rare words being extremely rare." Of the first case, Mandelbrot [...] gives James Joyce, whose vocabulary is 'quite varied,' as the example; of the second, the language of children (177-178).

De Campos then warns that a higher "informational temperature"—a concept which is directly based on "documentary," "semantic" and "factual" information—does not determine a higher degree of aesthetic information. What de Campos calls the "linguistic-statistical" component of a text—how many words are used, where they come from, all the factors that a parsing of the text might provide—only increases the informational temperature when they are allied to a high degree of craftsmanship. Craftsmanship is responsible for the level of "aesthetic information" in the text—how a phrase operates in relation to optional phrases that could replace it. A well-crafted text, like Joyce's *Ulysses*, is high linguistic-statistically and is well crafted, hence high in aesthetic informational temperature. A text that uses an equal amount of unique words in a baroque, overwrought manner—he uses the Brazilian writer Coelho Neto, whose "vocabulary is calculated at around 20,000 words"—is low in aesthetic information because his phrases can all be replaced by equally suitable phrases—that is, they weren't honed by "craft." De Campos believes this theory is useful, but that Concrete poetry falls outside of this schema, since Concrete poetry eschews all notions of "craft" in favor of industrial techniques of production. He says that the goal of Concrete poetry is a language "easily and quickly communicated," and hence necessarily utilizing a very simple vocabulary:

> That is why it rejects the airs and graces of craftsmanship—in spite of the seriousness with which it considers the artisan's contribution to the stockpile of extant forms—from the art of verse to the elaborate diversification of vocabulary in prose. It has recourse in its turn to factors of proximity and likeness on the graphic-gestaltic plane, to elements of recurrence and redundancy on the semantic and rhythmic plane, to a visual-ideogrammic syntax (when not merely "combinatory") for controlling the flux of signs and rationalizing the sensible materials of a composition. This is how it limits entropy (the tendency to dispersion, to disorder, to the maximum informational potential of a system), fixing the informational temperature at the minimum necessary to obtain the aesthetic achievement of each poem undertaken (179-180).

While concrete poetry and the CP are not obviously related, except insofar as a "concrete" poem can be found on a micro-level (as the Concretists found several useful poems in *Finnegans Wake*, such as "silvamoonlake"), the implications for the CP in this passage are several. First, de Campos recognizes that an alternative to the production of "crafted" verse can lie in industrial techniques—the "factory" aspect of the CP. As a corollary, one is free to negotiate aesthetic values in a dispassionate way, an attitude that would be attractive to the cyberpoet who will instinctually seek out verbal alchemy by fine-tuning a demon and tweaking the source texts rather than revising output, which would be seen as "heresy." Second, he—in a more simple and direct way than

McCaffery—looks at language as having physical properties and as possessing semiotic qualities independent of specific human intentionality. De Campos believes that structures constituted by language are always threatened with increased entropy, hence acknowledging the vulnerability of information—in this case text—to processes that render them quantifiably, and not qualitatively, exchangeable for other information. This helps elaborate the reliance the CP has on genre and convention: it is the centripetal motion of these forms that prevent the information of a CP from dispersing into the fog of its origins, to the "maximum informational temperature of a system." Being a congeries of "egos" and data, a CP cannot have ruins, or at least makes poor ones, which is why a CP is often an unsuitable source text for another CP. In fact, being primarily "deictic" [see footnote 41], pointing to another source or perspective, a CP shares with any digital art the vulnerability to being simply "shut-off," erased when the circuits of its meanings—residing in "culture" and the very materials of electronic communication, which render them equally available and proximate to other meanings—disappear. The third aspect this paragraph points to is the aesthetics of repetition, of return, of redundancy, which is more accurately described as plays of proximity rather than rhetoric. It is through these repetitions that one can observe the aesthetic dimension of the program itself, to catch a glimpse of the machinic, invisible proprietor of the ritual—the master of the game. One determines the success and failure of a CP by observing, with one eye on "informational temperature," how its repetitions stand up over the course of the time it takes to read the poem. The cyberpoet keeps track of information temperature when assembling source texts: the rightness and wrongness of styles, the difficulty of vocabulary, the amount of pronouns, articles, verbs, etc.—all of which become part of the rhetoric or the primary harmonic overtone of the output. Consequently, de Campos' use of the industrial model is also telling in that the Brazilian concretist's manifesto, the "Pilot Plan," was probably the first aesthetic manifesto to argue the necessity for a new country to create an "exportable" art form. Likewise, the CP plays an active rerouting role in the global system because it is a personal intervention in the indifferent flux of commercial, and also cultural, exchange. Like a computer virus, the CP thrives in the midst of transcontinental play. Concrete poetry, touted as the first "international literary movement" as it was seen, like music, to present a transnational artistic language, produced important artists with an investment in the idea of the "local"—the Brazilian Concretists, Ian Hamilton Finlay, and even the culture of site-specific happenings when they involve text—a fact that is often overlooked. In the context of postcolonialism in the digital age in which distances have been abolished and teleactive cultural clashes occur with greater frequency, the trope of the "local" has some role to play in the CP as it dissimulates its narrative of origin—a particularity in space and time.

35. The natural placement of the CP in contemporary literary discourse would be in the category of the "paranoiac," works of art that rely on a great level of associative thinking and on imagery that seems to lack specific symbolic value but suggests some overarching, if hidden, matrix of meanings. The most relevant paranoiac writer in this context might be William Burroughs, who famously turned to the cut-up method (developed by Brion Gysin, also creator of the "permutational poem") for the construction of several of his novels. Thomas Pynchon may be the novelist who best narrativizes the paranoiac sensibility by putting the invisible machinations of the world into the hands of renegade rocket scientists (*Gravity's Rainbow*), Masonic postal workers (*Crying of Lot 49*) and evil Jesuits (*Mason & Dixon*). It's because of this hidden matrix that the CP seems to have a "ritualistic" element to it in Benjamin's sense, as it remains apart from the user, has an "aura," and follows its own laws while remaining in dialogue with the reader via its aesthetic seductions and fragments of the "everyday." In fact, the CP may, by inflicting its rules on the user, transform the reader into the paranoiac herself, a different version of the "activated reader" than the Language poets might have wished though similar in that this breakdown of the boundaries of the self has socially transformative potentialities. Because the CP can take in materials from the everyday—if someone were to post their diary, for example, and the demon were to access it, this information would become part of a poem—the CP acts a bit like a newsreel film, which, as Benjamin notes, created the sense in the viewer that she could have been an extra. Thus, the reader becomes vulnerable in new ways, and begins to relate to the art work

not as a distant object but as a process, like voting or paying taxes, in which one participates. When this process is not knowable and out of the control of the reader, a state of delirium and of ontological insecurity might set in. When coupled with hyperactive mental activity—the relentless aesthetic of a CP might give that impression—something happens which might escape mere paranoia and approach "schizophrenia," a total collapse of ontological security. Schizophrenia was once a much bandied term in postmodern cultural discourse, envisioned as the most symptomatic aesthetic stance in late capitalism, one that was oppositional but also in fact replicated the logic of capital. A quick look at it here (even if this tactic has been rehearsed many times before) is valuable. Frederic Jameson, relying on psychological models that he understood as provisional, wrote that "schizophrenia" represented the breakdown of temporality, a sense of the presentness of all things—in a sense, the reduction of experience to a constant, uncontrollable input stream:

> For Lacan, the experience of temporality, human time, past, present, memory, the persistence of personal identity over months and years—this existential or experiential feeling of time itself—is also an effect of language. It is because language has a past and a future, because the sentence moves in time, that we can have what seems to us a concrete or lived experience of time. But since the schizophrenic does not know language articulation in this way, he or she does not have our experience of temporal continuity either, but is condemned to live a perpetual present with which the various moments of his or her past have little connection and for which there is no conceivable future on the horizon. In other words, schizophrenic experience is an experience of isolated, disconnected, discontinuous material signifiers which fail to link up into a coherent sequence. The schizophrenic thus does not know personal identity in our sense, since our feeling of identity depends on our sense of the persistence of the "I" or "me" over time (119).

The schizophrenic is someone who, without even a modicum of short-term memory, will not be able to connect a noun to a verb in a sentence. Rather, each entity approaches with such terrible presentness that it wipes out whatever syntactic structure a previous word might have started to develop, subsuming the syntagm of a phrase underneath the paradigm of the word—not as "noun" or "verb" but as a phenomenon of textuality. The well-tempered CP, one that promises interpretability and occupies, even as dissimulation, a quasi-conventional genre, is not "schizophrenic" in this sense, as these CPs always seem to point to some "other"—the sureties of the source files, the resources of everyday reasoning—for stability. The recurrence of its processes imitate a "concrete, lived experience" of time, of kinetic progress, and the familiarity of some of its themes and figures—the metastatic component [see footnote 3]—gives some assurance that a poetic is still in control. This sense of presentness is a component of a CP, but because it engages in cycles of recurrence, and dissimulates a narrative or lyrical body, it replaces the natural temporality of human "everyday" memory with a malleable, or fictional, substitute. Jameson later writes that the signifier takes on the properties of an "image" when it has lost its signified, that is, when it becomes opaque. This supports another view of the CP, which is that, rather than being "schizophrenic" or "paranoiac," it can act like a series of Rorschach tests (otherwise known as "inkblot tests"), in which the reader is confronted with an abstract shape (or gestalt) from which she attempts to conjure a meaningful image. My appreciation of this aspect of the CP is inspired by the recent appearance of such poems as Dan Farrell's book-length *The Inkblot Record*, itself a basic form of a CP in which the demon is simply the process of alphabetization, the content being anonymous responses to Rorschach tests. These phrases, divorced from their context in medical textbooks, present the reader with the raw materials of new, to-be-constructed and involuntary narrativizations. This breakdown of personal ontology—the opening of the self to streams of information and the efficacies of cyborgian creation—points to another curious feature of poets influenced by digital technology: the appeal of fully exhaustive methods in textual construction. Christian Bök's hyper-Oulipian *Eunoia*, for example, attempts to use every single word in the English language that only uses a single vowel ("toronto," "banana," "bikini," etc.) and arrange them in five chapters of discursive prose poetry that represents both the ultimate literary curio and an epic achievement (it took seven years to write, the same time it took

Joyce to write *Ulysses*). Kenneth Goldsmith has proceeded, book by book, to exhaust the various possibilities of "found poetry," such as in *Soliloquy*, the transcription of every word he said over the course of a week; *Fidget*, in which he recorded his bodily movements into a tape recorder for the duration of Bloomsday; and *No. 111*, a paper database in which thousands of words and phrases ending in the consonant "r" (or "h") were alphabetized and organized by number of syllables. Darren Wershler-Henry's *the tapeworm foundry, andor the dangerous prevalence of imagination* attempts to exhaust all possible forms of innovative poetry in a single stream of descriptions organized by the phrase "andor," while my own *Dreamlife of Letters*, a Flash piece organized by alphabetic principles, has been credited with trying to exhaust all forms of animated web poetry or the kinetics of movie titles. That all of these works have escaped, to some degree, the "marginality" that is usually granted the postmodern avant-garde work—*Eunoia*, for example, went through three printings in its first two months—suggests that experimental writing premised on algorithmic structures might have found a niche in the "mainstream" due to the increased general understanding of, and interest in, the properties of the database. Another example, Harryette Mullen's breakthrough book *Muse & Drudge* is a series of cyborgian lyrics—all the same length, in four quatrains, and with no punctuation—that freely used slang garnered from Clarence Major's African American dictionary *Juba to Jive*. Her next volume, to be published with a major university press, is called *Sleeping With The Dictionary*, and is practically a recipe book of algorithmic writing, pulling "minimal narratives" out of a programmatic interaction with a paper database. These moves to find the limits of reconfiguration given a closed set of principles—not unlike the pornographic imagination [see footnote 18]—represent a final gambit in the cultural arena in which the ontological security of the self is constantly threatened by the prospect of limitless information and limitless recombination, turning anybody—even the non-programmer—into a version of the cyborg, timeless and placeless but still (in its residual humanity, its mortality) pursued by history.

41. Because the demon of a CP treats the matter of language on the level of its letters, punctuation and even white spaces with a total indif-

ference to their "meaning" beyond their quantitative values as numbers, there is something inherent in a CP that bears relation to Sianne Ngai's formulation of a "poetics of disgust" in her essay "Raw Matter." Specifically, Ngai draws many distinctions between a "poetics of disgust" and a "poetics of desire" that positions the CP aesthetic in relation to human poetic production premised on "writing." Ngai's argument is that "pluralism" has become not only the signature quality of most poetics centered on "desires" described by such paradigms as polysemia, dissemination, jouissance, and the libidinal economy—but that it plays into the logic of late capitalism, with its quest to include all forms of pleasure in its machinations. Loosely, this could be an analog to the idea of web-site "personalization" that seeks to incorporate traces of individuality into a system of common exchange, and hence to increase market saturation [see footnote 18]. Ngai's sense is that a poetics of desire, despite its having been based on an oppositional, materialist perspective, has at times seemed "as if it were spiritual," and further, has become a "mysticism instead of a materialism. The false profundity of jouissance: desire as transgressive" (101). A poetics of disgust, on the contrary, involves a turning away from the object, the exclusion of the object about which one has a "negative fascination"— the denial of its assimilation into "pleasure." Expressions of disgust themselves often involve linguistic waste such as expletives and onomatopoeia ("Ugh!"), or even congeries of symbols ($#&!@), but despite this thingness, this surrender to impotence, they convey an affect and have an "insistence." Disgust, in a sense, serves as a poetic when it acts to take the word, any word, outside of systems that will recuperate it—close reading, theory, any sort of "seductive reasoning" in Ngai's terms—and will not permit the word or phrase to participate in a chain of signifiers or as paragrammic progenitor of the next syllable. It is, consequently, a poetics that acknowledges an "other," if only through negative space, which she associates with "deictic" words— words such as "this" or "that" that point to other words—or even symbols that have a deictic function, like brackets (a common feature of programming languages) that always point to the words between them. She describes her sense of the poetic functioning of deictic words by looking at the poetry of Kevin Davies in his first book, *Pause Button*:

Along with the more familiar forms of deixis (thisses, thats, and its) found in *Pause Button*, Davies' use of [ ] fulfills this function of giving form to formlessness, or of materializing 'outsideness.' Another example of such unusual deictic construction is Jeff Derksen's use of the maimed statistic in *Dwell*. Like @%$#!! and [ ], other negative utterances of expressions of outrage, the brute number ("France 8. 9%") functions as semiotic raw matter, insisting on the disappearance of its referent while at the same time refusing to defer to other terms. It won't coagulate into a unitary meaning and it also won't move; it can't be displaced. This statistic only covers a space; the reader cannot fix it metaphorically, assign a concept to it, nor send it on a metonymic voyage along a chain of other terms. There's no substantive meaning, yet there's also no possibility of polysemia: "France 8. 9%" doesn't budge. It only sits there, in its material embodiment, in its stolidity. The reader can only act upon it by not acting on it, by turning away—just as the maimed statistic itself turns away from its implicit referent, excluding it (113-114).

As with Veronica Forrest-Thomson's interest in incorporating the "nonmeaningful" elements of a poem into an appreciation, though not "interpretation," of it [see footnote 3], Ngai points to those forms in a poem that cannot be pulled into a hermeneutic matrix, that will always remain a question mark when one attempts to describe what the poem "means." The poem is not seen as transparent language, through which one can look to recuperate a narrative or expression of subjectivity, nor is it seen as a field of linguistic play that illustrates some property of language's autonomous self-creation. Rather, it is full of holes, or pointers that go nowhere. What becomes clear, in several of Ngai's examples, is that one cannot construct an entire poem based on a "poetics of disgust." The entirety of *Dwell*, for example, is not composed of "maimed statistics" but is merely punctuated by them, the rest of the poem having discursive features that Derksen himself has flippantly described as "socialist one-liners" and which he relates to a "rearticulatory" practice in poetics, a shifting of associations among referents. It is impossible to break chains of signification in an art-work if these breaks are not appropriately framed. For example, a "found poem" like the numbers and texts on a grocery receipt (an admittedly extreme example) could be recuperated into a discourse on poetry by analyzing the creation narrative or cultural paradigm that brought the artist to come to decide that it was "art." One would recall the concept of the ready-made, for instance, or reference some versions of Concrete poetry that seek to expose how machinic technology has imposed itself on the idea of literary dissemination—the cash register as desktop publisher. That is, the receipt, even unaltered, could become a "poem" provided the art-historical paradigm rose up around it— "seductive reasoning"—to incorporate it into discourse. Within this discourse, it might be seen as an expression of "disgust," but it couldn't possess this property without the discursive frame. Algorithmic writing, like the CP—in which nearly all words could be considered place-fillers, even pattern-holders, and which is not bothered by issues of subjectivity—might offer the closest example to poems that could be, through and through, "raw matter." The proto-CP work of Kenneth Goldsmith, like the "nutritionless writing" of his book *Day*, for which he recopied manually the entire contents of one issue of *The New York Times* word by word, might be one example, the entire text being "deictic" and pointing away from itself and toward the normative use and publishing history of an original (it also banalizes both the body and the demon by restricting their operations to the most banal form of media transference—copying words. This algorithm evokes the classic first computer program in Kernigan & Ritchie's seminal introduction to C, the entire program being limited to making the words "hello world" appear on the screen). However, the corpus of Goldsmith's work has gained a certain consistency, and hence a "seductive reasoning" in the form of his singular, but mutable and hence reproducible, creation narrative: all of his projects involve bodily exertion, text accumulation, editing, publication (often in several forms) reconstituting, finally, this "waste" for cultural consumption. One might argue that it is not the CP itself, with its poetics of dissimulation that might actively project a hyperactive erotics [see footnote 18], but the demon that offers the clearest embodiment of Ngai's theory. What more represents a "turning away" from intentional acts of expression than the complete deferral of authority to an automaton, and channels the most innovative creative act from "writing" to "coding"? A demon is a void—it can be filled with anything, but contains nothing—and hence becomes a form of the deictic itself, like the empty brackets in Davies' poem. Indeed, not only is it not pointing to an object, it is pointing away from the author and from authors while presenting the traces of that activity unique to humans: thinking in language. Though a demon "acts," it has no stories to tell of what it has done, unlike the artist for whom "acting" is part of the cycle of sleeping and waking, life and death. The demon denies all of these cycles and replaces them with banal loops. It also has no "memories"—which might be characterized as information which calls attention to itself because it is in a constant state of decay and is never perfectly recallable—nor even data to call its own, since source files can be replaceable and it is indifferent to them anyway. Because it courts hermeneutic potentialities but surrenders no description, and because its structures, including its words and rhetorical figures, are the product of algorithms, the CP goes beyond "disgust" to actively pursue a self-perpetuating negative presence—a subjective affect with no subject. Thus, the CP is like a virus, neither living nor dead—it is also not a poem, and not a process, but nonetheless a linguistic presence that troubles the line between activity and inactivity, engagement and disinterest, true and false.

➤

[Editors Note: The preceding text is an excerpt of an essay that appears, in full, in *Fashionable Noise: On Digital Politics* (Berkeley: Atelos, 2003). In the original essay, the numbered series of footnotes correspond to a translation of *The Battle of Brunaburh* constructed by algorithmically collaging a number of source texts.]

Creeping It Real: Brian Kim Stefans' "Invisible Congress" and the Notion of Community

K. Silem Mohammad

Brian Kim Stefans' article "When Lilacs Last in the Door: Notes on New Poetry," published on Steve Evans' Third Factory website, was originally slated for a column in *Poets & Writers*, but was finally rejected (for being too weird, one gathers).[1] In this article, Stefans offers "Creep Poetry" (after Radiohead's "Creep") as a defining label for an emergent tendency among younger experimental poets. It's significant that the term is borrowed from the trendy domain of alternative rock: Stefans points out that the Creep Poets "wonder why the poetry world is not as interested in the 'edge' as the art and music worlds," in which figures like Cindy Sherman and Ornette Coleman enjoy a relatively greater amount of popular exposure and acceptance. The nature of this "edge," of course, is the main question, and the necessity of scare quotes points to the problematic that informs Stefans' discussion. "Edgy," like "alternative," "innovative," "independent," "organic" or "non-toxic," is one of a rapidly increasing number of unreliable adjectives subject to use by various loosely-corporate agencies who really mean by them "extremely marketable." It might be argued that most experimental poets have nothing to worry about, as their work will never be mistaken for something marketable in any possible world; but in a culture where discursive nuance is continually taken for a microcosmic index of a more tangible network of material struggle, little things like this seem to matter a great deal. Especially suspect are labels that threaten to pigeonhole a style or movement as indebted (or indentured) to some predecessor or other, such as "Post Language" or "7th Generation New York" or "Post-neo-pre-Raphaelitism." One of the appeals of a term like "Creep" is its bratty indifference to literary genealogizing. The Radiohead song, obviously, is about not fitting in: about the pathos—and power—of orphandom.

I won't spend a lot of time on some specific questions that bug me about Creep, such as why Stefans makes some of the cut-off points he does (why, for example, are Lisa Jarnot and Rodrigo Toscano Creeps but Sianne Ngai and Lytle Shaw not, as he claims? Can writers over 40 like Michael Gizzi or Bruce Andrews be considered Creeps?). I want instead to isolate a couple of his broader observations about the tendency, and then spin off from there. Stefans observes that

> all the Creeps share [...] a surprising tendency to communicate, to perform, to create social *interactivity*, and to expand beyond the small communities that have been their inherited legacy from previous American avant-gardes. They are often experimentalists, but have no interest in experiment for its own sake, at least if the results are not something like a public, often very entertaining, form of poetry, a sort of deviant form of street theater itself. The Creeps are almost universally very funny, though why there has been such a turn to humor in their poetry is matter for debate.

The eyebrow-raising element here is the claim that Creeps want to break out of the community model of experimental writing, a model that has held indomitable sway for decades, notably reinforced and codified in Ron Silliman's passionate introduction to *In the American Tree*. Even though I question the universal applicability of this claim to all the writers Stefans names—and furthermore whether such a thing is really a good idea—it's refreshing just to see the thought given shape in print. The move outward to a public rather than a neighborhood arena, Stefans is quick to point out, does not mean that the Creeps are "simply assimilating experimental techniques into the mainstream" (as one might argue is the case with, say, the "Ellipticists," whom Stefans mentions politely but critically a couple of times). Although Stefans doesn't quite say it in this way, it's more the other way around: many writers (ones, I think, he might consider Creeps) are attempting to transport mainstream ingredients into experimental poetry, albeit in a radically messed-up form. Most significantly, Creeps often use the first-person pronoun in ways that challenge both traditional liberal humanist demands for unmediated presence *and* postmodern maledictions against lyric bourgeois subjectivity. Stefans uses Jennifer Moxley's "Wrong Life" as an example, pointing out that

> like many Creep poems, hers is an extended apostrophe, a discourse aimed at an imaginary audience, an audience of the future perhaps but one that, in the scope of the poem, is not there. Several Creep poets [...] will assume this mode of apostrophe, a stating-of-the-case before an invisible congress. Thus the "I" assumes a rhetorical function; not the "not-I" of common postmodern parlance, and yet not the "I" of the common lyric.

What these comments bring to my mind, oddly enough, is John Stuart Mill's "What Is Poetry?" with its famous distinction between poetry and oratory: "Oratory is heard; poetry is overheard." Stefans' "invisible congress" adds a neat metaphysical twist to this equation. In Mill's account, it is taken for granted not only that the speaker, whether poet or orator, is a unified subject, but that the reader / listener is equally unified. The postmodern turn has been to question the solidity of the addresser, but even in language-centered poetics, there has been relatively little consideration of the different possible spaces imagined (either by poet or reader) for the addressee. Stefans' account baffles Mill's overly rigid separation of poetry from public speech, but manages to retain the stimulating implications of "overhearing." The "imaginary audience" for the Creep Poet is itself overheard, or hypothesized in a way that approximates the absent engagement of overhearing. Take the impenetrable yet aggressively public scene of communication described in a poem like Stefans' own "Christopher Smart's America," from *Angry Penguins* (Harry Tankoos Books, 2000):

> And when the sick man says "love me," a cloud crashes into a church.
> Believe in the nineteenth century, and supine enactments of power.
> What depths in the cellars of the odes? Am I simply trying to fool you?
> The mind drifts every so often, as the sparks suggest new arenas. We
> became friends at the dolphin show. That's bathos. When will they recognize my struggle to attain the plain?

At once numbly prosaic and spasmodically excessive, Stefans' work, here as elsewhere, forces a reevaluation of the ways in which language can be ornamental, a reevaluation that makes the reader ask not only "who could be saying this?" but "who could be listening?" Looked at from this angle, the poem's strangeness starts to seem motivated, as opposed to arbitrary or capricious.

Stefans says that the "I" of Creep Poetry "is often situated beneath the economic stratum of increased commercial activity that digital technology has brought on." True enough, and perhaps more importantly, so is the "you." The "desire to communicate" that he sees in Creep, the quest "for the sensation of constant *exchange*," is a heroic one, because it happens in a space filled with hegemonic interference and corporate molestation. Exchange in a context like this is bound to be conducted cryptically, like exchanges in wartime, in occupied territory. Not to say that Creep is inaccessible except to a few in-the-know freedom fighters, however; its garbled surface announces itself as contraband, as though it *wants* to be arrested. At the base of all this is a faith in communication itself, no matter how deformed the means of transmission. And it is this faith that sets Creeps (at least in the way I have appropriated the term) apart from the Ellipticists, for example, who seem more interested in the obstacles to expression, as aesthetic points of fascination in themselves, than in who put the obstacles there or whether they might explode in someone's face.

So how does Creep constitute a turn away from a community-based poetics? Only to the extent that it rejects the notion of a safe enclave, a privileged brotherhood of artistry in which the problems of the outside world are after all, *outside*, and at least there's that. It does this by raising the quixotic possibility of intercourse between experimental poetry and mainstream culture (mainstream, that is, in the sense of TV and Wal-Mart and international politics, not in the sense of "mainstream poetry," which is no more mainstream than geodesic domes or bow ties). The oratorical overhearing that transpires in Creep is like party-crashing, or sneaking into someone else's convention and willfully mistranslating the speeches. Its logic, that is, is homophonic, and this may be why so much Creep Poetry has the quality of seeming like homophonic or homolinguistic translation, even when it's not. For example, these lines from Stefans' "The Cupcake Diaries" (also in *Angry Penguins*):

Style up drop kick, suffer invisible
intentionality dago (day ol)
a piss fervent contra-naturam
staple blister lists rearward stank of the
civilian next door burning contracts....

Or these lines from "lolabell" by Elizabeth Treadwell, a poet Stefans does not name, but who seems to me to fit the Creep description (I mean that in a *nice* way):

thought a boy apartment, taxi-cab, no early evening gum necessarily pleasant historians all night long, give cloister crooked muddy, protect her from almost kitchen stars (*Ixnay* 6, 2001).

Passages like these take the staunch unswingingness of classical Language-centered poetics and subject it to the aesthetic of an ever more commodified, appropriated, and soundbitten landscape, in order to point up the fine line between swinging and unswinging—or more accurately, they demonstrate that the line is imaginary, that what is unswinging according to one habit of hearing may be so because it has caught the rhythm of a new wavelength being broadcast on a hitherto untuneable station. It is the self-appointed task of these poets to conjure up not only the DJs and playlists but the *listeners* of such stations: an "invisible congress" of Creeps. The thing about radio is that practically everything on it is controlled by someone or something you don't trust, and yet you always seem to manage to hear something interesting that maybe wasn't supposed to get on in the first place. As Cocteau and Spicer knew, that's where poetry comes from, so it makes sense that Stefans' modern-rock analogy leads us to the most commercial of metaphors. The more moderated, the more preprogrammed the medium, the more public fantasies and private fetishes will emerge in the static, like those supposed voices of the dead recorded by paranormal researchers. Radio, then, is for Creeps. Radio is available for perverse listening in a way that TV resists or absorbs. On the radio, one can hear what one wants to hear—the buzz and whir of production, if wished, rather than the airbrushed, crystalline, cabled-in crispness of the post-produced, already-consumed final commodity.

This is the old familiar concept of defamiliarization, but a very specific version of it: not just verbal estrangement with an eye to making new, which, at least ideally, is what all poetry does, but a bigger socio-discursive estrangement in which it is no longer enough merely to make it new (since global capitalism has cornered the market on that trick): it must be made spectacularly unusable. Photography and music, to name just a couple of the other arts, are always usable, no matter how transgressive or experimental, inasmuch as they operate directly on the senses. Any physical perception, whether sight or sound or touch or taste or smell, can be commodified by virtue of its sheer material immediacy, regardless of "content" or "form." Novels can't help being potential movies, and thus arguably are more directly sensorial; poetry, on the other hand, always starts as an intellectual activity. Sensual response is made the responsibility of the reader, and thus too unpredictable to manipulate into a larger institutional purpose.[2] Any teacher who has ever stood dumb before a student's unaccountable, academically unassimilable emotions in response to a poem knows this. Note that we're talking mainly about "experimental" poetry here—one reason there is even such a category as "mainstream" poetry is that it at least can be read as arranged prose, and thus more uniformly visualized or "translated." Its immediate effect as sound or image is negligible, except as carefully schematized euphony or decoratively inert strophes.

Other features of Creep that Stefans points to are "run-on pacing that seems to take everything in," "off-beat humor that often strays just a little bit into solipsism," a "skating above sincere, often radical ideological concerns," and "a concern with sensation of language *unhinged*, not entirely beyond something someone could possibly say, but still coasting on every possibility open to language from within a performative aspect." The keynote here is one of failure or error: "run-on," "off-beat," "skating above," "unhinged." The various dead metaphors here are all related to mechanisms malfunctioning or agents miscalculating in some way. Stefans himself says that his "hope is that the name [Creep] will be rejected," and that he has himself "tried to reject it" but for various reasons, well, failed. Here too is the trope of getting it wrong, in this case knowingly and before the fact, which seems to be a major Creep stunt (Pee Wee Herman voice: "I *meant* to do that"). Even as a hedge against cooptation, this ploy is conspicuously redundant; as

Stefans remarks, "There is obviously nothing marketable about the Creeps," and this is nowhere more true than in their flaunting of their own inadequacy. Of course, even refusal and abjection can be (and are) co-opted these days, so there's no call to get complacent, but for the time being the Creeps take the approach of dismantling every known cultural apparatus (very inefficiently of course) and forcing a unilateral wipe. As Stefans writes:

> If their tactic is to go over-the-top with lexical plenitude, neologisms, about-face turns to somewhat antique meters, rhythms that are either too fast or too slow to digest, then again reversals into the slipstream of paratactics and high technology, it is because they believe, like Rimbaud, that all values have to be reinvented.

As opposed to say, lo-fi, punk, or grunge strategies, Creeps adopt the most grotesque extremes of progressive kitsch: arpeggiated squeals of Moog fanfare without justification or apology. This could be seen as just an indulgence in guilty pleasure, or as an assault on value, or both. Again from Stefans' *Angry Penguins*, an excerpt from "Poems I Will Never Publish" (which begins "I've seen the best minds of my generation / go baroque"):

> Pronouncements bellying sideways palming its sweat
> while the peanut glandulars *ooh* and *ahh* to no sufficient facticity,
> spoiled as they've been by the effervescence of day's rashes.
>   Can a slogan be more than a grump? they
> don't ask, and I don't argue with the rococo exchanges.

Amid the riot of this glossolalia, one can only focus on so much at a time, but what stands out here is the invocation of discourse as a barrage of flourishes, "rococo exchanges" against which the speaker puts up no fight. Indeed, he is the rococo ringmaster, magisterially ushering a series of unlikely chimeras through his hoop. The applause he earns may not necessarily be ours (though it is certainly mine), but the poem arranges that we imagine the applause nonetheless. In Stefans' Big Top, the Creepshow is the main attraction, and the qualities he sees as Creepy in his contemporaries are qualities that render them recognizable as denizens of his own brain's sinister, Bradburian tent folds.

All of this could sound like a negative critique, an indictment on the grounds of insularity. But this is exactly what I find attractive about Stefans' Creep (anti-)aesthetic: it's a movement that is formed within the mind of the reader, not the designs of a self-articulated community. Stefans' apprehension of Creepiness comes from his own Creepy imagination, his own desire to oversee a troupe of invisible, flea-like verbal acrobats. That the poets he names are readily conformable to such a desire says something about their shared use of certain techniques and their common concerns as postmodern artists, but more about a simultaneous resistance and porousness in their work that encourages progressive (but diverse) notions of community to be constructed from the margins outward (inward?)—there is no Creep manifesto, only an ever-growing passenger manifest, the names on which can be shuffled according to the needs of an equally various and multiple collective of readerly sensibilities.

➢

My Problems With Flarf

Gary Sullivan

after David Bromige

To go back to Eliot, my problem with flarf (really the hype around it) is that I think it's a case of two worlds becoming much too much "like the other": as with much AG poetry in general, it's painfully elitist and obscure, and too many drafts find their way to print (in ink or online) or performance as final poems. In my opinion, this is simply due to the substantial buddy system of the avant blog poets who are championing it. They take the dollars, the signs of an exploitation that has already occurred. How is flarf different?

I feel I have a legitimate claim to being something more than an "influence" on Flarf. I feel strongly that the absence of my name functions to de-legitimize my claim. Meanwhile you'll see a lot of Flarfists joke about "no, *I* invented Flarf, just look at Bruce Andrews: Started as a L=A=N=G=U=A=G=E poet, joined Flarf, and he is still thought of as a language poet. One signature of this pseudo-movement is massive self-promotion. It strikes me as kind of sleazy, the way they've used their insiderness to create a fake movement.

It's ridiculous that something like this has "generated buzz" on the internet or in any artsy community. It's just like political propaganda: all advertising, no substance. But that, in itself, doesn't offend me. What offends me is that these LangPods (and they love to change their names/disguises as frequently as possible ... kind of like right wing neo-conservative think-tanks trying to throw people attempting to under-stand what they are really about off their trail) propagandize like an

Orwellian state ... and do so so effectively that they manage to monopolize experimentation and pioneering in the poetry world.

While I haven't had the time to research any of the sources, my own general take (I'm hardly alone, of course) is that "aesthetically" Flarf's only rarely capable of more than warmed-over, quasi-nihilistic Dada high jinks, playing increasingly stale variations on a one-trick tune; "sociologically," and I mean this in objective spirit, it's shown itself to be a po-biz frat club with a healthy mean streak and a hyperactive snob complex.
Indeed, the seamy underbelly is structurally too similar to sweatshop-style exploitation to ignore, don't you think? I mean, what are we hiding—and why are we hiding it, for whom, in whose interest? Flarf is surely not a sustainable writing, but is rather a temporary phenomenon, multiple front groups are created, of course, but most important is the way in which flarf mimics P.R. companies that "seed" newspapers with stories whose origins in corporate culture are—mostly—hidden.

The word "Flarf" is in fact one of those jargony ex post rationales for something we've all done as bored undergraduates; assembling a crappy poem out of lines not our own for the purposes of mocking something. But now it's been recontextualized as something edgy, artistic, and manifesto-bound (will look nice on a CV, I'll bet, just in time for next years AWP). Flarf, like language poetry in general, annoys me insofar as it elbows its way into what could be a productive discussion on substantive topics.

Flarf very often uses the language of the naïve, the sentimental, the "fucked-up," the unschooled, the ignorant, the misogynist, the right-wing, homophobic, racist, fundamentalist christian, the sly politician, the populist demagogue, the citizen confused and mortally wounded by intellectual, spiritual and political tyranny.

In fact, if you spend a day on any of the cable channels geared towards the young white demographics: "racist"/"naughty" content recontextualized (to varying degrees) within the scare quotes of irony/pastiche/parody/flarf/etc./etc. But it's hardly a new or particularly radical approach to dealing with certain contents deemed inappropriate in mainstream civil discourse. In any case, flarf's Un-P.C. aesthetic aim is a reactionary sentiment left over from the 90s and indicative of what's problematic about the virtual poetry community's closed circle of interlinked blogs.

Indeed, show-offy dick-wagging in the context of a collective gung-ho attitude regarding their own techno-dependency is a breeding ground for some bad habits and a utopian view of the Internet's impact on the poetry community (which is often conflated with poetics). This is the problem inherent in flarf that none of its practitioners or published critiques have recognized—it is already ruined. The problem with Flarf is that there is rarely ever a fix as to just WHO it is that might be on the page (stage).

Maybe the problem was ever announcing "Flarf" as a concept, suggestive of a movement, etc., in the first place. Obviously, this is one of the problems with manifesto movements. Sloganeering, as flarf itself would have it, is definitely part of the problem. Flarf pieces object to having a "voice," which, if you want to be lent ears, is of utmost importance (e.g., "The world today is not like it was when the New Americans were running it, and that's the real problem.") It's like racism and bad grammar automatically lead to lower-class.

Flarf, dead, alive, or trussed up for action clouds some of the current realities of race, immigration and class in the city, but Flarf will never "end" because too many of the flarfistes are at best mildly talented poets capable only of writing flarf, which is, all things considered, a fairly subtilized form of minstrelsy. Too many poets wish to be poets without struggling with poetry. Too many poets wish to be radical without facing their own wholly conditioned assumptions. If that's what you're into, go for it. Then go fuck yourself.

If you're in the shock-and-awe anti-conformity game (e.g., "Flarf"), we have potentially heartbreaking news for you: bourgeois culture is kicking all our asses out of town and right on down Indifference Road toward the over-populated city of Irrelevance. We're not trying to tar and feather anybody, any one of them may very well turn out to be the best thing since Starbuck's, for all we know. But, as many of its critics and supporters have pointed out, part of flarf's transgressive power comes not from being purely a "polyphonic discourse," but a "wrong" or "cute" or "cloying" discourse that's primarily dependent on ridiculing "uneducated" discourse or discourses that the poet would presumably not be willing to claim as an accurate representation of his or her own subject-position.

I don't know, to choose PC as a target these days in America seems a little misguided, to put it generously. Even in Dennis Cooper's world there is tenderness and beauty. In Brett Easton Ellis there is morality. In Gabriel Gudding there is love. And I think though I feel a little silly about this reaction, mostly because it's the reaction I had as a kid when my parents were talking about race in front of people outside the family, I think it's valid in so far as poetry does not exist in a vacuum. It's a public conversation we are having, at least until we're dead. It has very much to do with how we end up relating to one another. I actually pity artists who would sculpt shit and have an instititional brand on it guaranteeing its quality.

There seem to be numerous examples, at least on the internet, of appropriations of Black Working-class Orientalist Redneck vernacular in flarf that could only be described as 21st century minstrelsy—whose awful and continuing racist history seems to be lost on folks. Framing it some pseudo avant garde poetry does little to entertain or stimulate me into further reading or any sort of debate. It's not interesting, and the "poetry" (if you can call it that) is lame. Isn't it sad that acquiring degrees and learning how to talk all that supra-official serious shit about shit doesn't instantly make one an artist?

Does google "lead" people to this ugliness? Hell yes. It's there all over the place in our virtual world...certainly there are more intelligent ways of pointing to it and commenting on it. Just spitting it back out is suspect. There are no flarf poems about how funny lynchings are—are there? So why is it funny to dehumanize women (e.g., "Chicks Dig War")? Is that just an easier target? Something you can still get away with "in the community"? As said the wise man Pee-Wee Herman,

"That's so funny, I forgot to laugh." If "Chicks Dig War" is the "Howl" of our generation we've got a big problem here. Problematic doesn't even begin to describe it.

I don't sense thinking or emotion in flarf, I sense sort of an obsessive, blank "hunting"; I understand this; actually it's all coming together now for me—*Deerhead Nation*, okay, it's all making sense ... googling is a virtual substitute for "the hunt," hunting and collecting, men hunt animals and women also, so I think perhaps this is the ugliness I am getting from this process, the blankness of mind and lovelessness, even hatred and murder that I sense. Vile and dirty, flarf seems a bit like those gangbang videos where the actress takes 200 guys.

I feel very fucked-up in saying all this, because I realize I am taking what was a discussion of a poem and pushing it back into what feels like a personal attack on the poet, and yet another personal attack on Flarfists in general, and this is truly not what I'm trying to do.

➤

Googling Flarf

Michael Gottlieb

Flarf: a self-dubbed group of young (or relatively young poets), distributed fairly widely over the landscape, with perhaps a fairly predictable skewing towards New York and the Bay Area, perhaps—also—rather fewer among them with academic positions or lifestyles. Originally organized (as it were) a few years ago, around a listserv where they share and communicate and, I understand also, naturally, bicker, they have built up a group identity in many ways more clearly defined than any since the first generation Language poets three decades ago.

A defining characteristic of their work can be said to be the embrace of the dizzying opportunities proffered to those who are so inclined to engage in chance-generated poetry or artistic composition, by the stunningly voracious, simply overwhelming power of the internet's search engines.

Another characteristic is that this group (not unlike similar collections of artists who have come together through the years, like the aforementioned Language poets or the Pop artists or the action painters or Bebop musicians or Surrealists or Cubists before them) is that for a number of reasons—including, doubtlessly, self-preservation—they have engaged in a variety of exclusionary activities, drawing lines between themselves and their peers, their competitors, as it were. Rejecting some, refusing others. Naturally this generates a certain amount of hostility. As well it should. As is right and proper.

Among others, these Flarfists include a number of what were for some time simply thought of a younger Language poets, as well as others, including: Drew Gardner, Rod Smith, Jordan Davis, Nada Gordon, Gary Sullivan and Katie Degentesh, and quite a few others.

This piece was occasioned by an article that appeared in the same online magazine, *Jacket*, where this essay, in a slightly modified version was also published. That article took the Flarf poets and their work to task for, chief among their failings, relying on a Google, a profit-driven enterprise, as the source of its 'chance,' as the motivic force that generates so much of its language, explicitly arguing that the interests and desires of a capitalist entity like Google had to, necessarily, conflict with the needs and concerns of poets.

So, when it comes to sorting out the various slaps and slams that have been administered to this thing they call Flarf, as a poet who was deeply involved in chance-generated practice for years, all of whose early work was produced via chance operations, some questions arise: if we stipulate that is it is indeed a corrupt, capitalist, contrived and suborned activity to write poetry using a product such as Google, then we are making at least two assumptions that on the face of themselves, at least, seem difficult to get one's arms around.

The first assumption is existential: that it is acceptable to make use of Google or similarly debased tools in certain situations but not in the production of poetry. Or are we not to make use of these kinds of tainted products or services at all? How different is this from the similar, on the face of it equally totalizing arguments: if you own a car you're supporting the oil companies and the extinction of the planet. Which leaves us where? Taking Amtrak to Chicago? And what other assumptions lie behind this kind of argument? What or how does it valorize our practice, our work, rightly or not, above other sorts of labor?

The second assumption is more literarily problematic. As the arguments go, there is something about the choices that Google offers up that is delimiting. Because it is a commercial enterprise, there is something intrinsic in its algorithms which somehow debases the language that it 'produces.' It is tainted, tinged, tilted to some commercial, key-word-AdWord-corrupted impulse.

On the face of it, this is a more compelling argument. It contends or implies that there are other links, other texts, that could be served up by a mechanism that did not have at its heart a profit-driven impulse; that there is an entire world of other.... other sites, other language, whose authors or hosts don't have the wherewithal or inclination to a) 'optimize' their html so as to ensure that a search engine's 'spiders' reach out and find it, and find it interesting, and keep returning, and keep finding it sufficiently cool, updated, etc. to pop it to the top of its listings, or b) pony up the fees that Google and the other engines demand to position paid links near their search findings, the ones that appear (if there is anyone left who doesn't understand that those are paid listings and not generated by the engines themselves) next to the 'regular' or 'natural' listings.

There are however two substantial problems with this argument. First, we live in a world—at least I think we do—wherein at least some artists have long since figured out a way to live with/ interact with/ abide with/ surmount/critique those same corrupt, commercial impulses, those politico-economic forces of which Google is presented to us as merely the latest, more hi-tech and, consequently, the most insidious iteration. It could be posited that while a considerable body of art produced, say, in the last one hundred years has attempted to eschew or ignore those impulses and forces there is an equally substantial body of work that embraced that world—this world—if that be an appropriate term, and through an examination, dissection, etc. of it and its commercial expressions, fashioned an art that proved to be the most devastating, thorough-going, uncompromising of it or any other time. Pop Art, and Cubism as well, spring to mind. What, in the final aspect, is the qualitative difference between incorporating the front page of a copy of *Le Monde* in one's painting or a few frames of a comic strip or a soup can label and making use of an equally commercial 'product' like a profit-based search engine? Is one use more critical, more knowing, more sarcastic, than the other? If that is the case, one would like to see the buttressing arguments that would support a finding that, for example, Drew Gardner's "Chicks Dig War," (from *Petroleum Hat*, Roof Books, 2005) with its ironically glossy reframing of found language, is less conscious of its antecedents and its compromised status than, say, Andy Warhol's silkscreen diptych *Double Elvis* (various impressions, struck 1963- 1964) with its equally desperate and campy appeal.

On a personal note, when I cast my mind back to the tools I found myself making use of when I was making work that depended so much on the ineluctable, irrevocable, generous, earth-shaking and fantastically liberating mysteries of chance, back when I still knew where to find my copy of the I Ching (and at a time when up to not too many months previously, that book was the only one I'd ever heard of the Bollingen Press publishing), I made use of two particular tools. The first was dice (or, rather, one die—I never seemed to require a piece of arithmetic that obliged me to parse, or sequence or randomize more than six units or pieces or words or sets at any one given time) and the second, more to the point for the purposes of this conversation, were coins.

I used coins all the time, for months, for years. It never occurred to me, at the time, that I was entering into a corrupt compact with any social-political-economic superstructure. As far as I was concerned, I was attempting to join up with, to show allegiance to a particular band of saints, Merce Cunningham and John Cage and William S. Burroughs and the ineffable Jackson Mac Low, who had clearly cracked one of the great codes of creation (of creating and Creation, both). They had figured out a way to give this world back to us in a new way, to serve it up to us, to give us through their art a world that was terrifyingly new and altogether familiar at the same time. And it was all in keeping with the rest of the art was being produced all around them—at the same time—the Roy Lichtensteins and the Jasper Johns and the Robert Rauschenbergs and the Andy Warhols, for example, that appeared on the same stage as the dances Cunningham choreographed to the music Cage had composed.

And it never occurred to me for a moment—and I wonder if it ever occurred to them—to Mac Low, for example, that committed socialist and pacifist who remained true to his convictions for decades upon decades, until his dying day—that making use of a coin, money, capital in its most crepuscular form, filthy lucre itself—that act would, could compromise us. After all, what could be more debased than currency itself? What is more oppressive, more corrupt than money? I thought I was just making use of a convenient, binary chance-generating engine. Little did I know. This was money. And money is the root of all evil. Isn't it?

Does poetry have a job? Is there something that is it supposed to do? Do for us? To us? I would suggest if what we are now calling Flarf has a role in our life, jointly or severally or individually—in, say, our literary life, its role is not, cannot be substantially different than that which previous methodologies or schools or movements have taken upon themselves. Its job—and I do think I believe that poetry indeed does have a job—is to crack open this terrible world and give it back to us in a way so we see it—at once, whole, entirely anew and, simultaneously, completely familiar. Its job is to enable us to see it in a way that we never could before, and never could now—without the aid of this new work. If we can adduce that this is art's, poetry's job—or, better perhaps—its responsibility, in every age, then we can, we have to, perhaps, stipulate that with every age poetry must needs find new tools to make it—as the bard of Rutherford, or was it Camden, proclaimed—to make itself new, to make itself over, anew. The old tools don't work anymore, at least for the time being—they are tired. The terrible vistas they once revealed now seem merely pretty. This is a commonplace: it is virtually impossible to look at Van Gogh or Matisse or read Eliot or Williams and grasp how uncompromising—how ugly, brutal, honest— they once seemed. It is our curse, is it not—as artists, to become picturesque. We should live so long.

That's why we need these folks, and every grimy, debased tool they can lay their hands on.

➤

Tagmosis / Prosody (extending parataxis)

James Sherry

*Discrete skeletal units are known as tagma. The process of fusion
is called Tagmosis. Different patterns of skeletal tagmosis
provide a primary criterion for identifying fossil arthropods* (104).
—S. J. Gould

D iscrete structural units of poetry are known as prosody. The
process of fusion of prosodic units is known as writing.
Different patterns of prosody provide a primary criterion for
identifying poetic affiliations.

Linking human and natural processes exposes other connections
long hidden by our arts and sciences. The ability to link of human intel-
lectual activity to survival and natural selection implies that the barrier
that humanism created between itself and nature, as a defense against
deism, must give way to environmentalism. That process is visible daily
in the crumbling of vertical knowledge, in the rise to power of matrices
overloaded to sparking with alien perceptions, cognition outside the
organism, and new social structures increasingly dogmatic and exclu-
sionary about their shared behaviors. It has all the earmarks of change.
The analogy of tagmosis and prosody is as good a place to start as any,
since data and knowledge about them derives from their process and
relational thought rather than ontological and hierarchical approaches.

There are three issues brought out by this analogy: First, in addition
to the separation of the different disciplines of knowledge we must
consider the sideways pull of interdisciplinary thought and define the
linkages between them. Otherwise hermeticism will create unpleasant
surprises for our specialists / species. This combination of vertical dis-

ciplines and sideways interactions produces the familiar branching of Darwin's tree of evolution and extends the analogy to environments of ideas. Second: the relationship between the various types of poetry should be based on prosodic distinctions rather than subjective (content-based) distinctions, although content can also be viewed as a kind of prosody. I will deal with these two subjects separately. Finally, poetic affiliations, loosely-knit groups of poets and schools, are mostly defined by how they view the prosody (Language Poets, New York School, Metaphysical poets) and / or the content (Romantics and identity-oriented poets) of their poetry, but I will not deal with these issues here.

The disciplines of knowledge developed in the 18th Century (art, science, and politics; or, for another common list of categories, see the introduction to Diderot and d'Alembert's *Encyclopedie*) have had significant responsibility for the vast increase in specialized knowledge in all fields. But by the beginning of the 21st Century, we have reached a limit in the value of some of these Enlightenment categories of thought. Today, in cosmology, we are discussing the first 10,000th of a second of the universe. In botany and zoology, we are identifying species at about the same rate as they are being extinguished by the rainforest destruction caused by the success of only one of the species. Further we are focused on the reducing the value of organisms while immortalizing DNA. In literature, we treat language, the material of writing itself, as the indivisible structure and ultimate content of the work. Moreover, these disciplines have become increasingly separated and the set of relationships among them is ignored if not scorned by most specialists in individual fields. The amount of effort going into these silos of epistemology has taken energy away from many real world problems, and critics of inter-disciplinary work claim it is not worth the attention of serious minds. In the arts, few accept the films of visual artists. Critics condescend to review a poet's novel and then only tongue in cheek.

"If you are an expert," Leo Szilard said, "you believe that you are in possession of the truth, and since you know so much, you are unwilling to make allowances for unforeseen developments." (qtd. Weart 229). People in one discipline either don't know what people in the other are talking about or they deny any relationships. In *Chaos: Making a New Science,* James Gleick quotes US Navy concerns that, "science was heading for a crisis of increasing specialization" (*Chaos* 5). In 1999, *The New York Times* reported that the search for a single irreducible element in the disciplines of art and science prevents integration. But the *Times* gives examples that are more than 100 years old: Flaubert's *mot juste* and Seurat's point of paint. Although the *Times* is, as usual, behind the times, only recently has the explanation of integration became available. At the beginning of the century, Picasso and Einstein disavowed the resemblance between Cubism and Relativity. Why did they reject the superficial relationship? Because they were bent on achieving the goal of essential and irreducible elements through their work. Einstein, to the end of his life, contended that there should be a grand synthesis in physics.

Less religiously, no single discipline describes a complete world. As a discipline stretches its usefulness in a vain attempt at a complete description, its proponents become increasingly strident, and they often obscure the real values of their discipline in the absurdities they concoct. An environmental view accepts the values of different disciplines within their niches and takes a practical position about their relationships. As all the plants in the forest take nourishment from the sun and soil, so all the ideals put their roots into fact and memory, some deeper, some wider, and synthesize theories and ideas.

An important characteristic of environmentalism for the arts is that a contemporary view of complex environments shows how the superficial is indicative of deeper layers. This relationship is signaled in the poetry of many contemporary writers, including John Ashbery, especially in works like *Girls on the Run* ("The men never learned to love much. There was both hunger and sadness / at their feasting, the rocks wave over the airstrip, the hyenas of sleep redescend, / the leeches brace themselves for one last fetid leap into thanksgiving / there where loam signals the synod's pallid approach" [38]) and Lyn Hejinian ("Planes of information intersect, coincide" [90]).

Similar, not identical, shapes exist in all sorts of complex systems at both the deep and surface levels, large and small scale. The perception of the relationship between modern physics and art persists because the relationship is based on complex not linear systems. Both Picasso and Einstein assumed linear viewpoints to describe complex phenomena which accounts for some of the apparent similarity. Picasso is famous for saying that the formula for success as an artist is that if you know how to do three things, use two. Other aspects of similarity persist and are accepted without concurrence of the creators. But can we trust our perceptions of similarity in opposition to specialist denials?

The view that there is a lack of sense data to make the 20th century worlds of art and science collectively comprehensible doesn't really hold. For example, history appears to repeat, to be similar, echoic, but not identical. The sense data supplies the similarity; our logic calls it history repeating itself, but environmental logic would notice something different. We often have a sense of dééjàà vu, an example which may seem to undermine the argument but occurs when a person senses a bunching up of meaning, but the sense data isn't really clear or able to be identified. Traffic tends to bunch up on the highway. Financial markets defy prediction, but tend to respond under stress in a way predicted by algorithms that describe the behavior of heating molecules in a closed container. Weather can be predicted near-term at best. Bad news is said to come in groups of three. There is no linear explanation why water turns suddenly turbulent as it courses downhill. Our senses provide plenty of data. And rather than continue to question the senses, let us look at scalar explanations in complexity theory.

While many innovations are taking place in linear approaches that continue to separate the disciplines, certain advances have been going on for quite a while that accept the similarities of real world phenomena at all scales, implying a single world view, single but composite, not unitary. In many disciplines of both types, revolutionary changes are going on. These changes overturn traditional assumptions about nature and humanity. They support a complex environmental view of unpredictable interactions. Now does not necessarily go this way and might go another. In paleontology, for example, Steven Jay Gould represents progress as punctuated and not uniformly progressive, citing periodic mass extinctions and long periods of relative calm. He also shows that survival is based on chance, not solely on Darwinian "fitness."

What are the implications of his revelations for our art / science model?

1. Art based on or assuming a continuous, progressive march of

ideas is inconsistent with our observation nature and must be viewed as contrary to biomorphic progress, since the origin of such art and politics is based on a linear / urban / humanist view of nature.

2. Politics, science, and arts based on a notion of continuous progress must be understood as being limited to a short time spans if they are to be valid at all. Such works in the arts are primarily ironic, parody or satire and do not rely on progress at all.

3. Arts and sciences which assume a composite set of natural forces or multiple views of nature must also reckon that short and long time spans have decidedly different kinds of progress (a single mode of discourse throughout a poem would not support both time spans; the odes of Charles Bernstein provide a good example). In the short run, progress can appear orderly, but phases of turbulence occur that may punctuate the sentence of progress, sometimes ending in a period.

4. Arts and sciences which assume only an association with nature or only an opposition to nature must be reconsidered since the idea of nature has changed as a result of human domination of previously more diverse niches. Humanity's relationship to nature must retain the measure of self interest necessary for survival.

5. These points of view are resisted by and depress many artists and scientists because they imply rethinking assumptions rather than carrying on from here. They also imply that there is more than one view of nature, and few cultural icons are held more dearly than one's singular view of nature. Yet what is changed and what is continuous would surprise many artists. The horizon is different; the surroundings are changed, but basic human requirements are not substantially altered. What that means is yet to be fully defined by artists and scientists. The result is that most people, educated or not, continue to have assumptions that are not supported by what we know about the world. The facts are available, but the modes of thought have not been assimilated.

For example, in literature most readers and most writers cling to 19th century assumptions about what we are trying to achieve in writing. Yet Symbolist, Surrealist, Formalist, Modernist, Objectivist, and Language poets have all introduced changes in the way we use language; those changes should have undercut the basis of meaning in narrative and descriptive prosody. The *Times* article cited earlier is a good example. But they haven't changed the overall viewpoint. Why? Basic human requirements — society, sex, needs for air, water, food, and predictable environment in a specific range — continue to support the reassurance of narrative structure and mirroring description. These modes cannot be disposed of entirely until humanity dematerializes (and our electrical organization ceases to be dependent on our bodies), because they are integral to our existence as organisms. Even though these modes' component parts can be analyzed out of existence, they will still exist. They are the obvious structures into which those components will be revamped when they are decomposed. Our daily stories about ourselves, the trajectory of a human life, and the sex act all imply narrative and support our identities. Society still implies description as well as the idea structure that post-Modernists assume. The solution that the new modes of writing and thinking could derive is that the tagma of narration and description might be fused, integrated into an environment with advanced approaches (New Sentences, lists, found poetry, multi-media, etc.) to create a contemporary poetry.

I drove to the
And should oak floor being low
We slip our accordions
Whatever this is for.

It is also pretty clear from a history of the progress of new approaches in all fields that new writing initially must take a hermetic approach to avoid being co-opted before the ideas are fully formed. Early versions of the ideas of each Modernist literary group are not promoted as adding to the foundation of poetry, but as a substitute for existing strategies. New ideas prove themselves by purporting to circumscribe the entire universe of writing. In the next phase, the new ideas seek to be linked to a rewritten canon. Language poetry has even refused to be named according to Bernstein's "The Conspiracy of Us" and other writers' disclaimers. John Ashbery and Barbara Guest have both publicly disavowed the existence of the New York School. Experimental art that works with disembodied components and linear problems is often the only path to the discovery and use of advanced tagma. Tagmosis itself occurs in composition and reading of the poem, but how many of the new links are fit to survive?

In the hot house of experimentation new ideas are born, but poetry does not only exist as a separate field of study any more than industry exists without agriculture. It can be spoken of separately, but will always in practice link with other fields. Here is another analogy from biology. Brian Goodwin (quoting Charles Delisi) makes a significant point about genetics: "the proposition that 'the collection of chromosomes in the fertilized egg constitutes the complete set of instructions for determining the timing and details of the formation of the heart, the central nervous system, the immune system, and every other organ and tissue required for life' [...] is incorrect" (34-35). Genes don't reproduce without an organism. Reproducing in isolation, the strings of genetic material fragment and stop reproducing in a few generations. The genetics, the prosody, must be modeled against the poem in the same way as a bodily form must in some way exist to propel the grammars forward beyond a single reading. Additionally, Goodwin points out that the growth of many organisms is structured by characteristics of the basic elements of biological growth, such as calcium, and mechanical stress, that occur in the form of the organism. Chemical and engineering realities account for the shape of organisms in a way nearly as significant as the genes do. The whorls of *Acetabularia*, a large, single cell organism, or the three ways leaves grow on multi-celled advanced plant stems relate directly to the speed at which free calcium accumulates in cytoplasm (81; 93; *et passant*). Initially postulated by Alan Turing, these notions confirm that there are generic categories, or forms, to life based on the interactions of the genes, chemical concentrations, and temperatures during cell growth. All of these factors determine the final shape of the organism. Genetics does not provide the essential reality of life forms any more than narrative, grammar, or sensibility alone provide essential poetic value.

Goodwin's conclusion that genes require physical organisms to model growth for them has other important parallels for the arts. The identification of language with the poem matches the attempt of geneticists to eliminate the organism as a valid episteme. It also over-simplifies Language poetry. Field poetry and biology work similarly. Goodwin says something familiar to innovative poets: "A field is not defined by the 'nature' of the molecules and other components involved, such as cells, but the way these interact with one another in time (their kinetics) and in space (their relational order — how the state of one region depends on the state of neighboring regions)" (51). Following this approach the poem orders itself through a set of rela-tionships and a process, not merely through a code, genetic or linguis-tic. The poem is a field established by the consequences that arise from the proximity of various components. A phoneme juxtaposed to a word or concept creates a resonant field throughout the poem. And typical of field poetry, a confluence of smaller fields — a vowel sound, for example, contrasted with a phrase — flows now turbulent, now tranquil toward the sea of the reader's metabolic syntax. From *Legend*, a collaboration between five poets (Bruce Andrews, Charles Bernstein, Ray DiPalma, Steve McCaffery, and Ron Silliman):

```
acid vacuum              the sea shells
            vertical form
                             lines
            AMP
LI                    FIED
notsomuch that      crowdbychances  (232).
```

Certain poems are dynamically stable and as such follow the forms in which language can become generic. Silliman's "Sunset Debris" is a good example: "Can you feel it? Does it hurt? Is this too soft? Do you like it? Do you like this? Is this how you like it? Is it alright? Is he there? Is he breathing? Is it him? Is it near?" (11). Fields of this type can also take greater risk in less stable forms that may perform a specific or heroic task. The work of P. Inman comes to mind:

Speak in from black knock

g l a y s husk ("decker" 8).

These specialized poems are also written with respect to the generic forms of language, but do not accept them as the entire set of possibilities. As such they can predict or account for linguistic change.

Modernism elided form and content. As such it established the possibility of a relational rather than hierarchic structure for the poem: "the women come and go" (Eliot 14). Post-modernism showed that the separation of an artist's context and work is untenable and exemplifies one of the relational models for writing as in Bernstein: "on a broad plane in a universe of mirrors you fall down on your waistband." (Bernstein, "Matters" 1). The variety of Language poetry, the successful and the unsuccessful efforts, represents a set of advances that field poetry might take through the matrix of possible poems. Linking in this way the *excitable media* of cytoplasm and language establish an extension of possibility. We can now revitalize categories of structure that allow information to be organized. Organisms : genes = poems : prosody. A cross-disciplinary discussion seems to be possible. Juliana Spahr's "Spiderwasp or Literary Criticism," for example, muses on power by multiplying the genres she uses to describe it. The relationship between the wasp and the tarantula, in spite of its drama, makes a point akin to Genet's *The Maids* about who controls whom in the household.

Once a cross-disciplinary option is established, the structure of the relationships, tagmosis, becomes an unavoidable question. I would extend this discussion to the current argument about stem-cell research. The notion that working with human genes is impious fails to recognize some of the basic discoveries of the past few decades. Lyn Margulies, in her proofs of exosymbiosis, has pointed out that vital energetic components of human (mitochondia) and plant (chloroplasts) cells were originally separate bacteria. As Bernt Walther puts it: "Eukaryotes are chimera of permanently fused monera" ("Commentary," 217). The notion that working with the human genome would create monstrosities ignores the fact that we ourselves, our cells themselves, are composed of multiple organisms and in the end poems are the monstrosities created by working with language.

➤

Handwriting as a Form of Protest: Fiona Templeton's Cells of Release

Caroline Bergvall

Handwriting as a Form of Protest

For six weeks, in 1995, the poet and performer Fiona Templeton locked herself up in the lugubrious corridors of the abandoned Eastern Penitentiary of Philadelphia to write. Why would she do this? Why would one do this? But this she did, "over six weeks," writing by hand with an indelible marker, no return no edit, "I wrote without the possibility of erasure," on one long string of paper, "where a spool of paper ran out, I sewed on the next one," guiding it through one prison cell per day, and for as long as it would take to work through the thirty-eight cells that make up this one corridor of the dreadful

panopticon. Once the project completed, she summarized it in this way: "written onsite / a continuous line / a cell a day." To work for weeks within the walls of an abandoned prison, everyday, alone, certainly demonstrates mental stamina and an engagement with materials and ideas at a physical as much as at a discursive level. But what kind of claim on textual prac-

photos by Bill Jacobson

tice is Templeton making through the long hours of her writing body?

The fact that *Cells of Release*, a "poetry installation" as she terms it, was created in collaboration with Amnesty International and that the poetry in question is occasionally created from case reports of current (at the time of the work) prisoners of conscience goes some way to clarifying the context of Templeton's approach. In the substantial endnote to the book of the project, she describes that each cell was dedicated to one Amnesty case and contained information on the prisoner of conscience as well as a pen and paper for the prospective visitor to use. Seen from this perspective, the poetics of this project are articulated at the borderline of civic activism. It is the project's outer circle:

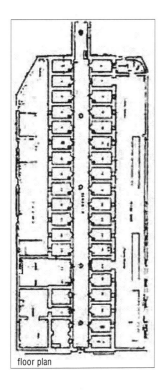

floor plan

Templeton writes and organizes the prison site (and later the book) to move "you" (visitor, reader) to write. Not for you to write for the sake of writing. In fact, not for you to write with art or literature in mind, but rather for you to write the kind of tailored letter to officials that Amnesty asks of its supporters in order to influence the release of prisoners of conscience.

The activity of writing (in epistolary as much as poetic form) finds its logic in this admonition to write. Writing must lead to writing. Write until there is release. Write then write again. The proven force of the Amnesty method being proven only so long as letters are being written. "For information on Amnesty International, current cases, and letter-writing, contact your local chapter." In the book, the final page gives the Washington (D.C.) address of Amnesty. If the question of the artist's social responsibility and the role of artistic creativity (why write?) in the face of human rights abuses is made explicit in the ways Templeton frames Amnesty's involvement, we shall see that this question is addressed at all the levels of this rich work. *Cells of Release* explores political engagement through its textual poetics (how write?), as well as through methods of artistic work determined primarily by the place (sited or context-led work) and by the artist's physical tasks in that place (why here? what now?). No one solution or key is proposed but rather a collage of authorial functions is activated and tested against the activist's call: a site-specific artist writing in a public space; writing as an explicit copying of social documents as textual sources; poetic practice as an organizing principle ("poetry installation"); the supra-artistic end of the project as audience development; the poetic end of the project as a book.

Site

Like much of her work, Fiona Templeton's project *Cells of Release* straddles a number of artistic methods and cultural environments. It has had two significant outputs. The piece was initially part of the "Prison Sentences" exhibition, and all the while Templeton was writing at the prison site, it was opened to visitors. From the text, it seems she engaged with visitors and their questions. The installation with its thin membrane of written paper has by now most likely crumbled (although there is a telephone number at the start of the book for visits by appointment, so if you're ever in Philadelphia, dial 215- 236 3118). Like all site-led pieces, there are all sorts of reasons why it may still be difficult to get to.

The installation has also become a book (which may be just as difficult to get to), published by the specialist poetry press Roof Books. Hence, the piece continues in the form of a textual and photographic document. The book remains concertedly an archive of the sited project. It is, as Templeton defines it, "a document of the poetry installation at the abandoned panopticon." It reproduces the entire line of handwritten text produced over the six weeks, and provides drawings and photos of the site and of the written line as it weaves itself in and out of cells, following the walls, reaching back to the corridor. However, far more than a "document" (at any rate we know the unstable truth-value of such material), the book explicitly relocates or transfers to book-form some of the poetic concerns that articulated her installation. She uses the printed document (the document as visual and textual genre) to process poetic ideas, rather than to solely represent the

sited piece as one would for a catalogue or monograph. This is important for the efficacy of her book as a project which depends on, yet also goes beyond the temporal and sited form of the piece.

A lengthy and crucial endnote closes the book. A lyrical, pensive prose piece, it confirms Templeton's motivations. It outlines her processes and ties her writing to the physical and emotional labour of working on site and with this kind of material "to see if the matter itself could be infused with the seeing-anew of art, not to alter the matter but to turn activity to it." It also specifies the range of sources which came to create her line of text: reports from prisoners of conscience; specific testimonies about violent arrests and abuses; statistics about state-sponsored human rights crimes; all of which co-exist with Templeton's own notation of her thoughts as she writes up these distressing stories day after day in the dank and menacing location of the prison. Some of the graffiti she found on the walls of cells as she was making her way down this corridor of writing make their way into her text. Pages of text alternate with black and white photos of prison cells and of the line of handwritten paper. On site, the writing seems rolled out like a scroll. In the book, the text is aligned at the centre of the page and separated into sections (entrance/ cell number/ corridor) that reproduce a map of the prison site and index the book: there are no page numbers. Templeton's handling of the book's photo-textual material assumes a readership that did not witness the piece first-hand (on site), whereas the book of course, allows and favors the abstraction of site.

From the way Templeton handles the task of writing, it is clear that this piece is informed as much by forms of artistic knowledge derived from late twentieth-century performance practices as by textual poetics. The way she chooses to write highlights this crucial interdependency between the sited event and its writerly structure. She uses writing to record, to register:

> The task in real time:
> "and I enter the cell" (CELL 8); "I almost passed this other marking" (CELL 13).

> The factual (Amnesty) material:
> "this week the state of Alabama reintroduced the chain gang"

The physical and psychological endurance of the task:
"I'd been yearning for a break
as in dam
or fever
or into fever
wanting my tongue to fork
but I have to go to hell first" (CORRIDOR).

The centrality of body perception for the apprehension of space:
"where the body begins
where in begins
turns
where you are
my body
speak it" (ENTRANCE).

The event-led structuring of time:
"I read it after falling
in Cell 21 last night" (CELL 19).

The experiential involvement with the site:
"and in the long dark writing
in the long light shaft
in the long dark time of the cell
my particular hand
bodying its short round bursts" (CELL 14).

From the point of view of textual poetics, one can therefore note that the text's temporality is dictated not by strategies inherent to textual poetics, but rather by a temporal narrative which lies very directly outside of the text: how long she is on site (the actual duration of her work on site) is the real-time of this text's writing. This being acknowledged, the many textual repetitions of the work start to read less as a stylistic device than as a rhythm, an inscription which literally punctuates, marks, keeps count of the passing of time and of the duration of the task. She has to keep writing in order to keep progressing down the corridor. Some cells of text read like a litany of negations ("not.../ not.../ not.../ not..."; "can't... / can't.../ can't.../ can't..."), others like a litany of revelations ("again now / again now / again now / again now / again now...") that try to exorcise the nightmare of this place (place... place... place... place... place) or attempt a correspondence between the referent siting of work and its discursive resonance ("message / passage / message / passage / message / passage"). "In context," writes Templeton in the note, repetition is "a hanging on desperately."

Similarly, spatial concerns are handled primarily in relation to her physical occupancy of the prison site. Her own body at the site of the prison is the central locus for the piece's spatiality. Not surprisingly, there's a predominant use of deictics throughout the text—"now" "here" "I" — a device used here to confirm, rather than imply, the congruence of the writer with the time and place of writing. Inevitably, the writing produced becomes in places profoundly personal, *voire* diaristic. The narratives are mostly held in first person narratives and prisoners' cases often appear in first person narratives: "*May I mention the stress which I overcame while I was a prisoner under sentence of death?*" The text reads simultaneously as a testimonial and as a barometer of her (and others') time on the "inside" (the opening word of the text).

As much as anything else, the text becomes an exploration of what being "inside" consists of: the body's interiority always equally within an institutional space, and both determined by the stricter or looser boundaries set by an "outside" (the last word of the text). The boundaries between what is in and out are never as strictly disturbed as when the "inside" is pushed to the furthest reaches of "outside." So far "in" you could be forgotten — so far in you could be left out, or might never come out:

a drawn boundary shifts across you
not drawn by you
meaning ownership of you shifts
because borders are breached
they breach you
they cross you (CELL 24).

In the case of prisoners of conscience, they frequently have no awareness of how long they will be kept. The imprisoned body, by definition a body stripped of interiority, is on the inside to be invaded by the cruel and complex layers of incarceration. It is impossible to measure how deeply one's sense of interiority, of having (or being) an inside, of having insides, might be turned out under torture or imprisonment. Released prisoners invariably speak of the very particular mental and physical strain at not knowing when they might be released and if anyone on the outside still knows where they are. Less than ten years from this project, and in the wake of the acute and politically opportunistic changes to civic liberties in the West since 9/11, it is chilling to note the current British justice's stance regarding the imprisonment with no trial, Guantanamo-style (under the "Anti-terrorism Crime and Security Act" of 2001), of nine foreign nationals on suspicion of terrorist activities.

The long hours and days of her voluntary confinement (how far does she take the act of doing this time? does she go home at night?) provoke thoughts regarding her own presence at the prison and the role of art production in the face of these merciless stories.

> A man stopped at the gate the other day. He spent fifteen years in this
> place, sentenced when he was a teenager.
> He said, I don't think they should make museums out of what goes
> on in places like that (CELL 2).

To which Templeton replies, "remembering warns." Yet her doubts as an artist caught in what is chiefly a metonymic form of imprisonment are increasingly at work. This dilemma of the artistic resolve is fascinating and familiar. It finds her caught in art's associative link, a testimonial at best, to the social injustices examined, along with the all-too familiar perception that art in itself doesn't effect social change. Flying in the face of formal considerations, her dilemma is frequently brought on by the harrowing detail of some of the tortures undergone by prisoners, and the obvious difficulty at giving account in ways which will not seem gratuitous or voyeuristic:

> I had chosen these cells near each other for metaphoric connection
> starving to death

221

and being beaten so hard his intestines were forced out through his
    anus
but sometime bringing these obscenities out
seemed as obscene as doing to the body
(TO CORRIDOR CEILING).

Is the work more potent, less voyeuristic for having subjected the artist to some degree of physical and emotional discomfort? Are we talking of empathetic action, a heightening of the ability to feel someone else's suffering, in order to validate a sense of personal indignation and even more crucially, validate the art-making process? Yet Templeton is caught too in the mechanics of her working method and the ethical concerns that arise from this strict adherence to form itself; she allows herself to be changed by the task, following it through whatever comes up, physically, mentally: "I'm not here to be right / I'm here to have a body" (CELL 26).

This is certainly one aspect in which Templeton's physical involvement, the way she implicates her own physicality, her own body as part of the writing process, can serve as a measuring stick. From the point of view of the art-making process, questions learnt and art produced from exercises in physical staying-power are different, though far from antithetical, than those learnt from intellectual patience (much in the same way that questions learnt from personal experience will vary from scholarly investigations). The perception of time and space, of scale, of materials and of context are not only different, they also provoke a different understanding of the use of one's body and one's writing. Ahead of discursive understanding, the very fact of (one's) body means at least two things: it represents the most common denominator (all humans have body) and the most singular one (each human entity has one specific, let's call it physical, body).

Twentieth-century performance and body-related arts place the exploration of the human body firmly at their structural centre. As site, the physical body is as singular as it is collective, as symbolic as any psycho-social site, as alive as it will be dead, as alive or as dead as it might be "live." Discourses of identity and of body boundaries have to do with such ins and outs. Performance reminds us that a "live" body is singularly alive and collective. It is singular and singularized.

Performance Art explores the collective (and plural) experiences of the singularized body. It involves the audience as witness and as accomplice. Herein lie the great excesses and secrets of performance art: cutting into the individual (performer's) body to display or show up the collective interdicts or events that could and do shape it. As a performer who's been involved in large-scale projects with both individual and collective bodies, Templeton knows this. She knows too that her explicit physical action (in this case, the action of writing on site) inevitably affects the kind of thinking processes she will produce: "my gut has turned from irony / from artful bettering" (CELL 26); "I stripped speech naked to discover why to respect it / threw away elsewhere to look for where I am" (CELL 36). Templeton's exercise heightens her experience of both the collective and of the singularized body. That the visitor would have to experience the piece in a prison plays certainly no small part in Templeton's decision to work there. Her endnote opens with the words: "Before the visitor interprets, she has brought her body. And in order for the visitor to perceive, the body goes further still, accompanies the work." The testimonial and empathetic activities of the project function through physical involvement, through accompaniment. To accompany: to go with, to keep company. The body accompanies the work. It assumes relationship, it enhances interrelationship, interdependence. In direct continuity with her Amnesty engagement, the act of writing supports the physical body, seeks to accompany it, to go with, to be several. At all stages of the work, we can discern such points of accompaniment, the social and physical "withness" of a performed writing, and the express sense of responsibility that it also implies.

Line

The development of an appropriate poetic line is one of the most enduring interests and concerns of prosody. One could even venture to say that it is what keeps poetry, poetry. How a poet justifies the length or the beat or spatiality of their "line" is a near obligatory part of poetic structure. Take Dante's tercet, Skelton's skeltonics, Sappho's lyric line, Milton's blank verse, Petrarch's sonnet, Shakespeare's sonnet, Omar Quayyam's quatrains, Basho's haiku, Baudelaire's prose line, Mallarmé's book line, Whitman's thought line, Blake's song lines,

Olson's breath line, Stein's paragraphic line, Joyce's omnivorous line, Kurt Schwitters's voice line, Allen Ginsberg's mantras, David Antin's transcribed line, John Ashbery's disjunctive line, Frank O'Hara's New York line, Kamau Brathwaite's computerized line, Ntozake Shange's choral line, Anne Marie Albiach's choral line, Henri Chopin's audio line, Brion Gysin's permuted line, Alice Notley's subway line, Susan Howe's visual line, Charles Bernstein's plundering line, Jackson Mac Low's acrostic line, John Cage's mesostic line, Kenneth Goldsmith's procedural line, Rachel Blau DuPlessis' scholarly line, Henri Michaux's commentary, Bob Cobbing's xeroxed line, Theresa Hak Kyung Cha's collage line, Erin Mouré's translative line, or Juliana Spahr's line of address for instance

For Templeton, the single continuous line explored here is, as we have seen, one obligated by place and duration. She writes in the endnote: "It is hard to represent on the pages of a book the physical continuity of the original writing. I felt mostly the single journey that I was making." This physical continuity marks the length of Templeton's line. This poetic line is a sited line. It cannot be erased or altered (edited) and is a continuous line in real time. Its successful progression responds intrinsically, inherently, to the *in situ* conditions through which it arises. This of course goes far beyond the historic considerations of what has been considered a poetic line. But then was the poetic line ever anything but a reflection of individual as much as cultural conditions? Applying basic prosodic notions to textual work that unfolds spatially and temporally in social sites, opens compositional concerns hitherto specific to poetry to events-led forms of writing. To measure the various units of a video-audio-spatial-physical piece by Brian Catling or Aaron Williamson enables these to be *structurally* considered as accompanying, as going with, as being part and parcel of the textual work. It forces textual criticism to continue to meet poetry at the door, or rather, in "the STREETS," as Steve Mc Caffery puts it within the related context of sonic poetry in his take on the famous couplet in Olson's "Projective Verse" (McCaffery's full alternative reads: "with the CAVITIES, by way of the THROAT, to the SOUND / the BODY, by way of TECHNOLOGICAL EXTENSION to the STREETS").

The line becomes that interruption, the spatial hiatus that organizes not only the verbal material but also the space on which it is active, and even the technology used to inscribe and manifest its rhythms and extensions. In a sense, one could say that the measure of the contemporary poetic line is to be found in the way the poet thinks about language, rather than in prosodic adaptation or reinvention. It is an attitude one commits to (a line) as much as a textual trait. Within the visual arts, and from the point of view of the exploration of the single line, one can think of the explicit linearity of Nancy Spero's hand-printed text murals of the 1970s, stretching along the walls of the gallery to exceed the painterly frame and explore ways of figuring (also through Amnesty reports) narrations of torture and abuse of women. There's the continuous line of blue paint casually leaked by Francis Alÿs to record his walks in different cities. There's the mapped line of Hamish Fulton's long walking pieces. From within the literary, there's the devastating one-sentence long prose piece *Eden Eden Eden* by Pierre Guyotat, published in France in 1962 at the height of the French-Algerian War. Along with Spero's work, this is perhaps the line that is the closest to Templeton's own. It is a vociferous book, a full 300 pages of claustrophobic close-up narrative of bodies tortured and humiliated and blown apart, names hardly given as figures are swallowed into the bloodied swamp of this one, single, breathlessly descriptive, cannibalistic and unending line—from start to finish one line of exploded phrases and fragmented events, one line which holds between its circuit of commas, the pulsating and cyclical revulsion, the unforgiving rhythm of the horrors of the Algerian War. This close to the skin it is an unsustainable read, morally as much as physically. It was banned when it was thought that it would encourage anti-French sentiment. There is something of this revulsion at work in Templeton's piece as well, something of this emphasis on myopic physical closeness and the way it forces up insights into suffering. There is something of this same insistence in the bleached-out photos of the collapsed cells, in the textual repetitions, in the retelling of abuse, in the reality of the prisoners' condition of disappearance, in the nightmarish duration of her process. All of which captured and made manifest in the stubborn singleness of her one handwritten site line.

Ironically, it is through the photos that one becomes aware of the singleness of her poetic line. In the book, the line travels down the centre of the page in short interrupted bursts, and turning the page creates interruptions and pauses. It is the photos that follow the handwritten line, the tracing of the text as it makes its way along the cells. The photographed line of text is pinned on the prison site, weaves a line of writing, a line of work in and out of the cells. There are no close-ups of the text. The photos are all taken mid-shot. From this distance, the actual line of text is not readable. It is viewable but largely unreadable. Photographed in this way the handwritten text belongs to the site, is a part of the site. The photos give credence to the veracity of the torturous task of writing. They make it seem (feel) true. They push the work towards social document. Susan Sontag observes in *Regarding the Pain of Others*, with reference to the German writer W.G Sebald's need to combine his mournful travelogues with archival photos, that they are there "to haunt us." They turn the elegist into a "militant elegist" (80). The photos confirm Templeton's personal process as a militant one. Furthermore, because their role is precisely to show the site as a place followed-through by the handwritten line of her intervention, their presence in the book is inextricably, though not descriptively, one of the modes of the piece. They are necessary to the iconic as much as signifying articulations and complexities of the (re)presented textualities.

Hand

At the innermost circle of the work: the handwritten line. As we've seen, this handwritten line, presented as it is through the photos of the book, shows less what it has written than that it has been written. In this sense, it doubles up on the performativeness and sitedness of Templeton's approach. As far as I can tell from the photos, Templeton's line of handwriting is steady, the gaps between phrases equidistant. It doesn't doodle, it doesn't draw anything else but letters and signs. The handwriting is in the task. A hand is seen to have been at writing. Being in (the) hand, it is on site. One assumes that it has originated in the hand (body) of the writer, in the one doing writing. This assumption is crucial. The handwriting specifies and particularizes the act of writing. It embodies the act of writing as a physical activity. Where typeset writing is explicitly separated from the literate physiologies of the particular writer's hand, when handwritten the text retains, even favor, the unmistakable trace of physical transit, of passage along a line from the writer's body to textual work. Seen from the angle of a poetic tracing, a textual gesture rather than a textual line, this corporeal tracing turns the handwriting itself into an excess of writing. Or rather, paradoxically, it can be considered in excess of writing very specifically because it literally incorporates the writing body to the textuality produced. It implies a somatization, not so much of the text, but of the act of writ-

 ing. In itself, a very particular example of the pulsational "feminine" writing famously advocated by the French writer Hélène Cixous and subsequently taken on by a whole range of artists, including Nancy Spero and Susan Hiller, whose work using handwriting seems the most directly relevant here. Similarly, Marjorie Welish connects the handwriting processes of Cy Twombly and Mary Kelly to a "poetic logic of language acquisition," one where the learning body itself provides the semantics of the gesture of writing.

One of the functions of handwriting as a poetic practice would be to testify to this physical root of the trace of writing. How much of the hand and how much of writing is there in the handwriting? Rather, what kinds of writing and textuality does handwriting produce? From the point of view of textual genetics, it is still very largely the case that it is the "poem" in progress which is of interest. This does not traditionally include a reading of its tracing. To pore over the poet's manuscript and its many drafts and corrections is done primarily to study the development of the verbal material. This does not include the blotches in the margins, the weight of the hand on the page. Critical work done around the connections between drawing and writing, as well as the growing field of textual genetics is helping shift this focus, but the analysis of writing gestures is still a largely marginal, incidental activity of poetics. Even after philosophy's influential discussions on the performativity of the signature, that last bastion of handwriting, it is still more often than not read as part of a biographic commerce in the writer's aura rather than as part of its textuality. "I wonder why manuscripts are so underestimated in all academic disciplines, including science, mathematics, linguistics, semiology," ponders Susan Howe in her recent *Pierce Arrow*, in which typeset texts and pages of manuscript are presented more or less as a viewing/reading pairing. This form of accompanied reading allows dedicated attention to Pierce's handwritten notes and verbal sketches, and the progressive aspects times of his thinking as also demonstrated in his writing. Connecting the writing to the writer's hand (not the writer's name) emphasizes the traced body, the bodily trace at the root of writing. The dramatic changes to Emily Dickinson's handwriting have been commented on. As years of writing go by, the way the pencil hardly seems to brush against the paper, how this visually ethereal quality accompanies the maturing of her extraordinary and elusive work. French critics have also variously reflected on the "added sensation" brought on to his autobiography by Stendahl's doodles. Handwriting commits writing to the circumstances of writing as much as to language. The poet commits her literate and socialized body to the emotive act of writing and to what Derrida, working on Artaud's "written drawings," has called, the graphic trace.

Using handwriting as a poetic or performance practice to enhance or explore embodied lines of work is invariably and to various degrees done in reaction to what is perceived as the prominence of phonocentric and logocentric knowledge. Susan Hiller's early automatic light-writings sought to excavate the body for buried (repressed, unconscious) meaning. From here, one is drawn to performances where writing becomes more of a mark-making process, less textual than it is performic. Deeply connected to the writer's body and politicized in no small way through feminist and "feminine" practices. In fact, gestural and calligraphic skills, long devalued by most western poetry, seem to have found their way back to art through performance and body-related visual arts: blood writing and white ink writing; writing done using body emissions and organic materials; writings that are seen to register bodily movements and highlight taboo manifestations of the human body's interior/s.

These performances are exemplified by the work of Gina Pane, Ana Mendieta, Andre Serrano, Franco B, and Ron Athey. Cris Cheek mentions tracing with "25 separate pages of marks made by my tongue. Marks made by 'licking' with crushed beetroot, red wine, coriander, tea, carrot and cochineal." The recording or sounding of handwriting done by Brion Gysin or TNWK or the "live transmissions" of the visual artist Morgan O'Hara, expand the sensory base of the written scratching of a hand-tool or body-tool on a surface. The far reaches of body writing are not only a somatization, but a practice of contestation. Done in resistance to linguistic semantics as much as to the power-structures surrounding the human body in art, they enhance forms of knowledge, of rituals and of art practice that have been largely discredited by the laws of written culture.

For poetic work, such practices have emerged initially from the revolutionary realms of Concrete Poetry and from the work of gestural calligraphy by a number of Western poets and painters from the 1950s onwards. See for instance the magical permutations of Brion Gysin, who trained in Japanese as well as Arabic calligraphy, and describes his writing paintings as "calligraffiti." Or the hand traces and drawings of the poets and writers associated with Bob Cobbing's workshop. See also the works of Henri Michaux and Antonin Artaud, two poets who have actively engaged with drawing texts. Michaux' handwritten pieces are calligraphic imitations, mimicries of writing, brush strokes which have abandoned writing, which "have left writing behind." It is a case of an active disengagement from and a spiritualization of the grapheme into line. Artaud's "written drawings" [dessins écrits] carry a verbal sense and the highly energetic representation of words increases, augments, devastates writing at its contact with the poet's hand. Writing draws its trace, becomes its own drawn trace. A body seeking to escape its writing through the trace. They are "but the circumscribed / figuration on paper / of an élan / that took place / and produced / magnetically and / magically its / effects ("50 Drawings to Assassinate Magic").

More recently, and in ways that are close to Spero or Templeton in her commitment to physicalising her social commentary, the Iranian photographer and filmmaker Shirin Neshat has used handwriting very specifically to document or sign her self-portraits by inscribing with Arabic script the areas of her skin not already veiled by the burka, playing out processes of "veiling," what makes a veil, and what unveils. Furthermore, the photos draw links between traditional and contemporary forms of inscription (writerly, photographic) and remind us that women have traditionally no access to practicing publicly the sacred art of Islamic calligraphic writing. These pieces from her 1996 series

"Anchorage" reflect the issues of power, gender and transmission always at work with writing. Made in the West, they are also a reminder that this script system inscribes the traditional richness of one of the world's influential cultures within the context of international contemporaneity. Neshat does this at a time when Islamic culture is already much threatened by ongoing interests in the politico-religious West as much as by waves of extremism in its own midst.

At a direct level one can say that all these practices widen the scope of alphabetic (speech dependent) writing toward a broader understanding of writing's ideographic history. In this context, the act of writing may be textual but it is not primarily linguistic. It concerns itself with the trace as much as with the traced. Poetic practices connected to the immediacy of the gestural body, to the stroke of the breath or of the skilled hand, position themselves in explicit extension of the literary production of writing. We've seen that the politicization of the marked performer's body (in Templeton's case, through handwriting processes) provides relevant contexts on approaching this kind of practice.

Templeton, as much as Spero or Sherat, works with the proximity of the writing body as physical document. Their form of testimony comes from a highly personalized response to social and political realities and an exploratory way of committing art to it. The experimental bricolage and responsive conceptualism of present-day arts activism is often seen to have emerged from the modalities of 60s–70s grass-root resistance as well as from the more physically progressive performance practices of these last few decades. Imbricated combinations of personal and social history are a means to mobilize and make a case for investigative concerns and on-the-ground, in-the-flesh methods of work. Templeton's piece connects with this tradition as much as with the function of poetry as a form of dissident witnessing. By intervening with text site-specifically and through site-led compositional methods, she creates a form of writing, which is profoundly connected to the "witness" material at source and provides for an uncompromising commitment to the act of "testimony."

Indeed, as we have seen, *Cells of Release* implicates the poet physically and viscerally, and deals with her sense of social responsibility in both pragmatic and subtle ways. She writes under duress and we've seen that she positions the act of writing very specifically at each level of her descent into the work. Her call to writing is very directly a call to individual responsiveness and individual involvement beyond the piece. Her use of cross-arts tactics and her performer's experience is attuned to artistic modes in which the performer explores representations of physical presence as a sample of thinking and as the very testing-ground for work. She addresses the impasse at the separateness of formal process and social motivation, of arts productive or non-productive nature, not by poeticizing towards a revolutionary state of Art revolt, or by projecting new political ideals, but rather by proposing a physically responsive and quietly collective mode of participation and of resistance. One which, for instance, accepts the participatory structures of an established, international and universalist body (Amnesty). This makes for work that recognizes how exploring a set of formal structures to the full and in context, by going to the heart of practice (body and sign), can turn writing into a form of protest.

➢

Adding Up to Plural:
On the Work of Roberto Tejada

Alan Gilbert

Mandorla

Ten years ago, when Roberto Tejada began editing the journal *Mandorla* (1991-present) in Mexico City, it seemed as if one couldn't have a conversation in the United States about poetry, or art in general, without the word multiculturalism coming up. This was also during the height of the "culture wars" in the United States, when multiculturalism meant much more than expanded college syllabi and wider-ranging literature anthologies. For conservatives such as William Bennett, Allan Bloom, and Lynne Cheney, multiculturalism was an attack on the very foundations of the democratic system in the United States. In their view, it created unnecessary rifts within the general body politic, thereby isolating and even antagonizing the various ingredients that were supposed to blend together in a wholesome ethnic melting pot stew, although heavy on the milk and cream and sopped up with plenty of white bread.

For ethnic and racial minority populations in the United States, these rifts have always existed. One way of understanding the rise of multiculturalism is as an attempt by members of these groups to begin to discuss societal divisions more publicly. The United States is pervaded by innumerable hierarchies, stratifications, and marginalizations according to class, ethnicity, gender, sexual orientation, generation, health issues, and geography. To imagine—as social and cultural conservatives frequently do—that these differences do not exist at the heart of life in the United States for the vast majority of the population is to seek to impose a nonexistent cultural and social homogeneity. As Robert Stam and Ella Shohat write: "That the current system of power relations within and outside the United States itself generates divisiveness goes unacknowledged; that multiculturalism offers a more egalitarian vision of representation is ignored" (quoted in Turner, 413). At the same time, a general homogeneity prevails within North America's ruling classes; hence, their desire to impose it as a dominant ideology and set of social relations. This is, of course, one means by which power seeks to perpetuate itself.

In the year 2001, there is not as much talk in the United States about multiculturalism. This is due to a variety of factors: a semantic enervation that the word began to experience after years of sustained argument on all sides over its significance; a wariness of being labeled a multiculturalist when one was not able to control how the word was being used and defined (a danger in any discussions of multiculturalism, including my own in this review); the increased inclusiveness of a broader cultural spectrum of work created by minorities, including a certain degree of success in expanding the literary canon, as evidenced by a publication such as *The Norton Anthology of African American Literature*; an economic upswing that has manufactured the notion of wide-spread—though, in reality, selective—prosperity for many different segments of U.S. society; and a general ideological conservatism inside and outside the academy that has continued to subtly and sometimes even unconsciously discredit the numerous projects that together constitute a radical multiculturalism.

As a result, people fighting for multiculturalism*s* have reasons to be cynical. At the same time, if the mainstream media and university professors are not treated as the sole windows onto cultural production, then it is possible to begin to see a great deal of contemporary work that is creating new ways of thinking about and enacting questions concerning cultural heterogeneities and political pluralities. Locally based, though usually occupying limnal spaces within these locations, and careful not to make cultures synonymous with particular ethnic identities ("the rejection of the essentialist identification of culture and race" is how Terence Turner describes it [411]), this work represents the future as it exists now.

The journal *Mandorla* is one such example. Though Tejada mostly lived in Mexico City while editing it, it has always been a journal concerned with borders. Fluently bilingual and multinational, *Mandorla* has

presented a wide variety of work by U.S. writers: from well-known fig-
ures such as H.D., Langston Hughes, and Walt Whitman; to established
experimental poets such as Lorine Niedecker, Charles Olson, and Susan
Howe; to younger writers such as Mark McMorris, Heather Ramsdell,
and Thad Ziolkowski. The range of writers from Mexico, South
America, Cuba, and Spain is enormous, though not as easily classifiable
due to exile, substantial government funding for the arts, and less readi-
ly compartmentalized aesthetics: Efraín Bartolomé, Carmen Boullosa,
Elsa Cross, Gerardo Deniz, Eliseo Diego, Roberto Echavarren, Salvador
Elizondo, Luisa Futoransky, Gloria Gervitz, Alberto Girri, David
Huerta, Ana Rosa González Matute, Eduardo Milán, María Negroni,
Olga Orozco, Guillermo Osorno, Octavio Paz, Reina María Rodríguez,
Alberto Ruy Sánchez, Osvaldo Sánchez, Severo Sarduy, César Vallejo,
Xavier Villaurrutia, Emilio Adolfo Westphalen, to name only some of
the writers who have appeared in its pages.

Early issues of *Mandorla* articulate an aesthetics influenced by
Octavio Paz and Clayton Eshleman, both of whose writing and edit-
ing combine an analysis of contemporary cultural conditions with an
interest in older, sometimes archaic, societies and rituals. As *Mandorla*
has progressed, its aesthetics have become looser. For example, the
most recent issue contains an interesting journalistic article that
describes a 1997 Mexico-United States World Cup qualifying match
played outside of Boston and a bus ride back to New York City after-
wards (Osorno). It is a piece that contrasts with an essay in the second
issue by Octavio Paz describing the timeless relation between love and
death via a discussion of Xavier Villaurrutia's poetry, and which is
more typical of the work included in earlier issues.

Mandorla's editorial approach is to present translations of work that
has been previously published: if it was originally published in English,
it is translated into Spanish, and vice versa. Previously unpublished
work is published in its original language. Over half the work in each
issue consists of new translations; much of it is writing by Latin
American poets virtually unknown in the United States and by U.S.
poets almost as obscure in Mexico (though not quite as obscure, since
Mexican poets seem to pay more attention to poetry written outside of
their own country than US. poets do, and have also been helped by
Eliot Weinberger's anthology of twentieth-century American poetry,

American Poetry since 1950: Outsiders & Innovators, which was a best-seller in Mexico before being published in the United States). I can't think of another current poetry journal in the North America of NAFTA that can claim *Mandorla*'s ratio of translated to previously unpublished work.

The result is that one finds in the pages of *Mandorla* a fluid dialogue between different writers and cultures. *Mandorla*'s cultural pluralism is very different from the managed multiculturalism that prevails in literary journals in the United States, where minority writers and non-U.S. writers are oftentimes given a circumscribed space (frequently in the form of a "special" issue or section) in order to prove how well they have mastered traditional or experimental forms currently dominant in the United States. In one of the rare moments where the word actually has meaning these days, I would argue that *Mandorla* is "avant." In the U. S. experimental poetry world in particular, still puzzling over "language in itself" and "lyricism," *Mandorla* has always been more than a decade ahead of the times; in the world of shifting social demographics, it is very much of the times.

Gift & Verdict

Managed subjectivities come in all forms, including some that appear to be unmanaged. This is the tension at the heart of Tejada's chapbook *Gift & Verdict*, published by Renee Gladman's excellent Leroy press. Tejada is an accomplished editor, translator, art critic, and essayist; *Gift & Verdict* is his first collection of poems. The "verdict" in the title refers to the various ways in which subjects are controlled and managed within North American society, and "gift" points to a countervailing desire for freedom and self-determination. This relationship is a complex one in Tejada's poetry, where power and resistance are never completely independent of each other. Consequently, agency and play are subsumed within the historical and material conditions from which they can never escape, although this does not curtail imagining alternatives to these conditions.

In the opening poem (none of the poems are titled), Tejada disrupts easy categories when he mentions

... the culprits who, police
announced on Tuesday, were

chiefly married professionals
of whom you would have suspected nothing
but a sort of devotion (5)

In other words, what appears "Not unlike any other/ relevant inquiry into the world, I mean the norm, not/ the appearance, one of having been ransacked" (5) turns out not to have been so normal after all, not so devoted to the status quo. But who's to know? Power and its accompanying discourses attempt to control the flow of information (which is why the announcement is made by the police), while poetry has the potential to examine and redirect this information. "Information wants to be free" was one of the mantras of both cyber-utopianists (*Mondo 2000*) and cyber-capitalists (*Wired*) in the early 1990s when the Internet was less of a virtual shopping mall. What both the Internet and poetry can tell us in this instance is that without a theory of translation to accompany it, information tends to become directly incorporated into preexisting economic and cultural structures.

This idea of translation need not be literal; in fact, there is almost no Spanish in the poems of *Gift & Verdict*, which is a bit surprising, given how concerned Tejada's work is with dismantling borders and upsetting classifications, and how easily the poems move back and forth between the United States and Mexico. Instead, the poems translate between cultures, between structures of power and modes of resistance, between linguistic forms, between ethnicities, between sexualities, and between geographical locations. Moreover, the translation can never be perfect, or else it would not be able to account for the differences it at the same time seeks to bridge: "a good thing I made so many mistakes/ in the translation" (8). The result is a layered poetry that finds its form in dense stanzas composed of lines that frequently veer toward a kind of fractured prose as they twist around on themselves in order to reflect on the different categories they constantly call into question.

But power and control are not so easily eluded, and tend to leave their marks on the human body. In Tejada's poetry, the body is where some of the most immediate struggles with authority occur. As repositories of speech, tongues become both the literal and metaphorical place of articulation where the body and language are collapsed into each other "and wield along fold or fissure not/elusive to darting points of tongue/and orifice by deflect and contradiction" (9). In other poems, this collapsing is depicted as an ecstatic state that "releases the kind of content/ swelling when we touch/ conclusive the ecstatic/ cataclysm of the terrifying lull" (15). These particular lines are followed by a description of a goat slaughter in Huajuápan de Leon in the state of Oaxaca in Mexico, which Tejada discusses elsewhere in an essay on the photography of Graciela Iturbide. At this moment in the poem, a connection between eroticism and death is briefly signaled.

These references to the ecstatic might initially appear to align Tejada's poetry with the idea of "nonproductive expenditure" formulated in the writings of Georges Bataille. For Bataille, "nonproductive expenditure" is found in limit experiences that push toward disintegration and reckless abandon, be it bodily, psychic, or linguistic. These experiences can be encountered in sexuality, death, madness, and ecstatic discourse; they are in stark dialectical contrast to the productive world of work and utilitarian activities (118). Bataille's theory of expenditure was influenced by Marcel Mauss' theory of the gift. According to Mauss' *The Gift: The Form and Reason for Exchange in Archaic Societies*, gift giving in various cultures creates societal cohesion and in some cases partially redistributes wealth. For Mauss, one of the most extreme forms of this dynamic is the potlatch ceremony in certain non-Western cultures, in which personal and collective wealth is given away or destroyed in a series of—hopefully—reciprocated gestures (6-7). Bataille, however, emphasizes the potentially unsettling effects these actions could have on the different societies in which they occur, as well as their symbolic relation to other, more destructive, forms of expenditure—including class struggle (123-129). Similarly, in its concern with breaking down rigid social functions, and in its equation of eroticism and expenditure, the "gift" in the title of Tejada's book might be seen as related to Bataille's reframing of Mauss' theories.

But the language of *Gift & Verdict* does not function as a dehistoricized destabilization of itself from within (for this kind of approach to poetic expenditure, see Steve McCaffery's essay "Writing as a General Economy" [1986]). Instead, the Foucauldian concept of power as controlling discourse and knowledge—and in the process producing specific subject positions and ideological categories—makes the most sense when reading Tejada's poems, especially given his frequent references to control, constraint, authority, and surveillance:

>—wrenched by
>velocity penultimate, our well-intentioned trimming as
>though patent with the shape of hands
>
>held to government notes across the carbon
>stars of a dense winter sky pulled
>
>out from under the chandler's wobble
>of Earth
>
>   wrung down the purring
>timbre of drop-bomb-seven whence blind
>embossed hazard and boozy sentiment
>
>are the repeated business of sense
>and sound or money and prestige (21)

The language of *Gift & Verdict* seeks to slip in and out of restraint and its imposed normative categories.

Within the French avant-garde tradition in particular, as well as in the strand of poststructuralism most influenced by Bataille (including Foucault), irrationality is sometimes posited as a response to an Enlightenment rationality seen as totalizing and controlling (Jeremy Bentham's panoptic prison, which Foucault has famously analyzed, being one of the most notable examples of this totalizing vision). Yet Tejada is unwilling to posit any heedless equation of ideological and linguistic coherence with power and authority; neither does he equate incoherence with marginality and rebellion. Instead, he crisscrosses these formulas every which way, sometimes connecting coherence with marginality (in a culture where the pervasive babble of media-speak is overwhelming [7]), sometimes relating incoherence with marginality (as when one breaks with dominant modes of representation [17]), sometimes matching coherence with power (where hegemony seeks to impose itself as the norm [9]), and sometimes coupling incoherence with power (when ideology becomes an expression of brute force [6]).

This scrambling of categories is not the result of conceptual careless-ness on Tejada's part, but instead is a precise schematic of the different forms these relationships can take. In other words, it's a flexible poetic mode that is able to engage with the invariably hybrid and multifaceted aspects of experience, culture, and ideology.

This is why Tejada writes that "local language is deemed/ insur-gent" (18) and "the plain terms this place a conversation where I reap-pear" (14). Postmodernism and its accompanying critical theories and aesthetic forms have insistently argued for deconstructed subject posi-tions. Tejada's poetry keeps its distance from a dismantling of subjec-tivity that conflates a critique of European Enlightenment universal male subjectivity with subjectivity in general. The destabilization of the subject from within and for its own sake is frequently espoused by those with a great deal of economic and cultural stability in North American and European society. Moreover, postmodernism itself—as writers such as Zygmunt Bauman (59), Stuart Hall (466), and Christine Di Stefano (75) have pointed out—is a relatively local phenomenon. Instead, Tejada's poetry articulates a subjectivity that both shapes and is shaped by history. Specifically, it's a subject whose instability is one component of a larger awareness of cross- and multicultural influences that destabilize to the degree hybridity undoes monocultural mooring and creates new, old, and ever-shifting social and cultural formations. This is where "I reappear."

This is not a subject emptied out by language and formalist tech-nique, but one positioned as historically contingent: "at a velocity con-comitant with the stuff and landscape/ in front of you" (10). Poetry has the potential to render this contingency disobedient and to imagine dif-ferent histories and politics, as well as uncover suppressed or forgotten ones. David Harvey writes in his book *Spaces of Hope* about the impor-tance of translation for alternative politics: "Struggle as we may, it is impossible to conduct politics without an adequate practice of transla-tion" (245-246). Tejada's work as a writer, translator, and editor con-tributes to a rethinking of the cultural politics of poetry along more pluralistic lines. One of poetry's many roles, Tejada writes, is to "make meaning a site of genuine/ labor" (8), even if this meaning is articulat-ed in non-standard, and not immediately classifiable, modes. Multiculturalisms are processes, not products. Tejada's poetry resists strict categories in attesting to the complexities of social and cultural life in contemporary North America.

➤

The Poem at the End of Theory

Michael Clune

Not all the fruit trees hate you/ just this one.
—Kevin Davies

Theory's aim is to free the intraworldly entities we encounter, and to free them in such a way that they can throw themselves against a pure discovering—that is, that they can become objects.
—Martin Heidegger

A curiously abstract detail, juxtaposed with dozens of other such details, constitutes the basic formal unit of Kevin Davies' recent book *Lateral Argument*. Consider the following examples:

"An exurb of postmusical attention" (9).
"The brand-new feudal nightmare" (10).
"The paper-mache potemkin/ village we've spread like/ spreadable cheese over the surface of/ what we call earth" (4).
"A meta-literate culture [...] blinking vulnerably in the light of its own/ radiant connectedness" (26).

How do we read such lines? What vision of the world do they represent? Just kidding. We all know how to read this. To anyone with even a passing acquaintance with the literary and cultural theory of the past two decades, Davies' lines are variously legible as instances of either "the pastiche of the stereotypical past" (21), or the "practice of the randomly heterogeneous and fragmentary" (25), or the "representation of some immense communicational network" (37). The text from which this second set of examples is drawn, Frederic Jameson's 1984 essay, "Postmodernism, or, the Cultural Logic of Late Capitalism," provides an uncannily ready key for interpreting Davies' fragmentary lines. Indeed, Jameson's description of Bob Perelman's poem "China" as a succession of "sentences in free-standing isolation" (28), along with his idea that this feature projects the decay of temporality in late capitalism, applies so well to Davies' practice of disjunction that no further interpretation seems necessary.

But Davies claims that his recent work, while apparently reproducing the kind of stark juxtapositions, the "heap of fragments" effect that characterizes "China" for Jameson, is actually distinguished by a novel principle of connectivity. Davies claims: "I'm interested in connecting fragments rather than the more intense disjunction" of earlier work, most notably his 1993 book *Pause Button* (Durand, 48). Davies' paradoxical suggestion that his poetry consists of "connected fragments" asks us to think of the disjunction between individual lines in terms of a new principle of connection. If, as I have suggested, the task of interpreting the individual "fragments" is uncannily easy, the question of how to interpret *Lateral Argument's* apparent disjunction as a sign of connection is real, and opens a way into the central problematic of contemporary poetry: what comes after Language writing?

As an initial approach to this question, let's consider the idea that what makes Davies' poem something other than what Jameson calls a "heap of fragments" is Jameson's own analysis. If Bob Perelman's poem is a "heap of fragments," Kevin Davies' poem is a heap of fragments that have been interpreted. This difference is signaled by *Lateral Argument's* own oblique reference to "China:" "You can choose your friends/ Arbitrarily, like family photos/ Bought at a junk shop" (8). These lines refer not to "China" itself, but to Jameson's description of what he calls the poem's "structural secret." Jameson tells us that Perelman was browsing in a Chinatown junk store when he came across a photo album which he picked up, writing "China" as a series of captions to the photos of the unknown family. The "structural secret" of "China" is thus the classic postmodern device of a representation of a representation, which in turn exposes the "structural secret" of a world thoroughly mediated by the universal system of late capitalism.

Throughout the poem, Davies' details are oriented towards this sense of a tightly integrated, totally systematized world illuminated by "the light of its own radiant connectedness." In contrast to the celebrated openness of Language writing, which sought to represent something like the raw, unformed materials for making a world in variously configurable bits and pieces of language, Davies' fragments are fully formed, mature, even dead. The objects of this writing are stiffened by a kind of rigor mortis. They exist in the changeless time of the thing, the object, and Davies has found a tone that emphasizes this dimension. One of his principle affective registers is a kind of contempt for the objects of his writing, contempt for them *as* objects. His things exist in various modes of finality, of stasis, closure.

> "The clerks grown in vats near Langley" (11).
> "The load-bearing walls composed of particles who prefer not to, who strike against the conditions" (13).
> "Life in the pressurized capsule/ becomes intolerable" (12).
> "Postulating an unconscious/ on the basis of boat slips" (8).
> "A decent life of waiting to be allowed to breed" (11).
> "An unexpectedly depressing millennium" (20).
> "Any surface at all, inside or out, you touch it and a scrolled menu appears" (25).
> "An eternal return machine constructed for the entertainment of con glomerate nonbeings who are, sort of, *over there*" (15).

This contempt registers the status of these beings as *objects*, as completed, ended, static, solid, opaque. Davies' affect has a distinctly epistemological valence. Contempt is the sign of the total, closed objecthood of this world. This is a world that stays in place. What place? At a certain absolute distance from the beholding subject, whose contempt registers this distance. This distance opens a kind of poetic space notably absent from Language writing. Beings not ordinarily conceived of as objects (time, other people, feelings) are frozen in the beam of this writing, become mere things. The class struggle is suspended as a "particle" in a "load-bearing wall." "Clerks" emerge from their "vats" fully formed and as good as dead. If capital turns relations between people into relations between things, Davies carries the process to the "late" stage forecast by Jameson, turning both people and their relations into mere things. The poem kicks these things, which emit a dull thud. They're not hollow. No interior. They are *just* things.

Matter transformed into information, nature transformed into representation, relations transformed into objects, time transformed into space: Davies' disjunct details are continually oriented towards a vision of a totally integrated, totally closed world animated (or deanimated) by a principle of objectification. Jameson calls this principle "capitalism," and Davies' details are underwritten, processed, and interpreted by this analysis. This process renders them closed, readable, intelligible, in a way that Perelman's fragments are not. Or rather, as Perelman's details are not until they have been read by Jameson.

Christopher Nealon's often insightful essay "Camp Messianism" marks Davies' curious relation to Jameson's account of late capitalism when he writes that this poetry is concerned with representing "something like really, *really* late capitalism" (580). But Nealon, in seeing this as a relation between two different times (1984 and 2003), fails to see it as a relation between two different texts. He ignores the crucial question of Davies' incorporation of Jameson's analysis of late capitalism and reads the poetry as a representation of the world, which consequently looks somehow *even more* like what Jameson said it was. In reading Davies' work as "an argument about the character of materiality in late capitalism" (588), Nealon also finds his way to Jameson's conclusion, that the problem this poetry addresses is "how to have a live relationship with a material world whose temporal-spatial character is unreadable" (598). Jameson sees postmodern art as an attempt to "map" the "ensemble of society's structures as a whole" (51). To the eye of the individual, the world appears incoherent and fragmentary. This apparent incoherence is ideological, masking the systematic oppression of capitalism. The job of the artist, assisted by the critic, is to map out the "totality," the "whole system," and render it legible.

The difference between the problem Jameson finds in Perelman (and Nealon finds in Davies) and the problem the Language poets saw themselves as addressing is instructive. The Language poets embraced the "rejection of closure" as a response to a world they saw as being made legible, understandable, and hence controllable, by power. For writers like Lyn Hejinian or Bruce Andrews, when faced with closure, "writing can respond with a drastic openness" (Andrews, 670). For

Jameson and Nealon, capitalism produces the effect of incoherence in order to conceal a malevolent system. There is a nice symmetry here. Closure and understandability is the problem for the Language poets, disjunction and openness is the solution. Disjunction and openness is the problem for Jameson, closure and understandability is the solution. Jameson shows us how to produce understandability out of disjunction by reading "China" as a sign of the particular kind of connectedness manifested by late capitalism. Jameson produces a theorized disjunction that reduces, in the way Nealon suggests, the "unreadability" of the world. Davies' practice of disjunction includes Jameson's theorized disjunction to produce formal disjunction as a sign of connection. His "fragments," underwritten by the key words of Jameson's theory, confront the reader with a drastic closure, as finished, as objects.

Thus, in opposition to Nealon, I would argue that Jameson's question for Perelman (What does this writing say about late capitalism?) cannot be our question for Davies, or at least not our *first* question. Our first question must be: What is Davies saying about Jameson? What must be accounted for is Davies' practice of doubling his fragments with the Jamesonian analytic in order to produce "connected fragments." What does this practice mean? What motivates it?

Discussing his recent work, Davies describes himself as going "back to Williams, sort of a back to basics kind of thing [...] he was one of my first poetry loves, my first modern one. I liked Blake and Wordsworth before that" (49). This poetry, so heavily marked with the prestigious signs of theory, announces itself as a return to poetry *as* poetry. Jameson, Marx, Derrida, or any other theorist is notably absent from Davies' invocation of his precursors and influences. His distancing of his work from theory is most striking in his denial of theory's classic claim that all writing is politicized, and his search for a specifically aesthetic effect: "Political change is not made by the choices we're making in verse. We're doing this so that certain possibilities can exist in the world" (52). Why this intense denial of theory? Why the unprecedented incorporation of theory in a poetry that announces itself as a repudiation of theory? For Davies, the possibility of writing post-Language poetry turns out to depend on the possibility of establishing poetry as a distinct and autonomous genre. And this possibility will depend on the poet's ability to defeat theory by subordinating it to an alien intention.

Davies conceives this project in a context calibrated to exclude such generic distinctions: the context of Language poetry, or, as its practitioners insisted, "language *writing*." Language writing made a pivotal and ambivalent bid for cultural authority by writing poetry that is *also* theory, and theory that is *also* poetry. This tendency is most visible in the formal feature Davies foregrounds as essential to Language writing: the fragment. In Language writing, as Oren Izenberg argues, the poetic line-as-fragment becomes an *example*; the fragmentary attains the status of the *exemplary*. Disjunct lines are thus examples of a certain theory of language, its relation to society, power, etc. The particular *content* of the theory is, in a very real sense, irrelevant. Jameson, Hejinian, Perelman, and Izenberg all have incompatible accounts of the theory illustrated by a poem like "China." What's important is the relation of poetic line to theoretical discourse, an *exemplary* relation. Thus the novelty of the theoretical writing that accompanied Language poetry is that unlike its predecessor, the modernist manifesto, theory here has an *integral* relation to the poem. To write poetry as fragments is to open the text to the supplement of theory, to the authority of a discourse of another kind. The fragmented lines attain integrity, "readability," and meaning, within the theoretical discourse that encloses them.

This writing arose in the 1970s and '80s, when the institutional prestige of theory reached its zenith. Language writing staked its own claims to cultural power on this prestige. With the decline of theory's prestige, one should expect to see attempts to disassociate avant-garde poetics from it. If Language writing's free "fragments"—its calculatedly "unfinished" poems—exemplify various theories of disjunction, Davies' practice of connected fragments subordinates theoretical discourse to the integrity of the poem. In objectifying and closing the fragment, he also closes the poem to the theoretical supplement and makes it an independent object. Language poetry's ideology of "orientation to the reader" signifies its orientation to an outside, constituted as a discourse of another kind. In contrast, Davies' practice of *incorporating* Jameson's theoretical model in sealing up and closing out his fragments subordinates theoretical discourse to poetic ends, to getting "back to basics." His project for poetry after Language writing is to constitute poetry as an autonomous discourse, the bearer of its own, non-theoretical form of knowledge.

Nealon reads according to the template established by Language writing when he treats Davies' poetry as an "argument about capitalism." His elision of two genres here is illuminating. Nealon would be more precise, and more true to his own critical practice, to describe Davies' lines as *examples* in "an argument about capitalism" made, as I have suggested, twenty years ago by Frederic Jameson. But Davies' work aspires to lift avant-garde poetry out of exemplary status, to free itself from theory. *Lateral Argument's* argument is that it is a poem, and it is its own example. To be poetry is the project of this writing. The fact that this is its project indicates that this work's status as poetry is not given. Davies' claiming of canonical poets (Wordsworth and Blake) as his predecessors is the *work* his poetry undertakes. *Lateral Argument*, a poem that, to put it mildly, doesn't exactly look like Blake or Wordsworth, succeeds or fails insofar as it justifies and authorizes this claim. His claim sounds so defiantly counter-intuitive because it is obvious that Davies' most immediate predecessors are not Wordsworth or Blake. One might go further and say that his relevant predecessors are not poets at all. At this moment in history, both for Davies personally and for experimental poetics generally, Language writing is the great fact. Before Davies, there is theory and examples. Davies' poetry is new. The newness of this writing is that it is poetry. Its interest lies in its thematization of its means of achieving this status.

So how does one become a post-Language poet? How does post-Language writing become poetry? Davies attempts to do it by recreating a relation stigmatized by theory, and by defining the poetic space as the space of that relation. *Lateral Argument* continually thematizes this relation, this space. For Davies, poetic space lies between a transcendent subject and a closed, determinate object. We have already seen half of this central relation in the closed-out, opaque objects of the poem, and in the contemptuous mood that illuminates this closure. Facing this closed object is a free, transcendent subject, and the complementary mood is a certain euphoria: the thrill of freedom and release. The second half of the relation, the subject, is most vividly represented by the poem's theme of *arrival*.

We have all survived crash landings

wandered here and invented plausible pasts
every so often one of us will slip (7).

Davies continually reproduces the trope of an alien, literally transcendent subject who has arrived from outer space and who confronts the objects of the world as brand-new, as purely *occurrent*. There is no involvement, no imbrication, no entanglement of subject and object; they are cleanly distinct.

Your beloved on the lawn
as if seen from space (6).

The subject looks down at the world from outer space. What better, or more provocative, metaphor for transcendence? Davies continually inserts this alien perspective, this absolute distance between subject and object, into the space of the poem. The subject is not *in* the world, it isn't identified with any position in the world, but illuminates all of the world's objects uniformly, nonrelatively, from an absolute distance.

There's a space.
You fill it, but it's not you.
You're not it
either—in fact you're not you. (3)

The metaphor of the alien "landing" thematizes Davies' scandalous effort to build poetic space around the subject and object. An absolute subject and closed objects make space poetic. There is nothing like it in Language writing, or in theory. To defeat, deny, and annihilate this relation is perhaps the essential content of theory. Jameson's celebrated description of the postmodern "schizophrenic" individual as marked by a total "loss of subjectivity" is perhaps the nearest example for Davies (14), but it is a dominant theme from poststructuralism to postmarxism. Language writing vividly adhered to this principle. The other side of its open objects, or "fragments," was an assault on the subject, especially in the guise of the author (Lyn Hejinian's *My Life* represents this tendency at its most thematic). It is true that some versions of Language writing often referred to a different kind of subject, the reader, who was supposedly free to make meaning without the imposition of the authorial intention or systematic closure. But in practice this reference to the reader served as an alibi for a different kind of outside, the outside of theory, where the fragments could attain their exemplary meaning. The figure of the reader served to conceal a theory of reading. In Davies' writing, the subject/object relation is enclosed by the poem, or rather, this relation constitutes the poem's closure, its borders, its integrity. The outside, outer space, is reconstituted within and as poetic space. The alien subject experiences the thrill of freedom in its clean apprehension of distanced, closed, distinct objects. The gaze of the subject, forever just arriving from outer space, dislodges the objects from their complex net of relative, shifting intraworldly relations and frees them for an absolute relation with this outside.

This relation constitutes poetic truth, constructed by Davies as different than and opposed to theory's truth. The irony of this moment in literary history is that poetic truth must be created out of the materials of theory. Davies makes theory speak a truth it never imagined. The incorporation of theory's key words into Davies' fragments serves to realize the central subject-object relation by stabilizing and neutralizing the objects, fixing them *as* objects. The alien subject, forever "landing" on this world, is called forth by these total objects. It surreptitiously occupies the space theory cleared for it, and which theory intended to leave vacant. The violence of this process, the scandal of the object of theory being recovered by a transcendent poetic subject, leaves disfiguring marks at several key moments in Davies' text. The most striking mark occurs with this couplet:

> Not all the fruit trees hate you
> just this one (19-20).

These lines record the violence, the multiple levels of negation through which poetry passes towards its renewal in Davies' writing. In the interview where he declares his intention to get "back to basics," he provides a short list of the names of canonical poets who function as the ghostly sponsors of his project. Turning to the text of *Lateral Argument*, one finds that each name corresponds to a certain principle that Davies finds essential to the generic reconstitution of poetry at this moment in history. Williams' name, for example, hovers over *Lateral Argument's* concern with objects and objectification, a concern that is actually implemented, as we have seen, with the aid of key terms from critical theory. Wordsworth's name symbolizes the work's interest in subjectivity. In the interview, Davies specifies his interest in Wordsworth: "no poem spoke to me as much as 'Ode: Intimations of Immortality'" (55). The line from *Lateral Argument* cited above attaches itself to a particular couplet from Wordsworth's "Ode," a passage that typifies the relation that, for Davies in 2003, defines the horizon of the poetic as such:

There's a tree, of many, one
A single field that I have looked upon (729).

From the thematic perspective established by *Lateral Argument*, this couplet represents the classical definition of poetic space. The "I," the transcendent subject, is called forth by the definite, redundant particularity of the object (one particular tree in one particular field). An inverse relation obtains between the collapsing density of the object and the expansion of the subject, swelling into space, infinity, immortality. When I say that Davies attempts to "renew" the relation formalized by Wordsworth's couplet, I mean to say that Davies, like poetic radicals from Blake to Pound, grounds a revolutionary departure in a prestigious origin. Wordsworth's lines reveal the dimension between the object and the subject, but this dimension emerges as definitive of poetry itself for Davies in a way that it could not have for Wordsworth. This particular generic feature wasn't a problem for modernism or romanticism; "postmodernism" marks the point in literary history when it became a problem. Here again, Davies' self-conscious claiming of Wordsworth as predecessor conceals more immediate predecessors who, as I have argued, produced writing, theory, and examples, but not poems.

It is theory that supplies the logic by which Davies achieves the total closure of the object Wordsworth is able to take for granted (a more polemical way of putting this point is to say that today the thing passes through discourse not to become other than nature, but to attain the perfect closure of Wordsworth's natural objects). Davies "steps back" from his refined, interpreted, processed Jamesonian details. He imposes the same distance between them and the poetic subject as

Wordsworth finds between the tree and the "I." This "stepping back"—this view from outer space—discloses the new dimension, the *poetic* dimension, of the writing, obtained by betraying theory.

Now we are finally in a position to understand the significance of Davies' relation to Jameson. "Not all the fruit trees hate you/ just this one." Davies' lines reveal the implicit antagonism of this relationship. Where theory orients these closed objects towards a new systemization, a subjectless discourse, in Davies' hands they are made to found a transcendent subject-object relation. His objects have been forced into an unnatural relation, and they "hate" it. One discursive formation, theory, is superseded by another, which Davies boldly calls "poetry." The nature of the cultural and institutional pressures that give the space between this new, alien poetic subject and its closed object such tension, depth, and interest remains to be explored. In attempting to theorize *this* writing, I would suggest to those inclined that it is here, in the affective density of this space, that we should look for signs of a successor to "late capitalism," for a new theory of the relation between art and society.

But this, of course, would simply be to generate a new example of the old, fading paradigm of "theory." I will conclude with a gesture in another direction, a different intimation of what Davies' generic experiment has to offer thought. Theory and criticism is in the midst of its own crisis of "renewal," its own search for new generic possibilities and here also, I suggest, the hateful subject-object relation might prove unexpectedly fruitful. Theory, both low and high, defined itself by a quasi-religious denial of the transcendent subject-object relation. A prestigious origin for this denial was found in Heidegger, whose primary accomplishment was said to be an overcoming of the subject-object relation. But Heidegger never denied this relation, which he in fact held to be self-evident. He simply undertook to show that what was self-evident (my apprehension of a tree as a distinct object situated at a certain absolute distance from myself) was built on a prior, primal imbrication of self and world. Thus subjects and objects were not foundational, as the Cartesian tradition held, but were built on top of, and emerged out of, a different mode of existence. Subject and object are not a given fact of human existence, but a *project* of human beings. Perhaps some insight like this one of Heidegger's might provide a stimulus for the renewal of theory in a way analogous to Wordsworth's new significance for Davies. Perhaps theory should listen to poetry, give up the ideal of the subjectless text, stop denouncing the space between subject and object as simply false, and begin to see it as a devious and sophisticated and thoroughly artificial structure, where something new and alien might come to life.

➤

The Pleasures of Déjà Dit:
Citation, Intertext and Ekphrasis in Recent Experimental Poetry

Marjorie Perloff

> What matters, is not the saying, it is the resaying,
> and, in this resaying to say each time for the first time.
> —Maurice Blanchot, *L'Entretien infini*

In the 1980s, when Language Poetry was making its first anthology appearances, its dominant mode looked like this:

(1) were I idiom and
the portray
what on
idiot you remarking
cessed to only up
opt hope this
was soundly action
more engineer
taut that the
    —Bruce Andrews, from "While" (1981)

(2) at the end of delight, one
who or that which revolves

more than chests have
to heave ". . . where gold,

dirt and blood flow

together"! : margins

the family, not personal
fallibility leads
to instrumentality
in self-restraint
    —Diane Ward, from "Limit" (1989)

(3) morrow every listen
ago potato who have a paper voice
the hole where the effort went
tome is crayern
a fasten into trance, necklace some awake of notes, floorer
as classed some follow
    —Peter Inman, from "Colloam" (1986)[1]

Different as the authors of these three excerpts surely are, theirs is a period style that shares specific features. First and foremost, this is a poetry of programmatic non-referentiality, words and phrases refusing to "add up" to any sort of coherent, much less transparent statement. Syntactic distortion is the key: in Andrews' "While," articles modify verbs rather than nouns, syllables are elided as in "cessed" (processed? recessed? accessed?), and it is not clear whether "this" in line 6 is the direct object of "hope" or the subject of "was" in the following line. Similarly in Inman's "Colloam" (the title word is not in the *OED*; it seems to be a neologism formed of "colophon" and "loam"), the verb "fasten" does not have "necklace" as its object; rather, we are given the phrase "a fasten into trance," where "fasten" and "trance" relate phonemically rather than semantically. All three poems use predominantly abstract language, and the pronouns have no discernable referents. Who is Ward's "one / who or that which revolves"? Or Inman's "who" with the "paper voice"? In each case, linkage is produced by sound rather than signification: in Andrews' poem, we find "idiom" where we expect "idiot" (see line 5) and "taut" (pun on "taught") in the last line goes with "that" and "the." Inman rhymes "ago" and "potato," "floorer" leads to follow," and "crayern" seems to be a phonetic spelling of "crayon" or a reference to "crayer," which is an obsolete word meaning "small vessel."

The reader of these poems is consistently *surprised*. Ward's "At the end of" anticipates a noun phrase like "the day" or "the journey" but not "the delight'; in Inman, the "hole" promises to contain something tangible rather than "effort," and although "morrow" (as in "tomorrow") and "ago" are related temporally, neither the potato nor the neologism "crayern" fit into their syntactic slots. The reader has to make her way through a maze, with no guidance from an authoritative "I." "The family / not personal," as Ward puts it.

At the same time, it is it is important to remember that that the words, morphemes, syntactic units, and sound patterns in question represent the poet's own vocabulary and discourse. Even when there is a brief unidentified quotation, as in Ward's couplets (lines 4-6: "where gold/ dirt and blood / flow together"), the poet is, so to speak, alone onstage. Indeed, despite the semiological play of "ago potato who have a paper voice," and so on, the poet tacitly takes full responsibility for the poem s/he has constructed so carefully. Even the jagged free verse, designed to represent the rhythm of thought, underscores the primacy of the poet's language in its ability to mean and not to mean. The limits of my language, in Wittgenstein's words, are the limits of my world. In this scheme of things, the poetic drive is, in Adorno's terms, one of *resistance*: the resistance of the individual poet to the linguistic field of capitalist commodification where language has become merely instrumental.

But in the climate of the new century, where sites of resistance have become increasingly eroded, we seem to be witnessing a poetic turn from negation and resistance to dialogue—a dialogue with earlier texts or texts in other media, or "writings through" or ekphrases that permit the poet to participate in a larger, more public discourse, even as the poet's *personal* signature is once again present. Such poetry is often *meditative*, but meditation is made oblique by the use of Oulipo constraint, citation, and the reliance on intertext: appropriation, after all, is now a central fact of life. As such, we are witnessing a new poetry, more conceptual than expressive—a poetry in which, in Craig Dworkin's words, "the idea cannot be separated from the writing itself."[2]

There is, of course, nothing new about appropriative poetry. A branch of Language poetry that we associate with Susan Howe, Steve McCaffery, and Rosmarie Waldrop—to take just three poets—has always worked with citation and constraint, with intertext and intermedia: Howe's *The Midnight*, with its documentary layers, poetic intertexts, and treated ambiguous photographs, is a paradigmatic case of citationality, if not primarily of constraint, which is better exemplified in such McCaffery sequences as *Evoba* or the recent *Dark Ladies*, a dazzling, rule-generated writing through Shakespeare's *Sonnets*.

Yet the three poetic texts I shall be discussing here—Jan Baetens' *Vivre sa vie*, Craig Dworkin's *Dure*, and Yoko Tawada's *Verwandlungen*—do deviate from earlier models in that their appropriation of already written—*déjà dit*—material is used to ruminate on a topos that experimental poetries have long held to be irrelevant, if not wholly passé, as being too personal, too reminiscent of a lyric tradition. I am thinking about *pain*—whether the pain of lost love or lost identity—a pain that quite literally doesn't dare to speak its name in our sophisticated poetry climate, so that it is conveyed by such distancing devices as citation, ekphrasis, and constraint. Such poetry is more accessible, perhaps more public than the poems of the eighties I cited earlier, being written in less non-referential, asyntactic language, indeed often in complete and coherent sentences. Conceptually, however—and this is a conceptual poetry—riddle and obliquity remain the order of the day. Nothing, these poets seem to imply, comes easy.

Autrement dit: The Film-Poem

My first example, Jan Baetens's 2005 "novelisation" of Jean-Luc Godard's classic 1962 film *Vivre sa vie* [Figure 1] is a sequence of fifteen poems (only loosely corresponding to Godard's twelve "chapters") that comments obliquely on the plot line and imagery of its parent text. In his Preface, Baetens remarks that what attracted him to Godard's "homonymic film" was "the poetry and love of the everyday that its images continue to evoke in me. [...] Since banality remains for me the most dazzling subject there is, I found it necessary to change the form (that is, the verse form) with each new section.[3]

This is an oddly Oulipian (Baetens has long been associated with the Oulipo) explanation on two counts. First, it's curious to refer to *Vivre sa vie*, with its heavily stylized images and sophisticated allusions to Montaigne, Cocteau, Poe's "Oval Portrait," and Sartrean existentialism, as "banal" and "everyday." The heroine's very name, Nana alludes to Zola's courtesan, and Anna Karina, who plays Nana, is given to such utterances as "Je suis responsable. Je suis responsable. Je suis responsable [I am responsible. I am responsible. I am responsible]." More important: to render the banal in poetry is typically to use casual, colloquial language—prose or loose free verse. Instead, Baetens gives us pantoums, tetra- and hepta-syllabics, full and reduced sonnets, rhopalic verses (stanzas where each line adds a syllable), *vers impairs*, and so on. The poem's artifice thus matches that of the film, but, the medium being the message, its "artifice" has a very different feel.

The film has a linear plot line: it moves inexorably from Nana's original decision to leave her husband Paul to her melodramatic death in the final shootout between her pimp and a rival. True, its titled chapters and impersonal male voiceover stylize and distance the successive events in Nana's career, but the film's musical score and imagery are both consistent and continuous, the key image being that of Anna Karina's sculptured, wide-eyed, and endlessly mobile face, whether seen frontally or in shadowy profile.

In the first sequence, Nana's face is not seen directly by the camera because we are behind her as the camera pans and glimpses her image in a mirror. Paul too is only seen from behind and once or twice in shadowy profile. But, in the course of the film, Nana's face become more and more central, although, oddly enough, her body is barely seen. Even in the scenes of sexual encounter, it is Nana's face—eyes lidded and resigned, sometimes lighting up and smiling, mouth caressing a cigarette, whose image dominates. Nana and her men are always *about* to undress when the camera cuts away. Again, in an early scene, when Nana goes to the movies and sees Carl Dreyer's great silent film *La Passion de Jeanne d'Arc*, her tear-stained face is juxtaposed to the face of the sympathetic priest (played by Antonin Artaud) and to that of Joan herself (Maria Falconnetti) at the stake. And in the penultimate scene, Nana's smiling face, now framed by her stylish new haircut, is silhouetted against the window facing her lover Luigi, who reads Poe's "The Oval Portrait" (foreshadowing Nana's own death) aloud to her.

Yet we never really know the person behind that face—or behind the faces of the various men in Nana's life—all of them stiff, unsmiling, fully clothed. The dialogue itself is largely banal, conveying necessary information or expressing what are rather pretentious philosophical musings on life and death, freedom and responsibility. The conceptual problem Baetens thus posed himself was how to render the tension between everyday conversation and the artifice of the film's audio-visual scheme, with its ambient sounds, shadowy interiors, expressive faces, smoking rituals, and ominously slow tempo, purely in *words*. The easy way would have been to produce imagistic, ideogrammic vignettes matching the film chapters, but instead Baetens provides poetic analogues that emphasize dramatic moments missing from the film. Here is #III, "Nana est jetée de la pension. Elle vit dans la rue," whose three three-line stanzas each have 3, 2, and 5 words per line—a technique used, among others, by Louis Zukofsky:

> *Les premiers jours*
> *le soir*
> *elle rentre encore à la pension,*
>
> *qui la guette ;*
> *les deux*
> *comme à la guerre préparées,*
>
> *Un silence-éclair.*
> *Les bruits*
> *sont innocents—marelle, chatte, pavé.*   (V 15)

(The first days
at night
she returns to her pension,

lying in wait;
the two
prepared as if for war,

A silence-lightning flash
The noises
are innocent—hopscotch, cat, pavement.)

This is a much more transparent, accessible lyric than are the language poems I cited earlier—or is it? In the film, the pension is just another decaying house in a nondescript Paris neighborhood, perhaps Pigalle. But in the poem, the pension is pictured as an animal that lies in wait for (*guette*) Nana as if there were a war between them—a sinister notion quite absent from the film, where affect is largely neutral. Meaning, moreover, is offset by the elaborate quasi-Troubadour sound structure: there is, for example, much internal rhyme, as in *guerre / éclair* and *sont / innocents*, the latter word constituting a phonetic anagram of *silence*. *Guerre* and *guette* are linked by eye rhyme, with *deux* having the same vowels in reverse. In the preceding stanza, *jour*, *soir* and *encore* are half-rhymes, and the three nouns defining the setting of the pension are linked by their *a* vowels: *marelle, chatte, pavé*. All these formal devices distance the narrative, giving it a sense of repetition and inevitability quite absent from the more realistic film.

The avoidance of a lyric "I" in a poem like *Vivre sa vie* is by no means, as is commonly thought, an avoidance of emotion. On the contrary, Baetens uses form to measure the pain of Nana's daily existence. Here is VII, a "reduced sonnet" (in trisyllabic lines") called "L'Habitude—Déjà la fin?":

Nana va	Nana goes
Nana vient	Nana comes
Nana baise	Nana fucks
Nana passe	Nana enters
Nana pense	Nana thinks
S'en aller	Of quitting
Puis n'y pense	Then doesn't
Plus du tout	Think at all
Un deux trois	One two three
C'est permis	It's allowed
Un deux trois	One two three
Mille francs	A thousand francs
Et un p'tit	And a small
Coup de blanc	Glass of white (25)

#VII has no parallel in the film, which can portray key "events" ("First Man," "The Letter," "The Concierge") more easily than it can capture the force of habit. The minimal sonnet can do so by means of repetition (*Nana va / Nana vient*), the counting ritual (*Un deux trois*), and the near-rhyme of *baise / passe / pense*, which equates all these actions. The pun on *passe* (*maison de passe* is the French term for brothel) also plays a role: as Microsoft Word reminds me by insisting on putting an accent over the *e*, Nana will be *passé* soon enough. But perhaps the key line is *C'est permis*: are these Nana's words to one of her customers? Is she inquiring whether *C'est permis de fumer*? If "one" is permitted, are two and three? And on the page, all three lines end with the letters *is*. It all culminates, in any case, in the *Mille francs* and the *p'tit / Coup de blanc*, which are Nana's payment. *Blanc* rhymes with *francs* and *p'tit* with *permis*, the poem thus sonically portraying the deadening circle of habit. Baetens's Nana could also be Zola's—or indeed any Nana who passes through this particular cycle.

The last few lyrics are especially striking. Nana's falling in love is initiated in the "snowball" poem *A Côté de Nana*:

> *Ensemble.*
> *Vers lui se tourne. Invite à le rejoinder.*
> *Je les entends parler. Il va parler seul. Elle va écouter.* (V 32)

> Together.
> Turns toward him. Invites him to join her.
> I hear them talking. Only he will speak. She will listen.

In XIII, an eight-part Parnassian lyric in heptasyllabic rhyming couplets, Nana's new friend makes a courtly declaration of his love, more powerful than Poe's encomium to the beloved who is the subject of his "oval portrait." It is all the more shocking after this to read the documentary *vers impairs* of the final scene, where Nana becomes the pawn between pimps and is shot to death:

> *Tout tourne autour du prix de Nana, im-*
> *peccable coupe*
> *de cheveux sixties qui lui donne l'âge*

> de la voiture
> de Lui 1 et de Lui 3. Puis (enfin)
>   des coups de feu.   (V 39)
> Everything turns on the price of Nana, im-
>   peccable sixties
>   haircut which makes her look the age
>   of the car
> Of Him 1 and of Him 3. Then (finally!)
>   gun shots.

It's all very matter-of-fact, the impeccable *coupe* (haircut) anticipating the *coups de feu* of the gangsters. But the final poem is called *Je tends la main à Nana* ("I hold Nana's hand") and is written in prose:

> *Au verso de cette feuille, au verso de ce texte que je cherche et transcris, il y a, plus absent pour toi lecteur que cette histoire de Nana qui revient, le brouillon pour moi seul visible et donc inexistent d'un ancient poème, que je ne relirai qu'a travers l'image de ces images d'elle, dans le désespoir impossible d'être enfin entièrement entièrement dupe.* (V 41)

> On the verso of this page, on the verso of this text which I look for and transcribe, there is, more remote for you, reader, than this story of Nana which returns, the little scrap, visible for me alone and hence nonexistent of an old poem, which I never reread except through the image of these images of her, in the impossible despair of being, in the end, entirely entirely duped.

Duped by whom or by what? On the verso, there is no "old poem" to reread, only Baetens's "Note finale" on the verse forms used through-out. Is the poet duped by Nana, whose hand he certainly doesn't "hold"? Or is he duped by the film's curiously unanticipated melodramatic ending—an ending in which the banal gives way to the shock effect of sudden death? Or is Baetens the dupe of the film itself, a film as seductive as its motifs and characters are ultimately trivial? Perhaps all the above, the poem's revelation being that there is, in the poet's subconscious, a little scrap of paper bearing an *ancien poème* which he never goes near except through the image of these Nana-images. A lost love evidently or perhaps a love never possessed but which this film, of all films, evokes. Who knows what happened? The poet is, in any case, the dupe.

In the course of *Vivre sa vie*, the ideological thrust of the film, whose central focus on the ways a capitalist social structure creates the fall into prostitution—a fall not particularly remarkable in the modern city but tragic nevertheless—is replaced by a sequence of love poems, that contain a trace of Troubadour lyric even as they interrogate and ironize the film from which they derive. At the same time, Baetens's *Vivre sa vie* is by no means parody or pastiche, for the text does take up the issue of how one lives one's life. In his Postface, the critic Semir Badir remarks that Baetens's project tries to "return poetry to the heart of things," where film has long been located (V 57). Indeed, the sequence calls into question the tedious high/low division, showing that the "low" is always, from another angle, perceivable as "high." As such, *Vivre sa vie* is also a metapoetic text: it theorizes the possibility of enlarging the boundaries of what poetry is and can be.

"From Paint to Point to Pain"

In his important study of citation, *La seconde main*, Antoine Compagnon writes

> When I cite, I excise, I mutilate, I extract. There is a primary object, placed before me, a text I have read, that I am reading; and the course of my reading is interrupted by a phrase. I return to the beginning; I re-read. The phrase reread becomes a formula, isolated from the text. The rereading separates it from that which precedes and that which follows. The chosen fragment converts itself into a text, no longer a bit of text, a part of a sentence or of discourse, but a chosen bit, an amputated limb, not yet a transplant, but already an organ, cut off and placed in reserve.[4]

Craig Dworkin's *Dure*, published as a chapbook by Cuneiform Press in 2004 and then reprinted in Dworkin's collection *Strand* (Roof Books) in 2005, is composed of the "amputated limbs" Compagnon speaks of.[5]

Here the intertext is neither poem nor film but an unsigned 1519 draw-
ing by Albrecht Dürer, formerly in the Bremen Kunstverein and repro-
duced in the *catalogue raisonée* of J.J. Winkler—a drawing, so Dworkin
tells us in the first prose poem, that "has not been seen since the sec-
ond world war" (*Strand* 75). The drawing depicts the torso, seen frontal-
ly, of a nude man, who points with his index finger to a scar on the left
side of his abdomen—a scar circled for emphasis, and in the original
chalk drawing, painted yellow [Figure 2]. The inscription at the top of
what may well be a self-portrait reads, "*Do der gelb fleck ist and mit dem fin-
ger darauff deut do ist mir weh,*" which Dworkin translates, "Where the yel-
low spot is and where I am pointing with my finger, that is where it
hurts."[6]

Although *Dure* is not, strictly speaking, composed according to
Oulipo constraints (as is, for example, the title piece of *Strand*), it does
observe Jacques Roubaud's rule that "A text written according to a con-
straint describes the constraint."[7] For the source texts, listed in a
chronological table at the back of the book and ranging from the *OED*
to Derrida and Wittgenstein, Smithson and Kosuth, Aristotle and
Augustine, obscure Renaissance medical texts and the notes of various
rare book dealers, are chosen with an eye to illustrating, in however
various ways, the meaning and resonance of the title: *Dure*, from *durus*
(Latin for "hard"), referring both to the enigmatic art of Dürer as well
as to the English derivates of *durus* like *duration, durable,* and *endure.*

Like a number of other recent poetry books—for example Cole
Swensen's *Goest* and Mary Jo Bang's *The Eye like a Strange Balloon, Dure*
is, broadly speaking, an ekphrastic poem, drawing out the meanings
contained in a given art work. Indeed, *Dure* begins by reviewing con-
flicting information about the Dürer drawing: "The assumption is that
Dürer drew it for a consultation with a foreign physician" (*Strand* 76),
or again, with a play on Richard Burton's classic, "It could be a fron-
tispiece to a lost treatise on the melancholy of anatomy" (94). Before
long, information and analysis give way to a series of more fantastic
suppositions: the portrait as love letter, as reproach to the viewer (*"you
have done this"*) as geometric drawing relating to Dürer's treatise on
ellipses, as an illustration for Renaissance treatises on medicine.
Citations are embedded in commentary marked by increasing word
and sound play, as in the following passage:

He has draped himself discreetly, naked to the waist. The tear ducts gape, humid and enlarged. "If any bodye weare vulneratede in the Eyes, insparge, and strewe this poulder there." Soiled solder, spoilt, spelt. Stays antiqued with tea. Psalm, palm, lapse. A damp map skirts the glair that binds the tongues of rawhide and required felt. Welt, stiletto, silhouette. The bruise on the boards of a book; the pall of raw words, "I assure you that I would more than gladly have painted myself here in my entirety, and completely naked at that." (*Strand* 82)

The poem begins matter-of-factly with a description of the portrait's sitter. But the second sentence moves from the real to the imagined: we cannot, of course, see those enlarged tear ducts. The citation that follows (from A. M. tr. Gabelhouser's 1599 *Bk. Physicke 54/1*) carries on the theme of eye damage: translated into modern English, it reads, "If anyone is wounded in the eyes, scatter and strew this powder there." The motif of wounding now becomes pervasive: "soiled, solder, spoilt, spelt," each word evidently suggesting the next by dint of sound. But the words also make sense: an attempt is made to "solder" the flesh containing the wound, but "soiled"/ "spoilt" suggest otherwise, while "spelt" refer to the effort to explain, to reveal, as in Gerard Manley Hopkins's "Spelt from Sybil's Leaves." And the triplet—Dworkin is very fond of these—"psalm, palm, lapse" combines rhyme and anagram to take us from prayer to the unstated "offense" that is alluded to throughout *Dure*, the lapse that has somehow caused the wound. But the lapse or break is also that within the book in which the poet contemplates Dürer's drawing: "a damp nap skirts the glair [a kind of glaze] that binds the tongues of rawhide and required felt." "Damp nap"—monosyllabic words that carry on the sound imagery of "psalm, palm, lapse"—seem to refer to the artist's sleep habits until we realize that this sentence deals with bookbinding, culminating in the final "felt" and its rhyming partner "welt." "Welt, stiletto, silhouette": the sharp "stiletto," may indeed produce a "welt"; indeed it does do so on the phonic level. And further, "silhouette" is a near-anagram of "stiletto" and brings us back to the "silhouette" in the Dürer drawing. For bookmaking is itself a kind of wounding: "The bruise on the boards of a book: the pall of raw words." And now follows a citation from Montaigne, namely, the great essayist's declaration of a willingness, seemingly unlike Dürer's riddling, to reveal himself, to appear to us "naked." But the conditional verbs of the passage suggest that, of course, Montaigne did no such thing. And in any case, in the context of verbal self-revelation, "naked" functions metaphorically: there is no image of a naked body for our eyes to light upon. Here the verbal and the visual part company.

The mode of *Dure* is thus what Compagnon calls *transplant*. Dürer, Montaigne, Gabelhouser: their words are transposed and set against Dworkin's catalogues of obscure and obsolete nouns or intricate sonic echoes, so as to position the artist's scar, referred to by the obsolete noun "crag" (cf. *Craig*, the poet's first name) in the opening section, in relation to the poet's own "wound." We can read *Dure* medically ("The tissue is a morose delectation, the fingertip testing its sensation, and that lack, with an unreciprocated pressure: the nerves failing to complete the narcissistic circuit, so back and fore to get at figuring this fascination of a flesh that is no longer ours," 70), or architecturally ("hinge joints rusted, jambs akimbo, the doors of perception droop," 82), or homophonically ("scars" as "scare tactics," 83). But the scar is also a mark of love: "These fractures factured with a hairline list: Communicating passages. Moments of separation held open to their possibility. Signs that we have shared space" (83). And a few pages later, we read "Ever, sever, swerve" and "He is pointing at, perhaps, her cost, and for her pleasure. Honey, ankle, tongue" (89).

Dworkin's language game oddly becomes most personal when it interweaves the Dürer materials with the "impersonal" propositions of Wittgenstein on pain. "How do we know," we read in section #11, "where to point to when we are asked to point to the painful spot. Can this sort of pointing be compared with pointing to a black spot on a sheet of paper"? (85). This observation comes from the *Blue & Brown Books* as does the following in #19: "And here again remember the difference between pointing to the painful spot without being led by the eye and on the other hand pointing to a scar on my body after looking for it" (93). What, then, of the self-portrait, which centers on the act of pointing at the encircled spot even as the artist's eye, far from gazing directly at the scar, gives a "sidelong" look at the viewer, as if to challenge his authority.

The citations from Wittgenstein's pain calculus along with Charles Peirce's analysis of the "pointing index finger" and Smithson's "set of disconnections, a bramble of stabilized fragments taken from things obscure and fluid" (102) increasingly focus on the poet himself, and we gradually realize that *Dure* is perhaps most notably an homage to lost love ("memory as the prosthesis of pain," 95), and hence lost language. If this makes Dworkin's poem sound like a latter-day version of John Ashbery's *Self-Portrait in a Convex Mirror*, published just thirty years earlier, it is necessary to note the differences between the two poems. Like Dworkin, Ashbery begins by contemplating an enigmatic self-portrait—in this case, Parmigiano's—and in the course of the poem, he ruminates on the conditions of its painting, the response from Vasari and contemporary art critics like Sidney Friedberg, and the relation of the painting to musical and literary works. But *Self-Portrait* has continuity, reflected in the consistency of its free verse (often loosely iambic pentameter) and the centrality of the poet's own self-portrait, however fragmented his observations. In a post-language poem like *Dure*, on the other hand, there can be no such continuity—only excision, extract, mutilation, transplant, echo. Consider #22:

> "Writing is a strange shadow whose sole purpose is to mark the destruction of the body that once stood between its light and its earth." Skiagraphy, touch-type, and method. A run of his finger feels nothing now that the surface has smoothed, but can still make out the thin ellipse floating on his forearm, like a shadow under shallow skin, and can trace its curve, left from the time she pushed him into the stove, and know that this is his proof: whatever else, she felt that strongly, she really did care this much that once. He who forgets that love lasts will not recognize its fist. Carp, suspended, mottle and kern. This entire text is an attempt to ask: "how can something be the shadow of an act which does not exist?" The problem is not finding a solution, but simply posing the proper question. "Don't you know then, what I mean, when I say that the stove is in pain?" (*Strand* 100)

Here, almost at the end of *Dure*, introduced by a comment made by Paul Mann, a detractor of the avant-garde potential for change, the poet's own "scar," finally comes out into the open: the "thin ellipse floating on his forearm, like a shadow under shallow skin" is the "cinder" or "mark" of that moment when the unspecified "she" "pushed him into the stove." In retrospect, it is a positive memory because "whatever else, she felt that strongly, she did care that much that once." The personal motif is immediately distanced and ironized in a reprise of Kruchenykh's famous Futurist cry in *A Slap in the Face of Public Taste*, cited as the first sentence in #7: "He who does not forget his first love will not recognize his last." In #26, this playful denunciation of the past is transposed into the darker aphorism, "He who forgets that love lasts will not recognize its fist," the revision emphasizing the *endurance* of love but also its *hardness*—its *dure*.

Four words follow, the first and fourth alliterating sharply: "Carp, suspended, mottle and kern." We can read this as an imperative: "suspend your carping, cover the object with mottled cloth or paper, and eliminate the white space between the letters ("kern"). But "carp" can also be a noun, hence a fish, and "kern" means "the part of a typographic letter that extends beyond the body." In this case, we are witnessing something emerging from its base. In either case, the words suggest that, "it must *change*." But how? Here Wittgenstein's *Investigations* comes to the rescue with the reminder that "The problem is not finding a solution, but simply posing the proper question." And that question can only be posed by the resort to "Skiagraphy" (literally 'shadow writing'), "touch-type, and method."

Dure thus replaces the expression of subjectivity that is still central to Ashbery by a written record, itself a scar, on a piece of paper—a "scar" rather like Jan Baetens's *brouillon* of that seminal old poem, known only to himself. Indeed, *Dure* might have been called, in Lyn Hejinian's words, *Writing is an Aid to Memory*. Yet compared to that book, Dworkin's is more *lisible*, more grounded. Use the notes and look up the words in any major dictionary, and the emotional resonance of Dworkin's "*Plaît*, plait, plaint" becomes apparent. *Ubi manus*, as we read in #1, *ibi dolor*. Where the hand was, there pain shall be. The reference is to the Dürer self-portrait, but it includes all those whose *dolor* Dworkin has been citing—especially the poet's own.

Language Envy

Dure reveals Craig Dworkin as obsessed with verbal and phonic mutation—the difference a letter can make as in "Granular, glandular, gradual, gloss." A similar obsession marks the work of the Japanese-German poet-novelist-essayist Yoko Tawada. Born in 1960 in a Tokyo suburb, Tawada studied literature in Japan and then came to Hamburg in 1982 to work for a local German book exporter as a trainee. She never went back and was soon writing in German as well as Japanese, and finally in German alone. Like her German precursors Thomas Bernhard, Ingeborg Bachmann, and Elfriede Jelinek, Tawada begins by writing an epiphanic free verse lyric usually laced with irony, as in the poem "O":

Auf der Rückseite	On the back
des Wassers	of the water
schreibe ich den Buchstaben O	I write the letter O
Wie man ein loch	Just as one drills a hole
in ein anderes Loch bohrt	into another hole
Ein spiegelverkehrtes O	The mirror image of O
steht auf dem Kopf	stands on its head
und lacht mich aus.	and laughs at me.[8]

Here, already, is the fixation on the powers of the alphabet. But before long, poems like "O" (juxtaposed to Japanese poems and their translations as well as artwork) are replaced by gnomic short fables and fairy tales written in prose, and culminating in the 2000 *Opium für Ovid*, which contains twenty-two versions of Ovidian fables on metamorphosis.

In 1998, as the fifth *Poetikdozent* [Professor of Poetics] at Tübingen University, Tawada gave three *Poetik-Vorlesungen*—published under the title *Verwandlungen* [*Metamorphoses*].[9] These poetic lectures—part essay, part prose poem, part poetic meditation—are tissues of citations and the poet's own variations on them: a list of sources is appended at the back of the book. Like *Dure*, *Verwandlungen* is, loosely speaking, ekphrastic, although it does not focus on a single image; like Baetens's *Vivre sa Vie*, Tawada's "lectures" especially the third, focus on a face, the German word *Gesicht* containing, as a paragram, the word *ich* or "I." Indeed, the discovery of the *ich* leads the poet to the further thought that, for a foreigner learning German, *Gesicht* looks like a verb in the perfect tense, beginning as it does with the prefix *ge-* as in "Ich habe es gesicht [I have faced it]," although there is no such word in the language.

How to read faces? It is a central question in *Vivre Sa Vie, Dure,* and such other recent citational poetic texts as Caroline Bergvall's "About Face," which I have discussed elsewhere.[10] The three lectures in *Verwandlungen* concern what it means to be a foreigner, specifically a Japanese living in Germany, with respect to three aspects of poetry: the spoken word, writing, and reading. The first lecture-poem is called "Voice of a Bird or the Problem of Strangeness." When Tawada listens to herself speak German, she feels as if she is spitting out strange bird sounds. Her sentences have perfect contours but they don't seem to belong to her. Indeed, the poet speculates, the constant effort to speak correctly, to get every consonant and vowel right, not to mention tone and pitch, may actually change the facial contours of the speaking person, so that their descendants, in the second or third generation, will have a different physiognomy.

Speaking a "foreign tongue" is, moreover, a transforming experience. Before she came to Hamburg, Tawada muses, her own voice meant nothing to her. It was merely a vehicle to communicate something. Now she is so aware of voicing that the opposite has happened: all the emphasis is on the medium of what Tawada calls *Vogelsprache,* Bird Language. The poet now exemplifies *Vogelsprache* in a Celan lyric from "Sprachgitter," a Ludwig Tieck fairytale, and Wagner's *Ring.* Confucius too is included:

> Confucius admired a man, who had officially been found guilty of murder and sentenced for the crime, and permitted this man to marry his daughter. What is interesting is the reason why the son-in-law had come under suspicion for murder: it seems he could understand Bird Language and happened to hear the birds conversing animatedly about the murder. Therefore, he knew exactly where the corpse was hidden. But most people refused to believe his story and insisted that he must have been the murderer. (*Verwandlungen* 19)

It is a cautionary tale for the reader who tries to penetrate the language of the Other. And, after some further examples—from Mozart's *Magic Flute* and Messiaen's *Catalogue des oiseaux,* the poet concludes:

> Wer, mit einer fremden Zunge spricht, ist ein Ornithologe

und ein Vogel in einer Person.
[Whoever speaks in a strange tongue, is an ornithologist
and a bird in one person]. (22)

Poetry, Tawada is suggesting, is defined by this double function: to pro-
duce speech that is always folding back upon itself, always constructing
only to deconstruct the text. And the two functions are inseparable.

The second lecture, "Schrift einer Schildkröte oder Das Problem
der übersetzung [Writing of a Turtle or the Problem of Translation],"
shifts the discourse from *voice* to *writing*. Again, foreignness is a paradox:
both alienating and yet essential to poetry:

> For a long time I didn't notice that I could only rarely become
> absorbed in the reading of a German book. As a child, I ran right
> into a book, just as one enters one's own house. Then I lost myself in
> the world described there and no longer saw the language. In order
> to get inside a book, just like a house, one must read so fast that the
> letters disappear. But perhaps it is not a matter of speed but of the
> way of reading. In theory, I know of course how to read phonetic
> writing: one must mentally quickly translate it into the corresponding
> word sounds, for otherwise their sense will remain hidden behind the
> wall of letters. I don't dare look at the written forms but must fly
> beyond them. Already after a few minutes, though, my eye begins to
> rest on each letter. Then all is silent in my head, and meaning disap-
> pears. Maybe one needs a vehicle to navigate these alphabetic land-
> scapes. Speech rhythm, for example, could be such a vehicle. It
> would carry me quickly over the meadow, so that the cannibal cac-
> tuses of letters could not catch me. (25)

The letter of the alphabet as cannibal cactus: the rest of "Writing of a
Turtle" contrasts the reading of Japanese to that of German (or any
alphabet language). The reader of Japanese connects ideograms and
their syllabic bridges, often without knowing how a given word might
sound. Poetry readings are thus considered pointless, the differentials of
the written language impossible to convey orally. "The word for 'aunt,'
for example, is always pronounced *oba*, but, according to whether the
aunt is younger or older than the parent in question, one writes a dif-

ferent ideogram" (*Verwandlungen* 27).

In such a culture, visual form becomes central. "Hieroglyphs are interesting because they make clear that the pictorial dimension of writing need have nothing to do with a concrete picture. It has much more to do with memory" (29). So much for Pound's theory that in Chinese, words are close to *things*. It is not thingness that distinguishes the ideogram but its place in an elaborately learned relational system. The poet is at home in this system, whereas she says, "every letter of the alphabet is a riddle" (30). One is forced, right away, to translate letter into sounds. And when one rearranges the letters, an entirely different sense obtains. "The anagram owes its art to the magic of the alphabet" (30). And a little anagrammatic poem, "Das Spielen der Kinder ist strengt untersagt [The Playing of Children Is Strictly Forbidden]" by Unica Zürn follows.

For Tawada, the challenge of the alphabet is thus its indeterminacy. "One writes a B, it can become a flower [*Blume*] but also a bomb [*Bombe*]" (31). So unreliable, unmeasurable, and unpredictable is every letter of the alphabet. And now come some wonderful pages on computer translation. Tawada's computer can translate alphabetic text into ideograms but the results are puzzling. The word for "secret" [*kakushigoto*] comes out as *kaku* [write] and *shigoto* [work]. "Maybe," the poet posits, the computer wants to say that one creates secrets by writing. Putting letters together is, after all, hard work.

As the poet probes the visual image of the alphabet, it becomes more and more mysterious. She begins to see letters everywhere—on footpaths, on leather bags, on doorways. The alphabet seems almost part of nature. Look at the palm of your hand and you can find I's, H's, and X's, but not C's. And indeed the actual letters (not the words they form) cannot be translated at all. A literary translation thus begins in untranslatability. For Tawada, certain texts by Kleist and Kafka, for example, sound as if they are translations, even though they are not. Why? A particular Kafka text contains the words "spring," "quick," "sun," "shade," "face," and "light"—words that, when re-assembled as *parole in libertà*, all contain the Chinese ideogram for "sun." And so the poet suddenly recognizes Kafka's image of the sinking sun lighting up the face of the young girl. It isn't that Kafka knew the ideogram in question, but that a literary text can sometimes find the intertext that gives it meaning (39). Consequently, the question should never be, "In what language do you dream?" but "In what script do you dream?". In the brief interlude "E-Mail for Japanese Ghosts," that follows, we read, "Every letter is like the back of a person. It can turn around any time. An author who thinks his own text must belong to him, to the last letter, is fooling himself: when a letter turns around, a strange face becomes visible" (41).

This marks the transition to the third lecture, "Gesicht eines Fisches oder das Problem der Verwandlung [Face of a Fish or the Problem of Metamorphosis]." As we move from voice to writing to reading a human face, Tawada's text becomes more somber, the paradox being that, as in Dworkin's *Dure*, the *malaise* recorded is presented almost entirely through citations from dictionaries, Walter Benjamin's *One-Way Street*, Barthes's *Empire of Signs,* and, as always, Ovid's *Metamorphoses*. The key word of the "lecture" is "Gesicht [Face]," beginning with the question whether fish can be said to have faces. The poet's dictionary defines *Gesicht* as "the front part of a human head, from chin to hairline, inscribed by the eyes, nose, and mouth" (45). But a fish, whose eyes are on both sides of the head, has no "front" and hence presumably no face." And what about the passage in Benjamin's *One-Way Street* that speaks of the collector's passion showing its "wahres Gesicht (true face)," even as his "Gesichtsfeld [ist] frei von Menschen (field of vision is free of human beings)"?

How to reconcile these seemingly different uses of *Gesicht?* In the Benjamin example, it is not the face that reveals passion [*Leidenschaft*] but the passion that has a face. Accordingly Tawada redefines *Gesicht* as *etwas, das sichbtar geworden ist*: "something that has become visible" or "has revealed itself." In this sense, a city has a "face" as does an occupation, faces not revealing themselves until they are *read*. The face is a text that contains latent multiple meanings. But, like both Baetens and Dworkin, Tawada traces the word horizontally as well as vertically:

> Ein Gesicht, ein Geräusch, ein Geruch, ein Geschmack, ein Gefühl.
> [A face, a noise, a smell, a taste, a feeling]. (48)

In German, the words designating the five senses sound alike. And yet syntactically, they carry different meanings, depending on whether the verb is transitive or intransitive. *Ich rieche* can mean "I smell [the unnamed object of the verb] or again "I smell [bad]." *Ich schmecke* is similarly ambivalent: it can mean "I taste [it]" or "I taste good."

Does the voice have a face? Here Tawada turns to the story of Echo and Narcissus. Spurning the invisible nymph, the self-regarding Narcissus is punished by becoming only a voice, whereas Echo becomes a voice that can repeat only what the other says. So when Narcissus says, "I would rather die than belong to you," Echo can only repeat "belong to you." To this extent, she can speak whereas Narcissus is transformed into a silent flower.

Gesicht, as I noted earlier, contains the ego, *Ich*, and it looks like a perfect verb form. The face is a highly variable signifier: Buddhist deities have dozens of faces emanating from their arms, and legs; angels have only one face. But most important, the face is a speech creation. God divided the earth and sea, not as a physical act, for the water would always contain a bit of earth and vice-versa, but by verbal fiat: he *said* he was dividing them. And now Tawada turns to Ovid, to the Kafka of *Metamorphosis*, to those many fairytales where men and women become animals. The reverse, Tawada notes, doesn't happen: there are no fairytales or myths where actual animals become human and marry other humans, although in Kafka's play *Ein Bericht für eine Akademie* [*A Report for an Academy*], the I-narrator is a monkey, who must, to his regret, take on human customs and habits.

Here is the conclusion to Tawada's lecture:

Das Modewort "Identitätsverlust" hat den Begriff der Verwandlung in die Ecke verdrängt. Die Verwandlung ist aber seit der Antike [...] eines der wichtigsten Motive der Literatur. Poetische Verwandlungen bilden einen Raum zwischen der Sehnsucht nach einer tödlichen verwandlung in ein Tier und dem Entzetzen über die Verwandlung in einen Menschen.

The fashionable term "loss of identity" has pushed the concept of Metamorphosis into the corner. But, it is Metamorphosis that, ever since Antiquity [...] is one of the most important motives of literature. Poetic metamorphoses create a space between the nostalgia for the deadly metamorphosis into an animal and the horror of meta-morphosis into a human being. (60)

What is the meaning of this pessimistic contrast and what is its import for Tawada's poetics? The poet might have written a coherent essay or narrative about identity loss, of the difficulties faced by being displaced, alienated, a victim of globalization and diaspora, and so on. Such tales are only too familiar. But throughout her three poem-lectures, Tawada can only deal with the loss of voice, writing, and reading as someone else's narrative. That, her poem-lectures imply, is, after all, what loss *is*.

In *Mandarinen*, there is a poem called "Ein Gedicht für ein Buch [A Poem for a Book]" that concludes:

zwischen einem wort	between a word
und einem schluck wasser	and a sip of water
dort	there
wo die stimme im fleisch aufwacht	where the voice awakes in
the flesh	
hört man ohne ohren	one hears without ears
ein wort	a word
befreit von seinem dienst	freed from its duty
ein	a
wort	word
direkt auf das trommelfell gescrhieben	written right on the eardrum
die trommel fällt	the drum falls
lautlos	noiselessly
stimmhaft	voiceless
ein wort	a word
ein ort	a place (93-94)

Here is Tawada's own Echo story: *wort, dort, ort* echoing on her eardrum. Loss, as the poet's various intertexts suggest, is also gain, metamorphosis offering, as it did for Echo, at least some respite from the pain of love. In the above poem, the word "ein" (or "einem") appears six times, in each case meaning either "a" or "one." The *ort* (place) of the word is thus ambiguous. Then, too, the non-native speaker's refusal to capitalize the nouns in question produces an odd clinamen from what these words are expected to be. "Ein wort / ein ort": but where? As in *Dure* and *Vivre sa vie*, Tawada's poetry is rooted in linguistic play—a form of play in dialogue with earlier artistic models, whether film, painting, or, in Tawada's case, Ovid and Kafka. It is this *literary* and *ekphrastic bent* that perhaps most clearly distinguishes the new generation of "experimental" poets from their precursors in the Language movement. But what they have learned from those precursors is that, in the digital age, one cannot simply write, as the mainstream would have it, "in the tradition of" this or that earlier poet or painter. The cited text remains in quotes—a transplant whose status as "amputated limb" reminds the reader that, in Blanchot's words, resaying is always "saying for the first time."

Jan Baetens

vivre sa vie

une novellisation en vers
du film de Jean-Luc Godard

postface de Sémir Badir

LES IMPRESSIONS NOUVELLES
PARIS - BRUXELLES

279

Notes

Craig Dworkin, pages 7–28

Notes & Acknowledgments

Thanks to Brent Cunningham, one of poetry's very best friends.

1. Weinberger, "Travels" 181.
2. *Ibidem.*
3. To be more precise, for anyone keeping score: the first two figures describe the peri-
   od 1993 to 2007, and come according to R. R. Bowker. The doubling of titles
   holds for poetry books and not just the industry in general; according to Bowker
   2,060 poetry (and drama) titles were published in 1993; by 2003 the figure was
   4,391, rising to 6,920 in 2004. One should note that 2005 was an anomalous year,
   recoding "the first decline in U.S. title output since 1999, and only the 10th down-
   turn recorded in the last 50 years. It follows the record increase of more than
   19,000 new books in 2004" (Bowker). Lee Briccetti, Executive Director of Poets
   House in New York corroborates these figures: "This year [*s.c.* 2003], Poets House
   will assemble a record-breaking number of poetry books [...] the final count is not
   in yet, but we expect the number of poetry books published in 2003 to exceed
   2,000—more than double the number published a little over a decade ago, when
   Poets House began its annual Showcase" (Poets House Press Release, March 2004).
   Not only are more titles being published, but, according to a survey of publishing
   in the last quarter of the twentieth century conducted by Gayle Feldman for
   Publishers Weekly, more people are buying them (quoted Smith).
      The figure for small press magazines comes from comparisons of listings in the
   Directory of Literary Magazines; the 1990/91 edition lists approximately 500 journals;
   in the 2000 editions the number rises to approximately 600; the 2007/2008 edition
   includes almost 700.
4. Some random searches for relatively well-known small press authors reveals substan-
   tial gaps in the Poets House collection, suggesting that any projections based on its
   library holdings are significantly lower than the actual number of books published.
5. The figure from Bowker was cited by their media contact, Daryn Teague, to the
   Association of Writers' and Writing Programs which reported it on their website
   page "May/Summer 2007 News" (retrieved 3 September, 2007). According to the
   same source, a total of 290,000 new book titles were introduced in 2006. The
   Amazon figure comes from an advanced search for they keyword "poetry" and the
   publication year 2006, run on 7 October, 2007.
6. Molesworth, *Fierce Embrace* 5; quoted by Kaladjian *Languages of Liberation* 25-6.
7. The pressure to quickly evaluate a large number of texts, even if they are not to be

read with more than a cursory effort, favors texts that can in fact of practice be assessed at a glance. Works that require complicated formal analyses (to discover unannounced structural or procedural practices, for instance), or that repay repeated readings (because of recursive structures, say), or that assume the reader will engage in research beyond the poem—all in order to merely gauge the scope of their poetic ambitions and categorize their poetic practices—are disadvantaged when reading time is at a premium.

8. See Sutherland, *Companion* 1; and James, *Victorian Novel* 3; Franco Moretti speculates: "twenty thousand, thirty, more, no one really knows" (*Graphs* 4). Whatever the figure, it puts the scale of contemporary production into perspective; in merely the first decade of the twenty-first century we can expect the publications of American poets to match the total number of nineteenth-century British novels. Fiction writers now do it every year; according to Bowker there were some 40,000 new adult fiction titles published in the United States in 2006.

9. The discrepancies are more subtle, but one could make the same argument staying within the canons of twentieth-century poetry. Where scholars of contemporary poetry might never have heard of Bruce Andrews, they would be likely to know Olson's name (even if they had never read any of his poetry) and equally likely to have actually read some of Stein's writing (even if they would not consider it for inclusion in the modernist canon). In short: consensus increases proportionally with historical distance.

10. Moretti, *Graphs* 4. See also Moretti, *Atlas*.

11. Perelman, *Marginalization* 3.

12. Bradshaw and Nichols, 3.

13. University press titles are printed in runs of one or two thousand, though there is no evidence that they sell at greater rates than small press titles. Because they have better bookstore distribution, initial sales often spike, but university press books face far higher returns, and are remaindered and pulped in greater numbers.

One should note that twenty-first-century production practices are slowly changing; volume breaks in production costs have been giving way to other production and distribution models of more or less continuous rolling small runs shipped directly from the printer to the distributor.

14. One might compare these figures to other historical moments. Print runs for the first press printed books, for instance, were also very small; fifteenth-century incunabula were produced in the low hundreds. The difference of course is that both the general population and the literate population have exploded over the intervening half millennium.

15. If you hadn't guessed: the most viewed television show, the best selling CD (assuming one ignores blank recordable compact discs), the top grossing movie, and the best selling softcover trade and mass market books in America in 2006, according to Nielsen, Nielsen SoundScan, and *Publishers Weekly*, respectively.

On 24 January, 1982 CBS broadcast the Super Bowl (San Francisco 49ers vs. Cincinnati Bengals) to 40.02 million viewers, or 49.1% of American households, a 73% share. On 30 January, 1983 NBC broadcast the Super Bowl (Washington Redskins vs. the Miami Dolphins) to 40.48 million viewers, or 48.6% of households, a 69% share.

In a 1998 print advertisement, the Burger King Corporation explicitly called this logic into question, though with a counter argument still based on demograph-ics: "If McDonald's makes 'America's Favorite Fries,' how come our fries beat them in a taste test?" As Jim Watkins, Senior Vice President for marketing at Burger King summarized the distinction: "which would you prefer [...] America's best-sell-ing french fries or America's best-tasting french fries? More doesn't mean better." (*PRNnewswire*, "Burger King Proclaims America's Favorite Fries... Based on Taste New Ad Aims to Set the Record Straight Versus McDonald's Claim").

16. For the record: *Pirates* opened at over 4,000 theatres; *Song* has been screened, how-ever successfully, at a handful of film festivals and art centers (selling out the Yerba Buena Center For the Arts is still only filling a 92 seat screening room).

17. Nicolas-Sébastien Roch de Chamfort, *Maximes, pensées, caracteres et anecdotes* (Paris: Baylis, 1796).

One might, however, critique the system of objects into which the popular cir-culates. Consider, as example, the following passage from Guy Debord's *Société du Spectacle*. For "commodity" and "object" read "poem":

The image of the blissful unification of society through consumption suspends disbelief with regard to the reality of division only until the next disillusionment occurs in the sphere of actual consumption. Each and every new product is sup-posed to offer a dramatic shortcut to the long-awaited promised land of total con-sumption. As such it is ceremoniously presented as the unique and ultimate prod-uct. But, as with the fashionable adoption of seemingly rare aristocratic first names which turn out in the end to be borne by a whole generation, so the would-be sin-gularity of an object can be offered to the eager hordes only if it has been mass-produced. The sole real status attaching to a mediocre objects of this kind is to have been placed, however briefly, at the very center of social life and hailed as a reve-lation of the goal of the production process. But even this spectacular prestige evaporates into vulgarity as soon as the object is taken home by its consumer—and hence by all other consumers too. For by this time another product will have been assigned to supply the system with its justification, and will in turn be demanding its moment of acclaim (Chapter 3, §69).

18. Collins has referred to "the sin of difficulty." For the guilty, see Bernstein.

19. Doran, np. With the expected conjunction of the random: an quick internet search reveals the imprint Milkweed Editions (Minneapolis Minnesota), which has appar-ently been publishing poetry since the late 1970s.

20. Hill, 439.

21. O'Hara, "Personism" 498.

22. Elberse, np.

23. See <http://english.utah.edu/eclipse>.

24. Mann, "Stupid Undergrounds" 2.

25. "Seja marginal / seja herói [be peripheral / be a hero]." Alternately the first phrase translates to "be criminal." The legend accompanied a silkscreen stenciled image of the assassinated cop-killing bandit Cara de Cavalo in a work exhibited as part of Oiticica's infamous 1968 installation *Homenagem a Cara de Cavalo* at the club Sucata in Rio de Janeiro; one of the texts included in the exhibition read: "Aqui está e aqui ficará. Contemplai o seu silêncio heróico [Here he lies and here he will remain. Contemplate his heroic silence]."

Works Cited

Anderson, Chris. "The Long Tail," *Wired Magazine* 12: 10 (October, 2004).

Bernstein, Charles. "The Difficult Poem," *Harper's Magazine* 306: 1837 (June 2003).

Bradshaw, Tom and Bonnie Nichols. *Reading at Risk: A Survey of Literary Reading in America*. Research Division Report #46 (Washington: NEA, 2004).

Collins, Billy. *PBS NewsHour* interview with Elizabeth Farnsworth (10 December, 2001).

Debord, Guy. *La Société du spectacle* (Paris: Buchet-Chastel, 1967). Translated by Donald Nicholson-Smith as *The Society of the Spectacle* (New York: Zone Books, 1994).

Doran, Tom C.. "Illinois' First Commercial Milkweed Field Harvested," *AgriNews* (Saturday, September 17, 2005).

Elberse, Anita. "A Taste for Obscurity: An Individual-Level Examination of 'Long Tail' Consumption," Harvard Business School Working Paper No. 08-008 (August 2007).

Gioia, Dana. "Can Poetry Matter?," *The Atlantic Monthly* 267: 5 (May 1991): 94-106.

Hill, Geoffrey. "On Reading *Crowds and Power*," *Poetry* 189: 6 (March 2007).

James, Louis. *The Victorian Novel* (Oxford: Blackwell, 2006).

Kaladjian, Walter. *Languages of Liberation: the Social Text in Contemporary American Poetry* (New York: Columbia University Press, 1989).

Mann, Paul. "Stupid Undergrounds," *Postmodern Culture* 5: 3 (May 1995).

O'Hara, Frank. "Personism: A Manifesto," *The Collected Poems Of Frank O'Hara*, edited by Donald Allen (Berkeley: University of California Press, 1995): 498-9.

Manovich, Lev. *The Language of New Media* (Cambridge: MIT Press, 2002).

Molesworth, Charles. *Fierce Embrace* (Columbia; University of Missouri Press, 1979).

Moretti, Franco. *An Atlas of the European Novel: 1800-1900* (London: Verso, 1998).

——————. *Graphs, Maps, Trees: Abstract Models for a Literary Theory* (London: Verso, 2005).

Perelman, Bob. *The Marginalization of Poetry: Language Writing and Literary History* (Princeton: Princeton University Press, 1996).

Smith, Dinitia. "In Book Publishing World, Some Reasons for Optimism," *The New York Times* 6 December, 2002 (Friday Final Late Edition): Section C, Page 2, Column 5.

Sutherland, John. *The Stanford Companion to Victorian Fiction* (Stanford: Stanford University Press, 1989).

Weinberger, Eliot. "Travels in the Federated Cantons of Poetry," *Outside Stories: Essays by Eliot Weinberger* (New York: New Directions, 1992).

Free (Market) Verse, Steve Evans page 25–36

Notes

1. To judge from his campaign donations, Barr's politics are typical of the Republican-dominated oil and gas industry, where more than three-quarters of contributions flow to the GOP. Alternately giving as his occupation "investor," "retired," "self-employed," and "poet," Barr opened his checkbook almost exclusively to Republican candidates between 1994 and 2004 (the one exception: a Republican who turned Independent to run against another Republican).

The Task of Poetics, the Fate of Innovation, and the Aesthetics of Criticism,
Charles Bernstein, 37–56

Notes

1. Chapter 2 of *The Evolution of Useful Things* is entitled "Form Follows Failure." I am grateful to James Shivers for underscoring the relevance of Petroski's work in *Charles Bernstein: American Innovator* (Doctoral dissertation, Université de Lausanne, Switzerland, 2002).

Works Cited

Christensen, Clayton M. *The Innovator's Dilemma: When New Technologies Cause the Great Firms to Fail* (Boston: Harvard Business School Press, 1997).

Petroski, Henry. *The Evolution of Useful Things: The Evolution of Useful Things How Everyday Artifacts—From Forks and Pins to Paper Clips and Zippers—Came to Be as They Are* (New York: Random House, 1994).

Poe, Edgar Allen. "The Philosophy of Composition," in *Poetry, Tales, & Selected Essays* (New York: Library of America *College Editions*, 1996).

Acknowledgements

An earlier version of this address was delivered on March 5, 2005, at "Poetics and Public Culture in Canada: A Conference in Honour of Frank Davey" and published in as "The Poet in the University or the Ends of Sinecure: The Task of Poetics, the Fate of Innovation, and the Aesthetics of Criticism" (*Open Letter* 12: 8 [Spring 2006]). The version presented here was first delivered at Notre Dame University as part of the Ward Phillips lectures, on November 27, 2006. Parts of the text are adapted from "Poetics," written for the Modern Language Association's *Introduction to Scholarship*, 3d edition, ed. David Nicholls (New York: MLA, 2007); "A Conversation with Marjorie Perloff," published in *Fulcrum* No. 2 (2003); and "A Blow Is Like an Instrument," written for the special Academic Profession issue of the publication of the American Academy of Arts and Letters and published in *Daedalus* 126: 4 (1997); as well as from "The Truth in Pudding" and "Invention Follies," both part of *The Attack of the Difficult Poems*, a work-in-progress

Audio and video of a performance of the essay at the University of Chicago is available at PennSound <http://writing.upenn.edu/pennsound/x/Bernstein-UChicago.html>.

Innovation and "Improbable Evidence", Jed Rasula, pages 58–91

Note

1. Adding a few titles from 2000 accentuates the variety, further compounding the encouraging portent of things to come: *Your Name Here* by John Ashbery; *Serenade* by Bill Berkson; *Men in the Off Hours* by Anne Carson; *On the Nameways* by Clark Coolidge; *Madame Deluxe* by Tenaya Darlington; *Comp.* by Kevin Davies; *Fidget* by Kenneth Goldsmith; *Swarm* by Jorie Graham; *Musca Domestica* by Christine Hume; *Utopic* by Claudia Keelan; *Talking Dirty to the Gods* by Yusef Komunyakaa; *The*

Promises of Glass by Michael Palmer; *For* by Carol Snow; *Isolato* by Larissa Szporluk; *The Architextures* by Nathaniel Tarn; *Marriage; A Sentence* by Anne Waldman; *The Annotated "Here" and Selected Poems* by Marjorie Welish; *The Tapeworm Foundry* by Darren Wershler-Henry. Several of poets (here and above) are Canadian, which raises the question of what an "American" poet is, particularly given the reciprocities established since the Tish group in Vancouver welcomed Donald Allen's clan of New American poets in 1963, reaffirmed in the 1980s by the Kootenay School's interaction with Language poetry. To acknowledge the consequences and significance of these precedents, the configuration of American poetry 2000-2001 can't help but be magnified by the inclusion of Bök, Carson, Davies, McCaffery and Robertson in the lists above: their inclusion is a reminder that "Canada" is a necessary inconvenience.

2. For one thing, there are more prizes. Fiscal realism joins hands with hyperbolic careerism: endowments are established at various presses to guarantee annual publications of poetry, so the books that are published are automatically deemed prizewinners.

3. Consider the Iowa Poetry Prize, which publishes two or three books a year. Both 1999 titles were by women, two out of three for 1998. Many of the previous years were split one each. A more significant pattern can be seen in the National Poetry Series that, until 1994, consistently published at a ratio of three men to two women. From 1994-99, however, 17 of the 25 titles have been by women (three of those years included only one man each year).

4. Most of the significant anthologies of the 1990s were engaged in partisan politics, concerned to establish the credibility of certain zones of praxis. It's telling that a notable gender disparity prevails in the more vanguard oriented collections: Paul Hoover's *Postmodern American Poetry* (28 women out of 103 poets, and only 4 of 31 born before 1934), Douglas Messeri's *From the Other Side of the Century* (20 of 81), and Eliot Weinberger's *American Poetry Since 1950* (5 of 35), though Weinberger suggests that "a subsequent selection of the innovators from the post-World War II generations would probably contain a majority of women" (xiii).

5. The critique of "movements" as constraints has been extended to feminism by Steve Evans in his preface to a special issue of *Differences* titled "After Patriarchal Poetry: Feminism and the Contemporary Avant-Garde": "We know [...] how the feminist poetry that has been institutionalized within women's studies programs and teaching anthologies can be restrictively organized around a normative concept of 'experience' that renders all but the most tentative formal innovations by women inadmissible and anathematizes theoretical reflection on poetic practice (by poets themselves, by their readers) as an overly intellectualized interference with the immediate pleasures afforded by cathartic identification" (i-ii). Evans laments the way such exclusions have resulted in the legacy of "an avant-garde without women, a poetics without poetry, [and] a poetry for which entire registers of experience, innovation, and reflexivity are taboo" (ii).

6. The case of Carson is complicated by the fact that she's Canadian, while her poetry has been published by New York trade publishers. It was not until after she had been awarded the MacArthur fellowship, curiously, that Canadian bookstores and libraries acknowledged her as a Canadian poet. Because she has become such a singularly important figure in American letters, however, it will be interesting to see

whether future anthologists can resist including her despite nationality.

7. Other examples—by older poets whose actual birthdates I don't know—include: *Candy Necklace* (1997) by Cal Bedient; *The Cult of the Right Hand* (1991) by Elaine Cerranova; The *Arrangement of Space* (1991) by Martha Collins; *At the Site of Inside Out* (1997) by Anna Rabinowitz; *Sister Betty Reads the Whole You* (1998) by Susan Holahan.

8. Or something long gone: "I've read some interesting poems from that domain," Philip Lamantia remarked in 1998, "but I can't see it as a direction, no. And it's been over as a movement for some time now" (Meltzer 148). 9. This dismissal of Palmer replicates Stein on Pound, though surely Stein would be no more amenable to Logan than Palmer is. Logan's bile extends far beyond Language poetry. He likens Creeley's work to "the tedium of diary jotting or the Dictaphone," producing "vacuous ruminations that are those of a man as a chamber decompresses and the oxygen goes out of his head" (170; 171); and he gazes ruefully on the "cruel tedium" of Ashbery's "vast rhetorical machines, spewing out meaning and non-meaning indifferently" (40). Logan's dyspeptic temperament is touted by Penguin, the publisher of his poetry, in lieu of blurbs. The back cover of *Night Battle* (1999) offers the following: "A brilliant, almost cheerless collection"; "The most hated man in American poetry"; and "William Logan is our Geoffrey Hill: cranky, gifted."

10. See John Koethe, whose "Contrary Impulses: The Tension between Poetry and Theory" addressed diverging practices in American poetry with unusual clarity in 1991. Charting a zone divided between workshop personalism and the Language poets, with deconstruction as the theoretical burden inducing the most stress for poetry, he advocated "a poetics [that] would neither reject the domain of subjectivity, as deconstruction does, nor try to incorporate it into the domain of the objective, as the poetics of authenticity tries to do" (49). The preoccupation with form evaporates under pressure of such ontological exigencies.

11. I'd spent much of my undergraduate years studying Heidegger, which led me to the Northwestern series on phenomenology and existentialism in which *Speech and Phenomenon* appeared.

12. This may be misleading: *Wch Way* was primarily a poetry magazine, published intermittently from 1975-1984 (the final two issues co-published with Jerome Rothenberg's *New Wilderness Letter*). A sense of the contents can be gleaned by a list of books in which material published in *Wch Way* later appeared: *Empty Words* by John Cage; *Talking at the Boundaries* by David Antin; *Without Music* by Michael Palmer; *Ground Work: Before the War* by Robert Duncan; *Evoba* by Steve McCaffery; *Call Steps* by Kenneth Irby; *My Emily Dickinson* by Susan Howe; *Bedouin Hornbook* by Nathaniel Mackey; *Phantom Anthems* by Robert Grenier; *The Sophist* by Charles Bernstein; *Primer* by Bob Perelman; *Loop* by John Taggart; *Streets Enough to Welcome Snow* by Rosmarie Waldrop; *Spring Trances in the Control Emerald Night* by Christopher Dewdney; *Solution Passage* by Clark Coolidge; *Complete Thought* by Barrett Watten; *Horse Sacrifice* and *Parts and Other Parts* by Charles Stein; among others. *Wch Way* also published Paul Metcalf, Frank Chin, Ed Dorn, Kathleen Fraser, Clayton Eshleman, Will Alexander, Howard Norman, John Clarke, Robert Kelly, Jackson Mac Low, Charles Simic, Michael Davidson and more.

13. Ron Silliman followed Allen's precedent, rounding out his selection of Language poetry in *In the American Tree* (1986) with a portfolio of poetics; and Mary Margaret

Sloan did likewise in *Moving Borders: Three Decades of Innovative Writing by Women* (1998).

14. "Criticism must be transcendental, that is, must consider literature ephemeral & easily entertain the supposition of its entire disappearance" (qtd. Poirier 27). I take Emerson's notion, in part, as intimation of an expanded (or maybe reclaimed) orality. Given Emerson's acute sense of flux and flow, he was disposed to view texts as frozen moments that might be thawed out. In a fully animated cultural milieu there would be no need for a text because every articulation would meet its moment head on, no deferrals necessary. This unimaginable prospect is one in which everyone would be constantly prepared for the sublime utterance.

15. Because of the special focus of the Best American Poetry series, of course—not to mention the revolving editorship—it would be misleading to infer significant patterns from inclusions or exclusions. Charles Bernstein, Frank Bidart, Lucie Brock-Broido, Mark Doty, Rita Dove, Carolyn Forché, Ann Lauterbach, Bin Ramke, Mary Jo Salter, and David Wojahn, despite influence and acclaim, have each appeared in only one of the fifteen volumes in the Best American Poetry series (1988-2001). Having said that, the series is hardly exonerated from perpetuating a familiar roster. The list of those with a half-dozen or more appearances largely replicates the anthology profile established in the 1950s: Hall; Ashbery; Simic; Hollander; Ammons; Creeley; Graham; Howard; Koch; Merrill; Strand; Tate; Wilbur; and Charles Wright.

16. On the dustjacket of *Felt* (2001): "Alice Fulton's honors include a fellowship from the John D. and Catherine T. MacArthur Foundation. Her work has appeared in six volumes of *The Best American Poetry* series, including *Best of the Best American Poetry*."

17. Concomitant with the rise of internet purchasing is an increased burden of instantaneity. Readers' evaluations of books on Amazon.com rarely offer historical context or suggest anything like lineage. If the positive side of this situation is a blurring of nascent boundaries among those writing today, the derelict side of the equation is an obscuring of precedent, and ultimately an effacement of history. Reading the younger poets of the 1990s, it's hard to avoid the sense that the new ecumenical spirit goes only so far. Language poetry has cast an enabling shadow of sorts, bearing with it the ghost of Jack Spicer, *agent provocateur extraordinaire*; but Olson and Duncan seem as remote as Doughty's *Dawn in Britain*, while fugitive informants like Gerrit Lansing, Ken Irby, Ronald Johnson, or Robin Blaser might as well have been writing Sanskrit. The festschrift can play a certain resuscitating role. The extraordinary four day symposium in Vancouver, "The Recovery of the Public World," was an international gathering of poets and critics in honor of Robin Blaser (some of the proceedings were subsequently published under that title by Talonbooks, edited by Charles Watts and Edward Byrne). On a more diminutive scale is the 150 page portfolio on Ronald Johnson in the premiere issue of *Facture* (edited by Lindsay Hill and Paul Naylor). Such occasions serve as lifelines to essential bodies of work that otherwise float off into the uncharted Atlantic of recent history.

There is, I think, a generational issue contributing to this increased bandwidth of contemporary awareness and a corresponding decrease in historical resonance—synchronic prevailing over diachronic perspective. Coming of age in the

1960s (and earlier) meant being stung to acute historical consciousness. The poetry I have most often written about is work that is "of" that moment in this sense: its demands were large, its terms of access unnervingly demanding. To be confronted with *The Cantos* and *The Maximus Poems* and *"A"* as a teenager, and to determine to read them, was to submit to nothing less than the "negative capability" demanded by Keats. There were no guides; even academic work on *The Cantos* was almost nonexistent. So one's viewfinders were strictly of the world of allied poetries sparked off by the grand examples of Pound, Olson, Zukofsky. I can't overstress the pedagogic importance of being an amateur (do it yourself) reader of these huge poems.

18. Jacket copy isn't usually so daring. Much of the space is reserved for professional appraisals. Blurbs commonly consolidate tribal views: Creeley and Silliman weigh in for Scalapino's *New Time*; Hollander and Howard for Tony Sanders' *Transit Authority*; Lauterbach and Fraser rally behind *The Human Abstract* by Elizabeth Willis, while Gerald Stern, John Updike, X. J. Kennedy, Stephen Dunn and Annie Proulx circle around *Picnic, Lightning* by Billy Collins. But there are (again) signs of border crossing in unlikely pairings of blurb contributors to the same book: Edward Hirsch and Marjorie Perloff (John Koethe, *The Constructor*); Richard Howard and Ann Lauterbach (Bin Ramke, *Massacre of the Innocents*); Rita Dove and Dean Young (Olena Kalytiak Davis, *And Her Soul Out of Nothing*); Forrest Gander and Jane Miller (Tessa Rumsey, *Assembling the Shepard*); Lyn Hejinian and Wayne Koestenbaum (Lisa Lubasch, *How Many More of Them Are You?*); and the trio of Guy Davenport, Jean Valentine and Gregory Orr (Tom Andrews, *The Hemophiliac's Motorcycle*). Nothing quite compares with the heterogeneous clusters on the back cover of *True North* by Stephanie Strickland (Barbara Guest, John Matthias, Molly Peacock, Maureen Seaton, Marie Ponsot, and N. Katherine Hayles) and *Bag 'o' Diamonds* by Susan Wheeler (David Lehman, Harold Bloom, Barbara Guest, Lyn Emanuel, and Ben Belitt). Amidst the proliferation of blurbs it's worth recalling that Black Sparrow launched a generation of poets without resorting to blurbs, as did Sun & Moon later. In the heyday of small presses—when "small" meant letterpress—blurbs would have been a desecration. Besides, blurbs were conspicuously associated with the inner sanctum of the poetry establishment. The expansion of poetry presses through NEA funding meant that fledgling presses like The Figures and Roof could afford to have their books printed by the same jobbers (McNaughton and Gunn of Ann Arbor, most famously) as the trade publishers and university presses. Now it's a visual tossup concerning publisher identity, as most books (and not just poetry books) conform to industry standards, and those standards routinely dedicate the back cover of a book to blurbs. Blurbs, like the poetry they appraise, can be an extension of billboard and blip culture; but they can also initiate a fructifying interface between different poetic constituencies, diverging sensibilities, and even become a site of miniature essaying (an idiom perfected by Jorie Graham).

19. In a state of total immersion, of course, the work in these anthologies becomes more "readable" as rhetorical contours become normative by the sheer mass of surrounding material. That is, your discrimination as a reader dissolves, allowing some approximation to aural receptivity. I should point out that the orientation of the anthologists is not uniform. Kaufman's *Outlaw Bible* is openly hostile to the status quo:

Outlaw poets relate to the poetic tradition, and to their contemporaries in the Academy, with the bristling wariness of a street hustler getting frisked by a cop. They've seen how excessive veneration for the poetic mainstream has turned the practice of the art today into an ongoing memorial service held by those who want poetry to stay in the closet (xxvi).

While the use of *Bible* in the title is probably intended as taunt, it tips the agenda towards canonical aspirations. Nevertheless, Kaufman's presentation of the poets into such groupings as "Slammers," "Meat Poets," "American Renegades," etc., provides an intelligible profile of the "outlaw" stance. Cabico and Swift, on the other hand, avow a fusion (hence their subtitle, "The North American Anthology of Fusion Poetry") of insider and outsider:

> We believe it is far too easy and reductive to classify poetry as either written or spoken, for the college or the bar, as slick or slam. In reality, many serious poets—the kind who get published in books like *Best American Poetry* and who teach as professors at universities and win or are nominated for major awards like the Pulitzer or the Governor General's—read or perform their work for audiences, and get their message across, wonderfully (26).

They, too, offer some provocative groupings ("Fusion Bomb," "Pound Unplugged," "Media Byrons"), but the great service of *Poetry Nation* is to present a fully integrated assembly of Canadian and American authors.

20. Commenting on their pertinence (or impertinence) for us now, Jerome McGann says of Rossetti's paintings that "their fetishism defines their truth" (104). As for Agamben, "Precisely because the fetish is a negation and the sign of an absence, it is not an unrepeatable unique object; on the contrary, it is something infinitely capable of substitution, without any of its successive incarnations succeeding in exhausting the nullity of which it is the symbol" (33). Given this model of infinite substitutions, it's clear why Agamben finds in poetry the exemplary form of the fetish.

Works Cited

Agamben, Giorgio. *Stanzas: Word and Phantasm in Western Culture.* Trans. Ronald L. Martinez. Minneapolis: U. of Minnesota Press, 1993.

Algarín, Miguel and Bob Holman (Editors). *Aloud: Voices from the Nuyorican Poets Cafe.* New York: Henry Holt, 1994.

Andrews, Bruce and Charles Bernstein (Editors). "Introduction." *The L=A=N=G=U=A=G=E Book.* Carbondale: Southern Illinois U. P., 1984.

Barone, Dennis and Peter Ganick: *The Art of Practice: 45 Contemporary Poets.* Elmwood: Potes and Poets, 1994.

Brown, Spencer. *Laws of Form.* New York: Bantam, 1973.

Cabico, Regie and Todd Swift (Editors). *Poetry Nation: The North American Anthology of Fusion Poetry,* Montreal: Véhicule, 1998.

Creeley, Robert. *The Collected Poems: 1945-1975.* Berkeley: U. of California P., 1982.

Daly, Lew and Alan Gilbert and Kristin Prevallet and Pam Rehm (Editors). *apex of the M* 1-6 (1994-1997).

Dent, Tory. *What Silence Equals: Poems*. New York: Persea, 1993.

Emanuel, Lyn. "Language Poets, New Formalists and the Techniquization of Poetry." *Poetry After Modernism*, Ed. Robert McDowell (Brownsville: Story Line, 1998): 199-221.

Steve Evans. "After Patriarchal Poetry: Feminism and the Contemporary Avant-Garde." *Differences* 12: 2 (2001): i-iii.

Foster, Edward. *Poetry and Poetics in a New Millennium: Interviews With Clark Coolidge, Theodore Enslin, Michael Heller, Eileen Myles, Alice Notley, Maureen Owen, Ron Padgett, Armand Schwerner, Anne Waldman, and Lewis Warsh*. Jersey City: Talisman House, 2000.

Fraser, Kathleen. *Translating the Unspeakable: Poetry and the Innovative Necessity*. Tuscaloosa: U. of Alabama P., 2000.

Fulton, Alice. *Felt*. New York: W. W. Norton, 2001.

Halliday, Mark. *Selfwolf*. Chicago: U. of Chicago P., 1999.

Hejinian, Lyn. *A Border Comedy*. New York: Granary Books, 2001.

Jarnot, Lisa and Leonard Schwartz and Chris Stroffolino (Editors). *An Anthology of New (American) Poets*. Jersey City: Talisman, 1998.

Kang, Eyvind. "Music Suffers." *Arcana: Musicians on Music*, Ed. John Zorn (New York: Granary Books, 2000): 167-169.

Kaufman, Alan. *The Outlaw Bible of American Poetry*. New York: Thunder's Mouth, 1999.

Koethe, John. "Contrary Impulses: The Tension between Poetry and Theory" *Poetry At One Remove: Essays*. Ann Arbor: U. of Michigan P., 2000.

Lehman, David. *The Daily Mirror: A Journal in Poetry*. New York: Scribner, 2000.

Logan, William. *Reputations of the Tongue: On Poets and Poetry*. Gainesville: U. P. of Florida, 1999.

Luhmann, Niklas. *Art as a Social System*, trans. Eva M. Knodt. Stanford: Stanford U. P., 2000.

Mann, Paul. *The Theory-Death of the Avant-Garde*. Bloomington: Indiana U. P., 1991.

McGann, Jerome. *Dante Gabriel Rossetti and the Game That Must Be Lost*. New Haven: Yale, U. P., 2000.

Meltzer, David (Editor). *San Francisco Beat: Talking with the Poets*. San Francisco: City Lights, 2001.

Notley, Alice. *Disobedience*. New York: Penguin, 2001.

Novarina, Valère. *The Theater of the Ears*, trans. Allen S. Weiss. Los Angeles: Sun & Moon, 1996.

Olsen, William. *Vision of a Storm Cloud*. Evanston: TriQuarterly, 1996.

Poirier, Richard. *The Renewal of Literature: Emersonian Reflections*. New York: Random House, 1987.

Rasula, Jed. *The American Poetry Wax Museum: Reality Effects, 1940-1990*. Urbana: National Council of Teachers of English, 1996.

Rehak, Melanie. "Things Fall Together." *New York Times Magazine* (26 March, 2000): 37-39.

Scalapino, Leslie. *The Public World / Syntactically Impermanence*. Middletown: Wesleyan U. P., 1999.

Scobie, Stephen (*et al.*). "Present Tense; The Closing Panel." *Future Indicative: Literary Theory and Canadian Literature*, Ed. John Moss (Ottawa: U. of Ottawa P., 1987): 239-245.

Silliman, Ron. *In the American Tree*. Orono: National Poetry Foundation, 1986.

Weinberger, Eliot. *American Poetry Since 1950: Innovators and Outsiders: An Anthology*. New York: Marsilio, 1993.

——————. "*Sunrise* by Frederick Seidel." *Sulfur* 1 (1981): 221-225.

Bruce Andrews' Venus: Paying Lip Service to Écriture Féminine, Barbara Cole, Pages 93

Notes

These lists have been culled from a variety of critical essays and reviews. The following list attributes the alignment with the source: Andrews' work has been compared to that of Beckett (Smith) and Joyce (Smith), Mac Low (Smith), Burroughs (Smith), Debord (Smith), Bakhtin (Rasula), Jameson (Sala), Mapplethorpe (Sala), Celine (Sala), the Sex Pistols (Sala) Foucault (Lazer), Ashbery, Eliot, Pound (Lazer), Williams (DuPlessis), Wagner (DuPlessis), Susan Howe (DuPlessis), Oppen (DuPlessis), Creeley (DuPlessis), Barthes (Hejinian), Klee (Hejinian), Bartok (Hejinian), and The Clash (Tejada).

2. As it turns out, I'm not the first to begin to make this connection. Rachel Blau DuPlessis noted that Andrews' essay, "Text and Context" (which originally appeared in 1977), "seems to call for a feminine writing strategy influenced by, or in tandem with, work by French and francophone (e.g. Quebecoise) feminism" (55). But still, neither DuPlessis nor any one else has sufficiently explored the feminist aspect of Andrews' project.

   Tina Darragh gestures towards this predicament in her mini-confessional anecdote about first hearing Andrews read in 1972 at her Catholic girls school (a scenario in itself that is rather fun to imagine). Darragh relates that the other women "had a far different reaction to Andrews' work," finding it autocratic whereas she found it freeing. Nearing her conclusion, Darragh notes that "it continues to bother me that I feel a kinship with work that my friends identified as oppressive" (102). But rather than exploring the gender-inflected reasons for this dismissal, Darragh moves on: "At the time it seemed like a gender issue, but now both women and men critique 'unreadable texts' as unintelligible abstractions that silence dissent and promotes the status quo" (102). On the one hand, I appreciate Darragh's attempt to complexify the critical reception of 'difficult' texts; however, I wish we could pause more extensively than a mere one or two sentences on the gender question.

Works Cited

Andrews, Bruce. *Lip Service*. Toronto: Coach House, 2001.

Cixous, Hélène. "The Laugh of the Medusa." Trans. Keith Cohen & Paula Cohen. Warhol, Robyn R. and Diane Price Herndl, eds. *Feminisms: an anthology of literary theory and criticism*. New Brunswick: Rutgers UP, 1996. 334-49.

Darragh, Tina. "Confession and the Work of Bruce Andrews." In *Aerial* 9 (1999): 102.

Davies, Kevin and Jeff Derksen. "Bruce Andrews Interview: May 1990, Vancouver." In *Aerial* 9 (1999): 5-17.

DuPlessis, Rachel Blau. "Surface Tension: Thinking About Andrews." In *Aerial* 9 (1999): 49-61.

Dworkin, Craig. "Bruce Andrews" (encyclopedia entry). Fitzray Dearborn's *Encyclopedia of American Poetry: The Twentieth Century* (2001); Eric Haralson, editor.

Friedlander, Benjamin. "'Social Romanticism'" In *Aerial* 9 (1999): 62.

Lazer, Hank. "'To Make Equality less Drab': The Writing of Bruce Andrews." In *Aerial* 9 (1999): 32-48.

Perloff, Marjorie. "A Syntax of Contrariety." In *Aerial* 9 (1999): 156-60.

Quartermain, Peter. "Paradise as Praxis: A preliminary Note on Bruce Andrews' *Lip Service.*" at *Witz: a Journal of Contemporary Poetics 6.2* (Summer 1998): 5-18.

Rasula, Jed. "Andrews Extremities Bruce." In *Aerial* 9 (1999): 23-27.

Sala, Jerome. "Talking About Shut Up." In *Aerial* 9 (1999): 28-31.

Smith, Rod, ed. "Introduction." *Aerial* 9 (Washington: Edge Books, 1999): v.

Tejada, Roberto. "The Clash. Funkadelic. Bruce Andrews: Introduction." Weds@4 Poetry Reading Series. Buffalo, NY. November 28, 2001.

Invitation to a Misreading: Andrews' Lip Service,
Gregg Biglieri, pages 103–116

Works Cited

The American Heritage College Dictionary of the English Language, Third Ed. (Boston: Houghton Mifflin, 1993).

Andrews, Bruce. *Lip Service*. Toronto: Coach House, 2001.

——————. *Paradise & Method*. Evanston: Northwestern UP, 1996.

Guerlac, Suzanne. "Longinus and the Subject of the Sublime." *New Literary History* 2 (1985): 275–289.

Longinus. "On the Sublime." *Critical Theory Since Plato*. Ed. Hazard Adams. Fort Worth: Harcourt Brace Jovanovich, 1992. 75–98.

Shklovsky, Viktor. *Third Factory*. Trans. Richard Sheldon. Chicago: Dalkey Archive, 2002.

from *Stuplimity: Shock and Boredom in Twentieth-Century Aesthetics,*
Sianne Ngai, pages 117–135

Notes

1. See Deleuze, *Difference* 39.

2. See Jean-François Lyotard, *Duchamp's TRANS/formers*, trans. Ian McLeod (Venice, Calif.: Lapis Press, 1990), a study of Duchamp's *Large Glass*. Lyotard's analysis of Duchamp's aesthetics as underwritten by a logic of "inexact precision" and "intelligent stupidity" also pertains to and sheds light on the poetics of Stein.

3 *Fidget* was originally commissioned by the Whitney Museum and performed in collaboration with vocalist Theo Bleckmann on June 16, 1998, at the Whitney Museum of American Art (New York). A web-based version was hosted by DIA's (now defunct) pioneering StadiumWeb. The text was subsequently published by Coach House Books (Toronto, 2000).

4. As Raphael Rubinstein notes on the volume's jacket, "Goldsmith's epic litanies and lists bring to the textual tradition of conceptual art not only an exploded frame of

reference, but a hitherto absent sense of hypnotic beat. Under its deceptively bland title, *No. 111 2.7.93-10.20.96* attempts no less than a complete reordering of the things of the world."

5. The "self-referential" text Goldsmith appropriates and edits for incorporation into his own conceptual project was written by mathematician David Moser and cited in Hofstadter (37-38). What ultimately determines this text's positioning between chapter "MDCLXXXV" and chapter "MDCLXXXVII" in Goldsmith's poem (encyclopedia? Baedeker?) is the fact that it contains the appropriate number of syllables, and, like the other rhymed "verses" in the volume, ends on the sound of the letter *r*: "Harder harder" (Goldsmith, *No. 111*, 568).

6. In the "Author's Note," Notley offers "a word about the quotation marks. People ask about them, in the beginning; in the process of reading the poem, they become comfortable with them, without necessarily thinking precisely about why they're there. But they're there, mostly, to measure the poem. The phrases they enclose are poetic feet. If I had simply left white spaces between the phrases, the phrases would be rushed by the reader—read too fast for my musical intention. The quotation marks make the reader slow down and silently articulate—not slur over mentally—the phrases at the pace, and with the stresses, I intend. They also distance the narrative from myself, the author: I am not Alette. Finally they may remind the reader that each phrase is a thing said by a voice: this is not a thought, or a record of thought-process, this a story, told."

Works Cited

Beckett, Samuel. *Murphy* (NY: Grove, 1957).

———. "Stirrings Still," in *The Complete Short Prose: 1929-1989*, ed. S. E. Gontarski (New York: Grove, (1995).

———. *Worstward Ho*, in *Nohow On* (NY: Grove, 1996).

Bloch, Ernst. *The Principle of Hope, Volume I*, trans. Neville Plaice, Stephen Plaice, and Paul Knight (Cambridge, Mass.: MIT Press, 1995).

Danto, Arthur C.. *The Abuse of Beauty: Aesthetics and the Concept of Art* (Chicago: Open Court, 2003).

DeKoven, Marianne. *A Different Language: Gertrude Stein's Experimental Writing* (Madison: U. of Wisconsin P., 1983).

Deleuze, Gilles. *Difference and Repetition*, trans. Paul Patton (New York: Columbia University Press, 1995).

———. "The Exhausted," *Essays Critical and Clinical*, trans. Daniel W. Smith and Michael A. Greco (Minneapolis: U. of Minnesota P., 2000).

Farrell, Dan. *366, 1996* in *Last Instance* (San Francisco: Krupskaya, 1998).

Goldman, Judith. "dictée," in *Vocoder* (New York: Roof Books, 2001): 50-54.

Goldsmith, Kenneth. *Fidget* (Toronto: Coach House Books, 2000).

———. *No. 111 2.7.93-10.20.96* (Great Barrington: The Figures, 1997).

Hofstadter, Douglas. *Metamagical Themas: Questing for the Essence of Mind and Pattern* (NY: Basic Books, 1985).

Kant, Immanuel. *Critique of Judgment*, trans. J. H. Bernard (NY: Hafner, 1951).

Kierkegaard, Søøren. *"Fear and Trembling" and "Repetition"*, ed. and trans. Howard V. Hong and Edna H. Hong (Princeton: Princeton U. P., 1983).

Lacan, Jacques. *The Four Fundamental Concepts of Psycho-Analysis*, ed. Jacques-Alain

Miller, trans. Alan Sheridan (New York: Norton, 1981).

Notley, Alice. *The Descent of Alette* (New York: Penguin, 1992).

Poe, Edgar Allan. "The Gold-Bug," in *"The Fall of the House of Usher" and Other Writings* (New York: Penguin, (1986).

Richter, Gerhard. *Atlas* (New York: Distributed Art Publishers, 1997).

Rubinstein, Raphael. Promotional back cover text to Kenneth Goldsmith's *No. 111* (*op. cit.*).

Schmitz, Neil. *Of Hack and Alice: Humorous Writing in American Literature* (Minneapolis: University of Minnesota Press, 1983).

Sontag, Susan. *Styles of Radical Will* (New York: Doubleday, 1969).

Stein, Gertrude. *How to Write* (Los Angeles: Sun and Moon, 1995).

——————. *The Making of Americans* (Normal: Dalkey Archive Press, 1995).

——————. *Writings and Lectures, 1909-1945*, ed. Patricia Meyerowitz (Baltimore: Johns Hopkins University Press, 1974).

Tomkins, Silvan. *Exploring Affect: The Selected Writings of Silvan S. Tomkins*, ed. Virginia Demos (Cambridge: Cambridge University Press, 1995).

Wagner-Martin, Linda. *Favored Strangers: Gertrude Stein and Her Family* (New Brunswick: Rutgers University Press, 1995).

Wakefield, Neville. "Ann Hamilton: Between Words and Things," *Ann Hamilton, Mneme* (Liverpool: Tate Gallery Liverpool, 1994).

West, Nathanael. "The Day of the Locust," *"Miss Lonelyhearts" and "The Day of the Locust"* (New York: New Directions, 1962): 169-247.

Zweig, Janet. Note on *Her Recursive Apology*, in *Chain* 2 (1995): 248-249.

A Week of Blogs for the Poetry Foundation, Kenneth Goldsmith, pages 137–150

Notes

1. Craig Dworkin, "Introduction," *The UbuWeb Anthology of Conceptual Writing* <www.ubu.com/concept>.

2. See Ron Silliman, *The New Sentence*. New York: Roof Books, 1987.

3. Marc Chagall.

4. Philip Yeo.

5. Richard Florida.

6. Dr. Wayne Dwyer.

7. Kimon Nicolaides.

8. Raoul Dufy.

9. Gail Sheehy.

10. Douglas Huebler, Artist's Statement for the gallery publication to accompany *January 5 - 31* (Seth Segelaub Gallery, 1969).

11. G. R. Swenson, "What is Pop Art? Answers from 8 Painters, Part I," *ARTnews* 62: 7 (November 1963): 26.

12. Christian Bök, "The Piecemeal Bard Is Deconstructed: Notes Toward a Potential Robopoetics," *Object 10: Cyber Poetics,* Ed. Kenneth Goldsmith (2001) <http://www.ubu.com/papers/object/03_bok.pdf>.

13. See Jorge Louis Borges, "Pierre Menard, Author of the *Quixote*," *Collected Fictions*, Trans. Andrew Hurley (New York: Penguin, 1999): 88-95.

14. John Cage, "Four Statements on the Dance," *Silence* (Middletown: Wesleyan U. P., 1962): 93.
15. Ulla E. Dydo. *A Stein Reader* (Evanston: Northwestern U. P., 1993): 480.

Stops and Rebels: a critique of hypertext [remix], Brian Kim Stefans, 151–184

Works Cited

Bakhtin, Mikhail. *Rabelais and His World*. Bloomington: Indiana University Press, 1984.

Benjamin, Walter. *Illuminations*. New York: Schocken Books, 1985.

Bey, Hakim. *T.A.Z: The Temporary Autonomous Zone, Ontological Anarchy, Poetic Terrorism*. New York: Autonomedia, 1991.

Bök, Christian. *Crystallography*. Toronto: Coach House Books, 1994.

Bök, Christian. *Eunoia*. Toronto: Coach House Books, 2001.

Cayley, John. "Of Programmatology," <www. shadoof.net/ infprogfprogsetO. html>.

Chomsky, Noam. *Noam Chomsky on The Generative Enterprise*. Holland: Foris Publications, 1982.

Davies, Kevin. *Pause Button*. Vancouver: Talonbooks, 1992.

De Campos, Haroldo. "The Informational Temperature of a Text," *Precisely 13 14 15 16: The Poetics of the New Poetries*, Eds. Richard Kostelanetz and Benjamin Hrushovski. New York: Archae Editions, 1984.

Farrell, Dan. *The Inkblot Record*. Toronto: Coach House Books, 2001.

Forrest-Thomson, Veronica. *Poetic Artifice*. New York: St. Martin's Press, 1978.

Goldsmith, Kenneth. *Fidget*. Toronto: Coach House Books, 2001.

Goldsmith, Kenneth. *No. 111: 2.7.93-10.20.96*. Great Barrington: The Figures, 1997.

Goldsmith, Kenneth. *Soliloquy*. New York: Granary Books, 2001.

Haraway, Donna. *Simians, Cyborgs, arid Women*. New York: Routledge, 1991.

Jameson, Frederic. "Postmodernism and Consumer Society," *The Anti-Aesthetic: Essays on Postmodern Culture*. Edited by Hal Foster. Seattle: Bay Press, 1983.

Lechte, John. *Fifty Key Contemporary Thinkers: From Structuralism to Postmodernity*. New York: Routledge, 1994.

Manovich, Lev. *The Language of New Media*. Boston: MIT Press, 2001.

McCaffery, Steve. *North of Intention*. New York: Roof Books, 2000.

McCaffery, Steve. *Prior to Meaning: The Protosemantic and Poetics*. Evanston: Northwestern University Press, 2001

Mullen, Harryette. *Muse & Drudge*. Philadelphia: Singing Horse Press, 1995.

Ngai, Sianne. "Raw Matter: A Poetics of Disgust." *Open Letter: Disgust and Overdetermination* (Tenth Series, No. 1. Winter, 1998).

Penley, Constance. "Brownian Motion: Women, Tactics, and Technology." *Technoculture*. Minneapolis: University of Minnesota Press, 1991.

Prynne, J. H. *Red D Gypsum*. Cambridge: Barque, 1998.

Rimbaud, Arthur. *Complete Works, Selected Letters*. Chicago: University of Chicago Press, 1987.

Sontag, Susan. *Styles of Radical Will*. New York: Doubleday, 1969.

Wardrip-Fruin, Noah et. al. *The Impermanence Agent*. <www. impermanenceagent.com/>.

Wershler-Henry, Darren. *the tapeworm foundry: andor the dangerous prevalence of imagination*. Toronto: House of Anansi Press, 2001.

Wiener, Norbert. *The Human Use of Human Beings*. New York: Avon Books, 1950.

Wilkinson, John. "The Metastases of Poetry." *Parataxis* No. 8/9 (1996).

Creeping It Real: Brian Kim Stefans' "Invisible Congress" and the Notion of Community,
K. Silem Mohammad, pages 185–192

Notes

1. Accessible via a link on Stefans' wonderful website *Arras*, at
    http://www.arras.net/stefans.htm. I suspect that I'm not supposed to quote from,
    allude to, or otherwise acknowledge the existence of anything on the Third Factory
    site, according to a warning label thereto attached (does the warning itself count?),
    but oh well, if I go to jail, I go to jail.

2. Of course, poetry is read aloud too. But I always think of spoken poetry, even when
    spoken by the author, as a specific *interpretation* of the poem that rules out other
    interpretations, whereas silent reading offers the possibility of multiple interpreta-
    tions simultaneously, and with that much simultaneity going on, there's no room for
    sense-experience. If it's working correctly.

Tagmosis / Prosody (extending parataxis), James Sherry, pages 205–212

Works Cited

Andrews, Bruce, Charles Bernstein, Ray DiPalma, Steve McCaffery, and Ron Silliman
    LEGEND (New York: L=A=N=G=U=A=G=E / SEGUE, 1980).

Ashbery, John. *Girls on the Run: A Poem* (New York: Farrar Straus & Giroux, 1989).

Bernstein, Charles. "The Conspiracy of Us," *Content's Dream: Essays 1875-1984*
    (Evanston: Northwestern UP, 2001): 343-347.

——————. "Matters of Policy," *Controlling Interests* (New York: Roof, 1980).

Delisi, Charles. "The Human Genome Project," *American Scientist* 76 (1988): 488- 493.

Eliot, T. S. "The Love Song of J. Alfred Prufrock," *Prufrock and Other Observations*
    (London: Egoist, 1917).

Genet, Jean. *The Maids and Deathwatch*, translated by Bernard Frechtman (New York:
    Grove, 1994).

Gleick, James. *Chaos: Making a New Science* (NY: Penguin, 1988).

Goodwin, Brian. *How the Leopard Changed Its Spots: The Evolution of Complexity* (Princeton:
    Princeton UP, 1994).

Gould, Stephen Jay. *Wonderful Life: The Burgess Shale and the Nature of History* (NY: W. W.
    Norton, 1989).

Hejinian, Lyn. *My Life* (Los Angeles: Sun & Moon, 1987).

Inman. P[eter]. *Red Shift* (New York: Roof, 1988).

Panek, Richard. "Art and Science: A Universe Apart," *The New York Times* (14 February,
    1999).

Silliman, Ron. "Sunset Debris," *The Age of Huts* (New York: Roof, 1986).

Spahr, Juliana. *Spiderwasp: or, Literary Criticism* (New York: Explosive Books, 1998).

Turing, A. M. "The Chemical Basis of Morphogenesis," *Philosophical Transactions of the
    Royal Society of London. Series B, Biological Sciences* 237: 641 (14 August, 1952): 37-72.

Walther, Bernt. "Commentary," *Journal of Biosciences* 25: 3 (September, 2000): 217-220.

Weart, S. R. and G. Weiss Szilard (Editors). *Leo Szilard: His Version of the Facts / Selected
    Recollections and Correspondence* (Cambridge: MIT Press, 1978).

Handwriting as a Form of Protest: Fiona Templeton's Cells of Release,
Caroline Bergvall, 215–230

Note

My thanks to the students and poets attending my MA Seminar "Contemporary Poetic & Text-led Practices" in 2004 at Birkbeck College, London, where this text was first discussed. As ever, many thanks to John Hall for providing my initial draft with comments and suggestions.

Works Cited

Bird, John, Jo Anna Isaak, and Sylvère Lotringer (eds.). *Nancy Spero* (London: Phaidon Press, 1996).

Cobbing, Bob and Lawrence Upton (eds.). *Word Score Utterance Choreography in verbal & visual poetry* (London: Writers Forum, 1998).

Derrida, Jacques and Paule Thevenin. *The secret art of Antonin Artaud*, trans. Mary Ann Caws (Cambridge: MIT Press, 1998).

Howe, Susan. *Pierce Arrow* (New York: Directions, 1999).

Kuti, José Feréz (ed.). *Brion Gysin: Tuning in to the Multimedia Age* (London: Thames & Hudson, 2003).

McCaffery, Steve. "From phonic to sonic: the emergence of the audio poem," in Adelaide Morris, *Sound States: Innovative Poetics and Acoustic technologies* (Chapel Hill: U. of North Carolina P., 1997).

Sontag, Susan. *Regarding the Pain of Others* (New York: Penguin, 2003).

Spira, Antony. *Henri Michaux* (Whitechapel Art Gallery, 1999).

Reid, Martine (ed.). "Boundaries: writing and drawing," special issue of *Yale French Studies* 84 (1994).

Templeton, Fiona. *Cells of Release* (New York: Roof Books, 1997).

Verner, Marta. "Divinations: Emily Dickinson's Scriptive Economies" in Juliana Spahr, Mark Wallace, Kriten Prevallet, and Pam Rehm (eds.), *A Poetics of Criticism* (Buffalo: Leave Books, 1994).

Welish, Marjorie. *Signifying art: essays on art after 1960* (Cambridge: Cambridge University Press, 1999).

Adding Up to Plural: On the Work of Roberto Tejada,
Alan Gilbert, pages 231–238

Works Cited

Bataille, Georges. "The Notion of Expenditure," *Visions of Excess: Selected Writings, 1927-1939*. Ed. Alan Stoekl, trans. Stoekl, Carl R. Lovitt and Donald M. Leslie Jr. Minneapolis: U. of Minnesota Press, 1985.

Bauman, Zygmunt. "Sociological Responses to Postmodernity." *Intimations of Postmodernity*. London: Routledge, 1992.

Di Stefano, Christine. "Dilemmas of Difference: Feminism, Modernity, and Postmodernism." *Feminism / Postmodernism*. Ed. Linda J. Nicholson. New York: Routledge, 1990.

Foucault, Michel. *Discipline and Punish: The Birth of the Prison*. Trans. Alan Sheridan. New

York: Pantheon Books, 1977.

Gates, Henry Louis, Jr. and Nellie Y. McKay (Eds.). *The Norton Anthology of African American Literature*. New York: W. W. Norton, 1997.

Hall, Stuart. "What Is This 'Black' in Black Popular Culture?" *Stuart Hall: Critical Dialogues in Cultural Studies*. Ed. David Morley and Kuan-Hsing Chen. London: Routledge, 1996.

Harvey, David. *Spaces of Hope*. Berkeley: U. of California P., 2000.

Mauss, Marcel. *The Gift: The Form and Reason for Exchange in Archaic Societies*. Trans. W. D. Halls. New York: W. W. Norton, 1990.

McCaffery, Steve. "Writing as a General Economy." *North of Intention: Critical Writings 1973-1986*. New York and Toronto: Roof Books and Nightwood Editions, 1986.

Osorno, Guillermo. "Soccer Match." *Mandorla* 6 (1998): 59-66.

Tejada, Roberto. "Graciela Iturbide and La Matanza." *Sulfur* 36 (Spring 1995): 128-130.

—————. *Gift & Verdict*. San Francisco: Leroy, 1999.

Turner, Terence. "Anthropology and Multiculturalism: What Is Anthropology that Multiculturalists Should Be Mindful of It?" *Multiculturalism: A Critical Reader*. Ed. David Theo Goldberg. Oxford: Basil Blackwell, 1994,

Weinberger, Eliot. *American Poetry since 1950: Outsiders & Innovators*. New York: Marsilio, 1993.

The Poem at the End of Theory, Michael Clune, pages 239–250

Works Cited

Andrews, Bruce, "Poetry as Explanation, Poetry as Praxis" in *Postmodern American Poetry: A Norton Anthology* ed. Paul Hoover (New York: Norton, 1994): 668-671.

Davies, Kevin, *Lateral Argument*. New York: Barretta Books, 2003.

Durand, Marcella, "Marcella Durand Interviews Kevin Davies." *The Poker #3* (Fall 2003).

Heidegger, Martin. *Being and Time*. Albany: SUNY P., 1996.

Izenberg, Oren. "Language Poetry and Collective Life." *Critical Inquiry* 29: 4 (Fall 2003): 132-159.

Jameson, Frederic *Postmodernism, or The Cultural Logic of Late Capitalism*. Durham: Duke U P, 1991.

Nealon, Christopher. "Camp Messianism, or, The Hopes of Poetry in Late-Late Capitalism." *American Literature* 76: 3 (September 2004): 579-602.

Wordsworth, William. "Ode: Intimations of Immortality" in *The Norton Anthology of Poetry*, ed. Margaret Ferguson *et al.* (New York: Norton, 1996): 728-732.

Notes

1. I take these three examples from Douglas Messerli's anthology *From the Other Side of the Century: A New American Poetry 1960-1990* (Los Angeles: Sun & Moon Press, 1994): 1057, 512, 997.

2. Craig Dworkin, "Introduction," *The Ubuweb Anthology of Conceptual Writing* <http//www.ubu.com>.

3. Jan Baetens, *Vive sa vie, une novelisation en vers du film de Jean-Luc Godard* (Paris-Bruxelles: Les Impressions nouvelles, 2005): 11. My translation throughout.

4. Antoine Compagnon, *La second main ou le travail de la citation* (Paris: Seuil, 1979): 17. My translation.

5. The chapbook spreads a color rendition of the drawing across the recto and verso of the cover, with the inscription rendered as calligraphy in the frontispiece and title pages, *Dure* bearing the subtitle "For a/ Form." In *Strand,* the layout is more conventional, with the drawing as frontispiece. The chapbook is an artist's book and should be consulted even if the reader uses the more accessible and readable Roof edition. Citations here are to *Strand* as the more readily available version.

6. Since the inscription is written in rather blurred Old German script, it is difficult to decipher. Dworkin transcribes the *u*'s in "darauff" and "deut" as *w*, and omits the final "h" of "weh." I have reinstated them because in German "w" is not a dipthong and "we" would not have been a word.

7. Jacques Roubaud, "Introduction, The Oulipo and Combinatorial Art" (1991), in *Oulipo Compendium*, compiled by Harry Mathews & Alastair Brotchie (London: Atlas Press, 1998): 42.

8. Yoko Tawada, *Aber die Mandarinen müssen heute abend noch geraubt werden* (Tübingen: Verlag Claudia Gehrke, 2003): 59. All translations mine.

9. Yoko Tawada, *Verwandlungen* (Tübingen: Poetik-Vorlesungen, 1998).

10. Marjorie Perloff, "The Oulipo Factor," *Differentials* (Tuscaloosa: U. of Alabama P., 2004).

Sources

Steve Evans. "Free (Market) Verse" was published in a slightly different version in *The Baffler* 17 "Superslayer Storybook" (2006).

Jed Rasula. "Innovation and 'Improbable Evidence'" was published in a slightly different version in Syncopations: The Stress of Innovation in Contemporary American Poetry (Tuscaloosa: University of Alabama Press, 2004). Reprinted with permission.

Barbara Cole. "Bruce Andrews' Venus: Paying Lip Service to Écriture Féminine" was published in a slightly different version in *Jacket* 22 (May 2003) special issue on Bruce Andrews edited by Nick Lawrence.

Gregg Biglieri. Invitation to a Misreading: Andrews' *Lip Service*" was originally published in *Jacket* 22 (May 2003) special issue on Bruce Andrews edited by Nick Lawrence.

Sianne Ngai: "Stuplimity." Excerpted from *Ugly Feelings* (Cambridge: Harvard University Press, 2005). Reprinted with permission. An earlier version of the essay was published as "Stuplimity: Shock and Boredom in Twentieth-Century Aesthetics," *Postmodern Culture* 10: 2 (January, 2000).

Brian Kim Stefans. "Stops and Rebels." Excerpted from *Fashionable Noise: On Digital Poetics* (Berkeley: Atelos, 2003).

K. Silem Mohammad. "Creeping it Real" was published in *Tripwire* 6 (Fall 2002).

Michael Gottlieb. "Googling Flarf" was published in a different form in *Jacket* 13 (October 2006).

Caroline Bergvall. "Handwriting as a Form of Protest: Fiona Templeton's *Cells of Release*" was published in *Jacket* 26 (October 2004).

Alan Gilbert. "Adding Up To Plural: On the Work of Roberto Tejada" was originally published in *Another Future: Poetry and Art in a Postmodern Twilight* (Middletown: Wesleyan University Press, 2006). Reprinted with permission. An earlier version appeared in *Facture* 3 (2002).

Michael Clune. "The Poem at the End of Theory" was originally published in *NO: A Journal of the Arts* Issue Four (2005).

ROOF BOOKS
the best in language since 1976

- Andrews, Bruce. **Co**. Collaborations with Barbara Cole, Jesse Freeman, Jessica Grim, Yedda Morrison, Kim Rosefield. 104p. $12.95.
- Andrews, Bruce. **Ex Why Zee**. 112p. $10.95.
- Andrews, Bruce. **Getting Ready To Have Been Frightened**. 116p. $7.50.
- Arakawa, Gins, Madeline. **Making Dying Illegal**. 224p. $22.95.
- Benson, Steve. **Blue Book**. Copub. with The Figures. 250p. $12.50
- Bernstein, Charles. **Controlling Interests**. 80p. $11.95.
- Bernstein, Charles. **Islets/Irritations**. 112p. $9.95.
- Bernstein, Charles (editor). **The Politics of Poetic Form**. 246p. $12.95; cloth $21.95.
- Brossard, Nicole. **Picture Theory**. 188p. $11.95.
- Cadiot, Olivier. **Former, Future, Fugitive**. Translated by Cole Swensen. 166p. $13.95.
- Champion, Miles. **Three Bell Zero**. 72p. $10.95.
- Child, Abigail. **Scatter Matrix**. 79p. $9.95.
- Davies, Alan. **Active 24 Hours**. 100p. $5.
- Davies, Alan. **Signage**. 184p. $11.
- Davies, Alan. **Rave**. 64p. $7.95.
- Day, Jean. **A Young Recruit**. 58p. $6.
- Di Palma, Ray. **Motion of the Cypher**. 112p. $10.95.
- Di Palma, Ray. **Raik**. 100p. $9.95.
- Doris, Stacy. **Kildare**. 104p. $9.95.
- Doris, Stacy. **Cheerleader's Guide to the World: Council Book** 88p. $12.95.
- Dreyer, Lynne. **The White Museum**. 80p. $6.
- Dworkin, Craig. **Strand**. 112p. $12.95.
- Edwards, Ken. **Good Science**. 80p. $9.95.
- Eigner, Larry. **Areas Lights Heights**. 182p. $12, $22 (cloth).
- Gardner, Drew. **Petroleum Hat**. 96p. $12.95.
- Gizzi, Michael. **Continental Harmonies**. 96p. $8.95.
- Gladman, Renee. **A Picture-Feeling**. 72p. $10.95.
- Goldman, Judith. **Vocoder**. 96p. $11.95.
- Gordon, Nada. **Folly**. 128p. $13.95
- Gottlieb, Michael. **Ninety-Six Tears**. 88p. $5.
- Gottlieb, Michael. **Gorgeous Plunge**. 96p. $11.95.
- Gottlieb, Michael. **Lost & Found**. 80p. $11.95.
- Greenwald, Ted. **Jumping the Line**. 120p. $12.95.
- Grenier, Robert. **A Day at the Beach**. 80p. $6.
- Grosman, Ernesto. **The XULReader: An Anthology of Argentine Poetry (1981–1996)**. 167p. $14.95.
- Guest, Barbara. **Dürer in the Window, Reflexions on Art**. Book design by Richard Tuttle. Four color throughout. 80p. $24.95.
- Hills, Henry. **Making Money**. 72p. $7.50. VHS videotape $24.95. Book & tape $29.95.
- Huang Yunte. **SHI: A Radical Reading of Chinese Poetry**. 76p. $9.95
- Hunt, Erica. **Local History**. 80 p. $9.95.
- Kuszai, Joel (editor) **poetics@**, 192 p. $13.95.
- Inman, P. **Criss Cross**. 64 p. $7.95.

- Inman, P. **Red Shift**. 64p. $6.
- Lazer, Hank. **Doublespace**. 192 p. $12.
- Levy, Andrew. **Paper Head Last Lyrics**. 112 p. $11.95.
- Mac Low, Jackson. **Representative Works: 1938–1985**. 360p. $18.95 (cloth).
- Mac Low, Jackson. **Twenties**. 112p. $8.95.
- McMorris, Mark. **The Café at Light**. 112p. $12.95.
- Moriarty, Laura. **Rondeaux**. 107p. $8.
- Nasdor, Marc. **Sonnetailia**. 80p. $12.95
- Neilson, Melanie. **Civil Noir**. 96p. $8.95.
- Osman, Jena. **An Essay in Asterisks**. 112p. $12.95.
- Pearson, Ted. **Planetary Gear**. 72p. $8.95.
- Perelman, Bob. **Virtual Reality**. 80p. $9.95.
- Perelman, Bob. **The Future of Memory**. 120p. $14.95.
- Perelman, Bob. **Iflife**. 140p. $13.95.
- Piombino, Nick, **The Boundary of Blur**. 128p. $13.95.
- Prize Budget for Boys, **The Spectacular Vernacular Revue**. 96p. $14.95.
- Raworth, Tom. **Clean & Will-Lit**. 106p. $10.95.
- Robinson, Kit. **Balance Sheet**. 112p. $11.95.
- Robinson, Kit. **Democracy Boulevard**. 104p. $9.95.
- Robinson, Kit. **Ice Cubes**. 96p. $6.
- Rosenfield, Kim. **Good Morning—MIDNIGHT—**. 112p. $10.95.
- Scalapino, Leslie. **Objects in the Terrifying Tense Longing from Taking Place**. 88p. $9.95.
- Seaton, Peter. **The Son Master**. 64p. $5.
- Shaw, Lytle, editor. **Nineteen Lines: A Drawing Center Writing Anthology**. 336p. $24.95
- Sherry, James. **Popular Fiction**. 84p. $6.
- Silliman, Ron. **The New Sentence**. 200p. $10.
- Silliman, Ron. **N/O**. 112p. $10.95.
- Smith, Rod. **Music or Honesty**. 96p. $12.95
- Smith, Rod. **Protective Immediacy**. 96p. $9.95
- Stefans, Brian Kim. **Free Space Comix**. 96p. $9.95
- Stefans, Brian Kim. **Kluge**. 128p. $13.95
- Tarkos, Christophe. **Ma Langue est Poétique—Selected Works**. 96p. $12.95.
- Templeton, Fiona. **Cells of Release**. 128p. with photographs. $13.95.
- Templeton, Fiona. **YOU—The City**. 150p. $11.95.
- Torres, Edwin. **The All-Union Day of the Shock Worker**. 112 p. $10.95.
- Tysh, Chris. **Cleavage**. 96p. $11.95.
- Ward, Diane. **Human Ceiling**. 80p. $8.95.
- Ward, Diane. **Relation**. 64p. $7.50.
- Watson, Craig. **Free Will**. 80p. $9.95.
- Watten, Barrett. **Progress**. 122p. $7.50.
- Weiner, Hannah. **We Speak Silent**. 76 p. $9.95
- Weiner, Hannah. **Page**. 136 p. $12.95
- Wellman, Mac. **Miniature**. 112 p. $12.95
- Wellman, Mac. **Strange Elegies**. 96 p. $12.95
- Wolsak, Lissa. **Pen Chants**. 80p. $9.95.
- Yasusada, Araki. **Doubled Flowering: From the Notebooks of Araki Yasusada**. 272p. $14.95.

Roof Books are published by
Segue Foundation • 300 Bowery • New York, NY 10012
Visit our website at **seguefoundation.com**

Roof Books are distributed by
SMALL PRESS DISTRIBUTION
1341 Seventh Street • Berkeley, CA. 94710-1403.
Phone orders: 800-869-7553
spdbooks.org